JUXTAPOSING AUTONOMY AND PATERNALISM IN PRIVATE LAW

Selecting an appropriate balance in the law between autonomy and paternalism is an important and difficult task, requiring a careful consideration of moral, political and economic values. This collection deals with the task at both general and specific levels, locating itself within the broader context of the relationship between law and market forces. Concepts are defined and analysed, in particular the distinction between the coercive approach of 'hard paternalism' in the law, and the 'nudge' approach of 'soft paternalism'. Attention is then focused on how the tensions between the concepts are resolved in the law of contract, where deficient information and mistakes can justify an interventionist approach. Besides overviews of the issues within the general law of contract, and historical studies of the relevant principles in the common law and Roman law, the book also includes studies of specific areas, notably insurance contracts and consumer bankruptcy. The authors, from North America, the United Kingdom and continental Europe, include economists, sociologists and traditional legal scholars.

Juxtaposing Autonomy and Paternalism in Private Law

Edited by

Anthony Ogus

and

Willem H van Boom

•HART•
PUBLISHING

OXFORD AND PORTLAND, OREGON
2011

Published in the United Kingdom by Hart Publishing Ltd
16C Worcester Place, Oxford, OX1 2JW
Telephone: +44 (0)1865 517530
Fax: +44 (0)1865 510710
E-mail: mail@hartpub.co.uk
Website: http://www.hartpub.co.uk

Published in North America (US and Canada) by
Hart Publishing
c/o International Specialized Book Services
920 NE 58th Avenue, Suite 300
Portland, OR 97213–3786
USA
Tel: +1 503 287 3093 or toll-free: (1) 800 944 6190
Fax: +1 503 280 8832
E-mail: orders@isbs.com
Website: http://www.isbs.com

British Library Cataloguing in Publication Data
Data Available

ISBN: 978-1-84946-118-4

Typeset by Columns Design XML Ltd, Reading
Printed and bound in Great Britain by
Lightning Source UK Ltd

Contents

1

Introducing, Defining and Balancing 'Autonomy versus Paternalism'

WILLEM H VAN BOOM* AND ANTHONY OGUS**

1. INTRODUCING THE THEME

AUTONOMY IS GENERALLY regarded as the fundamental right of individuals to shape their own future through voluntary action. In private law, it is associated with freedom of contract and the concept of *casum sentit dominus* (the loss lies where it falls). As such, it is opposed to legal paternalism, briefly defined as instances in which legislation or the courts interfere with the individual's decision-making process on the ground that otherwise decisions will not be made in the individual's own best interests.

Traditionally, legislation protecting the estate of minors and mentally disabled individuals against the consequences of their actions is considered the prime example of paternalism.[1] However, a broader range of protection against the risks of succumbing to weakness and extortionary practices is nowadays ubiquitous in Western society. The level of protection differs from domain to domain. The prohibition of trading in humans as a commodity — ranging from slavery to prostitution and selling organs — seems to have little in common with restrictions on freedom of contract in marital and family issues or with gambling regulation, but the essential common denominator is the substitution of voluntary individual decision-making by a decision that the legislator or court finds most appropriate.

Obviously, there is no strict definition of paternalism. Indeed, the definitions used may provide an indication of the author's own views. If paternalism is defined in terms of governments assuming the power to determine what is best

* Professor of Law at the Erasmus School of Law, Erasmus University Rotterdam.
** Professor of Fundamentals of Private Law at Erasmus University Rotterdam; Emeritus Professor of Law at the University of Manchester.
[1] E Zamir, 'The Efficiency of Paternalism' (1998) 84 *Virginia Law Review* 238, fn 25.

for citizens because the latter cannot be trusted to make decisions in their own best interests, it may be concluded that the author is somewhat sceptical of such state intervention.[2]

Some define paternalism as coercive intervention with the behaviour of individuals in order to prevent them from causing harm to themselves.[3] Some authors focus on the grounds of justification for intervention as the defining element in paternalism: state intervention is paternalistic if it purports to increase the individual's welfare and happiness or to further his or her interests, needs and values.[4]

The authority for interfering is thought by some to lie in the mere coercive powers of the state,[5] whereas others take a more sophisticated approach by arguing that paternalism may be founded on a hypothetical contract with the individual,[6] where, in particular, the individual recognises his or her own fallibility and is assumed to delegate decision-making to another.[7]

2. DEFINING PATERNALISM

As far as terminology is concerned, different sub categorisations are used.[8] 'Pure paternalism' is distinguished from 'impure paternalism', where the former is aimed directly at the person assumed to be in need of protection, whereas the latter calls for the intervention of a gatekeeper. 'Impure paternalism', therefore, involves not only the protectee but also a third party who owes a legal duty to ensure the protectee is separated from a source of danger.[9] Here we can think of the bartender who is legally obliged not to sell alcohol to a person under a certain age or to an already intoxicated customer.

Another categorisation relates to the distinction between 'strong paternalism' and 'weak paternalism'. Weak paternalism refers to soft state intervention aimed at educating and informing and influencing the decision-making process, thus 'nudging' individuals towards what are perceived to be better outcomes. Law is often used as an instrument to this end — eg information duties and the duty to frame information in a certain fashion — and is considered an alternative to state information campaigns and so forth.

[2] A Ogus, *Costs and Cautionary Tales — Economic Insights for the Law* (Oxford, Hart Publishing, 2006) 83.

[3] EG Valdés, 'On Justifying Legal Paternalism' (1990) *Ratio Juris* 173 ff.

[4] G Dworkin, 'Paternalism' in RA Wasserstrom (ed), *Morality and the Law* (Belmont, CA, Wadsworth, 1971) 108. cf Zamir, above n 1, at 236.

[5] D Kennedy, 'Distributive and Paternalist Motives in Contract and Tort Law, with Special Reference to Compulsory Terms and Unequal Bargaining Power' (1982) 41 *Maryland Law Review* 563, 572.

[6] Ogus, above n 2, at 234.

[7] J Kleinig, *Paternalism* (Totowa, NJ, Rowman and Allanheld, 1983) 55–67.

[8] Further categories to be found in G Dworkin, 'Moral Paternalism' (2005) 24 *Law and Philosophy* 305ff.

[9] Dworkin, above n 4, at 111.

Strong paternalism is more interventionist. Its mission is not merely to inform or even to persuade but to ensure that individual behaviour that leads to adverse consequences is altered or stopped if necessary. It focuses on changing preferences rather than informing individuals of the relative advantages and disadvantages of their preferences.[10] As such, it is associated with mandatory law.[11] It is *ius cogens* rather than *ius dispositivum*.[12]

In the law of contracts and torts, weak paternalism seems to be on the increase. By nudging the protectee in a certain direction it is thought that the law helps to overcome bounded rationality and the influence of biases, heuristics and cravings.[13] Rather than forbidding certain activities, information rules or default rules are construed in such a way as to help the individual make the decision that maximises his or her welfare. By using powerful warning signs, the owner of dangerous premises can nudge potential victims into avoiding the premises. By using default contract law rules, a legislator can nudge contracting parties in a specific direction if, in practice, these rules are never the subject of contract negotiations.[14]

By way of example, consider the following sliding scale between autonomy and paternalism in private law:

Autonomy		**Weak paternalism: nudging**	**Strong paternalism: intervention**
Casum sentit dominus (D.50, 17, 23)	Duty to inform against risks	Duty to warn against risks	Prohibition of certain acts, duty to intervene in personal sphere of other person
Contracts are binding	information duties aimed at optimal informed decision-making	Cooling-off periods	Mandatory standards for content or conclusion of contract

10 G Dworkin, 'Paternalism' in EN Zalta (ed), *Stanford Encyclopedia of Philosophy* (2002) available at www.plato.stanford.edu, 1.

11 Ogus, above n 2, at 85.

12 B Rudden, 'Ius Cogens, Ius Dispositivum' (1980) 11 *The Cambrian Law Review* 87ff.

13 On the concept of nudging, see eg RH Thaler and CR Sunstein, Nudge – Improving Decisions About Health, Wealth, and Happiness (New Haven, Yale University Press, 2008) 1ff. Note that here we witness a cultural gap between the United States and Europe. Had Thaler and Sunstein originated from Europe, they would probably not have chosen the catchword 'nudging', as it would surely be associated with the cheeky 'nudge nudge, wink wink' Monty Python sketch.

14 CR Sunstein and RH Thaler, 'Libertarian Paternalism Is Not an Oxymoron' (2003) 70 *University of Chicago Law Review* 1159ff.

Related to paternalism, but perhaps conceptually best kept distinct from it, are measures that, though intended to enhance individual welfare, are also aimed at social welfare generally. This is because the decisions made by the individual have spillover effects for the rest of society, or externalities, as they are sometimes called.[15] Thus, for example, the mandatory wearing of seat belts in vehicles or the (usually soft) measures taken to curtail tobacco smoking may appear to be principally concerned with reducing the risk of harm for the individual concerned but can be justified by reference to the public purse, because most health care costs are borne by the community as a whole.[16] Individual autonomy may thus be curtailed for the benefit of the greater good.[17]

3. THE DEBATE ABOUT PATERNALISM

The appropriate role of paternalism, weak and strong, in legal policymaking has been the subject of a lively debate in the, predominantly American, literature. The traditional opposition to it, based on classical notions of individual autonomy, have been challenged by those drawing on the social psychology and behavioural economics findings referred to above. It has been suggested that it is a mistake to see as dichotomous the choice between individual autonomy and paternalistic intervention: rather, there is a spectrum between these two extremes, calling for more or less intervention, depending on the circumstances.[18]

While recognising this, others argue that the problems of identifying appropriate decisions which are sufficiently harmful and selecting the means of remedying them are simply too great, in particular because individuals are different and it is wrong to treat them as a homogenous group.[19] One response to this has been to sponsor 'asymmetric' paternalist measures, those which can potentially generate significant benefits for those who need protection, without imposing significant costs on those who do not need it;[20] or else weak paternalist measures which preserve freedom of choice.[21]

Even milder approaches such as these do not escape the criticisms of the hard-nosed, perhaps ideological, opponents of paternalism. It is said that once a move towards paternalism is made, policymakers find themselves on a 'slippery slope', finding it increasingly difficult to resist arguments for more paternalist

15 A Ogus, *Regulation: Legal Form and Economic Theory* (Oxford, Hart Publishing, 1994) 35–8.

16 However, care must be taken in using this argument, because, if, eg curtailing smoking prolongs life, this can add to rather than diminish the health care costs borne by others.

17 Cf Kennedy, above n 5, at 633.

18 C Camerer *et al* 'Behavioral Economics and the Case for Asymmetric Paternalism' (2003) 151 *University of Pennsylvania Law Review* 1211.

19 DG Whitman and MJ Rizzo, 'Paternalism Slopes' (2007) 2 *New York University Journal of Law and Liberty* 411.

20 Camerer *et al*, above n 18.

21 Sunstein and Thaler, above n 14.

measures.[22] Analogous, but different, is the contention that even soft paternalist interventions create disincentives for individuals to learn for themselves, so making them increasingly dependent on decisions being made for them.[23]

4. COST AND BENEFITS OF AUTONOMY AND PATERNALISM

Appraising the relative costs and benefits of autonomy and paternalism is fraught with difficulties, but establishing a framework for this purpose can at least facilitate good policy-making.[24] Take, first of all, the costs of paternalism. If mandatory paternalism is introduced without regulating price, the private party burdened with executing the paternalistic intervention (eg gatekeepers) will surely consider charging the protectee for the relevant measure.[25] Such transfer of cost may cause the price of the product to rise and ultimately render it unaffordable for individuals on lower incomes, in which case the object of the legal intervention is defeated.[26]

Some other important costs of paternalism should also be mentioned. As regards hard paternalism, there will be some individuals who will lose out by being deprived of the ability to make alternative choices, because their preferences are different from those assumed by the legal policy-makers. Quite apart from this, there is also the possibility that the latter will make errors in deciding what is best for the individuals concerned, perhaps because of undue political pressures.

Such costs may be difficult to quantify, and the same can be said of the benefits of paternalist measures. Fundamentally, these comprise any reduction in the losses which would have accrued to individuals if they had made free choices; and to assess these requires an estimate both of the amount of such losses that would have been sustained and of the extent to which the paternalist measure will be effective in avoiding that outcome. As regards this latter dimension, it will be easier to predict the impact of hard paternalist measures, which is a function of the effectiveness of the enforcement of prohibitions, than that of soft measures, since the latter will depend on how individuals respond to the 'nudge', a highly subjective variable.

Whatever may be concluded from a cost-benefit appraisal, it has to be recognised that political considerations may also be important. In modern times,

[22] Whitman and Rizzo, above n 19.

[23] C Hill, 'Anti-Anti-Anti-Paternalism' (2007) 2 *New York University Journal of Law and Liberty* 444.

[24] Zamir, above n 1, at 229 ff; A Ogus, 'The Paradoxes of Legal Paternalism and How to Resolve Them' (2010) 30 *Legal Studies* 61ff.

[25] Cf Kennedy, above n 5, at 625.

[26] Ogus, above n 2, at 31, 227–28 and 252. The mechanism in itself does not make paternalism the equivalent of redistribution, unless the cost increase is distributed equally among all those buying the product. On the relationship between paternalism and (re)distributive justice, see Ogus, above n 2, at 220.

paternalism may not be consistent with political correctness. Politicians, courts and policy-makers do not like their products to be branded as interventionist and meddlesome, and the 'p-word' is almost always used in a pejorative sense when used in public debates.[27] This is paradoxical because 'contrary to the prevailing rhetoric of policymakers (and much of the legal literature), the legal systems of all western liberal democracies contain innumerable paternalistic rules and doctrines.'[28]

In short, the extent to which a given society is willing to allow paternalist intervention tells us a great deal about the dominant political philosophy. Unsurprisingly, the legal debate on paternalism in the United States of America differs substantially from the debate in Europe,[29] perhaps because individual autonomy and freedom of decision-making have deeper cultural and constitutional roots in the former compared with the latter.

5. THE ROTTERDAM WORKSHOP

Participants at the Rotterdam Workshop were invited to relate their contributions to the themes discussed above. In this section, we briefly introduce their contributions.

In 'Mandatory Contract Law: Functions and Principles in Light of the Proposal for a Directive on Consumer Rights', *Gerhard Wagner* provides an overview of the relationship between autonomy and paternalism in contract law. From a comparative perspective, he finds it easier to locate a tradition of mandatory law (*ius cogens*) within the civil law culture than within that of common law. From the perspective of economic theory, he finds that strong justifications for mandatory law can be found, but not so easily in the case of paternalism. In the second half of the article, he discusses different instances of mandatory rules, considering justifications for them, particularly in the light of the proposed Directive on Consumer Rights, by reference to both paternalist protection and standardisation.

By analysing 'The Role of Information Deficiencies in Contract Enforcement', *Ann-Sophie Vandenberghe* essentially looks into the issue whether and to what extent duties to inform in contract law amount to paternalism. From the outset, it is clearly a difficult task to draw the line between information deficiencies of which the law will take account and those it will disregard. Vandenberghe sets out the economic framework for determining when it is appropriate to shift responsibility for information deficiencies from one contracting party to the other. She finds that intervention is warranted in cases where information deficiencies

[27] Ogus, above n 24, at 63.

[28] Zamir, above n 1, at 285.

[29] See eg the (US) academic debate between O Bar-Gill and RA Epstein, *Consumer Contracts: Behavioral Economics vs Neoclassical Economics* (New York University, Law and Economics Working Papers, 2007) 1ff.

interfere with a special relationship of trust between the contracting parties. It seems that, in these trust relationships, the mere duty to inform may transform into a duty to give advice and sometimes even to prevent unnecessary risk-taking. The economic justification for, and limitation of, such duties and other regulatory interventions in the contracting process is to be found, Vandenberghe argues, in consumers' tendency to 'sign without reading'.

In 'Consumer Bankruptcy: A Third Way between Autonomy and Paternalism in Private Law', *Nick Huls* links the friction between autonomy and paternalism to consumer bankruptcy, against the backdrop of the introduction of American ideas of consumer bankruptcy into European continental civil law systems. Huls analyses the history of 'bankruptcy waves' and reflects on the next regulatory wave that the recent credit crisis can be expected to create. He then goes on to argue that consumer bankruptcy in Europe has evolved into an overt battleground between the competing interests of creditors and debtors.

In 'Regulating Consumer Demand in Insurance Markets', *Daniel Schwarcz* concentrates on the problems of understanding consumer behaviour in relation to the choice of insurance contracts. Although he recognises that a limited understanding of the complexities involved in risk phenomena may justify interventionist measures by reference to paternalism, there is a need to develop a deeper understanding of the role that insurance plays in the emotional life of individuals. This topic has been neglected in the literature. Using examples, such as the demand for insurance against small risks and non-pecuniary losses, or for excessively low deductibles, he speculates on how appropriately designed disclosure rules might succeed in discriminating between those individuals who make these choices as a result of cognitive errors and those who might have good emotional reasons for them.

In 'Contracts and Capabilities: An Evolutionary Perspective on the Autonomy-Paternalism Debate', *Simon Deakin*, adopts a broad evolutionary theoretical approach to contracts. Drawing on the writings of Gintis, which foster such an approach, he considers that paternalism is only one strand in a more complex web of justifications for selectivity and discrimination in the enforcement of contracts. He argues that capability theory provides a surer way of understanding interventionist measures than the autonomy-paternalism dichotomy, because, rather than concentrating exclusively on the individual and rationality, it takes account of the evolution of the market and its functions in promoting general welfare. In other words, it is necessary to understand the interaction between the dual systems of market and law in order to apply norms of societal coordination to contractual relationships. To illustrate this thesis, Deakin examines the history of labour law and the justifications for the regulation of employment contracts.

The paper by *Stephen Waddams*, 'Autonomy and Paternalism from a Common Law Perspective: Setting Aside Disadvantageous Transactions', explores the roots and developments of various doctrines protecting disadvantaged parties in the English law of contract, with some reference to the Draft Common Frame of

Reference. He successively reviews the relevant principles, including those governing consideration, specific performance, relief of forfeiture in mortgages, penalty clauses, undue influence and unconscionability, and then considers possible rationalisations for them. He concludes that although autonomy and paternalism have been important factors, other considerations have influenced the courts, particularly public policy. Examples of the latter include considerations relating to the unreasonable restraint of trade, the requirement of legitimate interest to enforce contracts and, finally, the doctrine of unjust enrichment.

In their contribution, entitled 'Informing Consumers About Themselves', *Oren Bar-Gill* and *Franco Ferrari* focus on mistakes typically made by consumers that are often invoked to justify paternalist interventions, both hard and soft. They argue that insufficient attention has so far been given to what they call 'use-pattern mistakes', that is, mistakes that are made when consumers use products or services that are purchased. Such mistakes are often exploited by suppliers, leading to even greater losses. The authors discuss different methods of combating the problem and argue for better systems of mandatory disclosure, with suppliers being obliged to highlight information about aspects that are typically misperceived by consumers.

Finally, in 'Forms of Imposed Protection in Legal History, Especially in Roman Law', *Laurens Winkel* traces the origins of paternalism back to early Roman family law in the so-called Twelve Tables. Indeed, several forms of imposed protection can be found in legislation concerning gifts, in decrees of the Senate and in praetorian legal remedies. Moreover, Winkel shows that contract law was also a source of protective measures, in so far as good faith played a role in this area, and that the concept of 'mistake of law' gave birth to special rules of paternalism. Winkel then addresses the wider reception of Roman law, concluding that, although the oldest forms of imposed protection are to be found in family law, the broad idea of protection has, from the Middle Ages onwards, gradually spread to all parts of patrimonial law in continental legal systems.

Obviously, these fine contributions to this volume do not provide a definitive answer to the 'autonomy v paternalism' debate. What they do provide, however, is a thought-provoking addition to the debate and a deepened understanding of the considerations that underlie policy choices made in Europe and elsewhere in the private law domain and beyond. We would like to thank the contributors for the enjoyable discussions we had with them, the Erasmus School of Law research programme on Behavioural Approaches to Contract and Tort[30] for hosting the Rotterdam workshop, the Erasmus Law Review, where these essays were previously published, and its blind reviewers for meticulous refereeing, and, last but not least, Richard Hart and his colleagues for their assistance in bringing the product of the workshop to a broader public.

[30] See: www.behaviouralapproaches.eu.

2

Mandatory Contract Law: Functions and Principles in Light of the Proposal for a Directive on Consumer Rights

GERHARD WAGNER*

ABSTRACT

Starting from the theoretical underpinnings of contract law, mandatory rules should be the exception. In the reality of current European legislation, mandatory law is not the exception but the rule. The obvious explanation is that the EU has focused on consumer law, ie on the regulation of transactions between a business and a consumer. In a B-to-C relationship, the consumer is perceived as the weaker party which requires protection against the more powerful business.

THE FOLLOWING CHAPTER tries to dismantle the assumptions that consumers are weak and that the 'weakness' of consumers forms the normative basis for the body of Directives we now have before us. The *Draft Proposal of a Directive on Consumer Rights* is used as an object for analyses from the perspectives of comparative law and economic reasoning. The argument is that, while there are important areas where mandatory law is justified, the card of mandatory law has been overplayed in important respects. In particular, the petrification of the law of sales that began with the *Directive on Consumer Sales and Guarantees* seems to be unjustified. Within a system that allows for court control over standard contract terms, the need for mandatory law is negligible. Where court control over standard terms is perceived not to be sufficient, 'options' should be used instead of mandatory law. While options preserve party autonomy, they do limit freedom of choice to a set of immutable alternatives. And in doing so, they reconcile party autonomy with legal certainty.

* Dr Gerhard Wagner LLM is Professor of Fundamentals of Private Law at Erasmus University, Rotterdam, as well as, Professor of German and European Private Law and Civil Procedure at the University of Bonn.

1. INTRODUCTION

Contract law is generally thought to be based on the principle of party autonomy. The moral justification for the principle of party autonomy may be derived from any theory that embraces the value of individual freedom. For a Kantian, party autonomy is a consequence of the principle of treating persons not as objects but as subjects, and not as means but as ends.[1] Utilitarian theories do not start from ethical principles, but from the objective to maximise happiness.[2] It follows easily that the maximisation of the happiness of the greatest number of subjects turns on the advancement of individual happiness. Even though one may conceive a utilitarian theory that entrusts the maximisation of individual happiness to a benevolent dictator, the moral yardstick remains an individualistic one. From the premise that it is individual well-being that counts in the moral universe, it is but a short step to the notion of party autonomy. In all likelihood, individuals themselves know best what makes them happy or contributes to their well-being. Therefore, they should be allowed to take the pursuit of happiness into their own hands and to make the choices they think are best for them. As will be explained later, this is exactly the point of view to which neoclassical economics subscribes,[3] regardless of whether or not it qualifies as a special case of utilitarianism.[4]

Given that there is something of an overlapping consensus regarding the normative justification of party autonomy, it is surprising that, in reality, party autonomy is on the retreat. During the 1960s and 1970s it was believed that the principle of party autonomy was unhelpful in organising modern societies. The proclamation of the 'death of contract' was not merely meant as a diagnosis, but as an affirmation of a new paradigm in private law that would supersede the outdated institutions of ancient times. Today, the 'death of contract' movement seems to be dead itself.[5] With the demise of socialism, market economies that rely on the aggregation of individual choices through the market appeared to be left without a serious alternative. Contracts are an indispensable cog in the market mechanism. Without a functioning law of contract, parties would be unable to engage in transactions or they would have to take costly measures of self-protection against the opportunistic behaviour of their counterpart. In summary, voluntary agreements, and the body of law enabling and protecting them, are indispensable institutions for a market economy.

[1] I Kant, *Grundlegung zur Metaphysik der Sitten*, Akademie-Edition (1785) 429.

[2] J Bentham, *Introduction to the Principles of Morals and Legislation* (1789); H Sidgwick, *The Methods of Ethics*, 7th edn (1907) 413.

[3] See section 3 below.

[4] On this issue, see RA Posner, 'Utilitarianism, Economics, and Legal Theory' (1979) 8 *Journal of Legal Studies* 103; RM Dworkin, 'Is Wealth a Value?' (1980) 9 *Journal of Legal Studies* 191 215ff; JL Coleman, 'Efficiency, Utility, and Wealth Maximization' (1980) 8 *Hofstra Law Review* 509, 515. For a recent account of the methodological underpinnings of economic analysis of law, see L Kaplow and S Shavell, *Fairness vs. Welfare* (2002) 15ff.

[5] G Gilmore, *The Death of Contract* (1974).

2. THE DOMAIN OF CONSUMER LAW

In spite of this finding, the legislation of the European Union in the area of contract law is almost exclusively in the mode of mandatory rules. The many directives dealing with consumer contracts regulate various aspects of contract formation or even the substantive terms of commercial agreements. These rules are optional for the consumer in the sense that she may agree contractual provisions more favourable to her.[6] For the other side, the business enterprise contracting with the consumer, they are mandatory in the sense that the business entity must not derogate from the statutory provisions to the detriment of the consumer.[7] As the choice for mandatory rules operates only unilaterally, one may call this mode of legislation 'unilaterally mandatory'.

Today, consumer law is firmly established, as evidenced by the Proposal for a Directive on Consumer Rights. After decades of piecemeal legislation in the form of various directives that each deal with a particular aspect of consumer contract law, the Commission has come to the conclusion that some harmonisation is needed.[8] Accordingly, the Proposal for a Directive on Consumer Rights does not break new ground in the sense that new subject-matter is being explored. Rather, its aim is to draw together four existing directives, namely the directives on doorstep selling, distance selling, unfair terms in consumer contracts, and consumer sales and guarantees. The provisions on contracts of sale being the only ones regulating the contents of a particular type of contract, the Draft Directive follows a 'horizontal' approach rather than a 'vertical' one. The principle of unilateral force of statutory provisions — in the sense that the parties must not undercut the standard of protection accorded to the consumer — is being generalised as well. The proposal for a Directive on Consumer Rights subscribes to the principle that the statutory framework is binding for the business but not mandatory for the consumer. Pursuant to its Article 43, 'consumers may not waive the rights conferred on them by this Directive'.

For the theory of contract law, the Proposal for a Directive on Consumer Rights represents a major challenge. The time has come to ask if the rules of contract law, whether they are created by lawmakers or judges, should be mandatory or of a default nature. This question has a particular bearing on

[6] For purposes of gender neutrality and convenience, this paper envisages a female consumer and a male trader, professional or businessman.

[7] Art 6 of Council Directive 85/577/EEC of 20 December 1985 to protect the consumer in respect of contracts negotiated away from business premises, OJ 1985 L 372/31; Art 12(1) of Directive 97/7/EC of the European Parliament and of the Council of 20 May 1997 on the protection of consumers in respect of distance contracts, OJ 1997 L 144/19 ff.; Art 6 of Council Directive 93/13/EEC of 5 April 1993 on unfair terms in consumer contracts, OJ 1993 L 95/29 ff.; Art 7(1) of Directive 1999/44/EC of the European Parliament and of the Council of 25 May 1999 on certain aspects of the sale of consumer goods and associated guarantees, OJ 1999 L 171/12 ff.

[8] Proposal for a Directive of the European Parliament and of the Council on consumer rights of 8 October 2008, COM (2008) 614 final, at 3 and Rec 2.

business-to-consumer transactions. However, conceptually, it must not be confined to the area of consumer law. As long as the reasons and justifications for the continuing growth of mandatory contract law remain unclear, it is impossible to tell whether mandatory rules are a hallmark of consumer law, or whether they must be generalised, as they rest on general normative principles.

3. COMPARATIVE OVERVIEW

Analyses of mandatory rules in contract law are rare, if they exist at all. With the notable exception of scholars subscribing to the economic approach, the interest in conceptual clarity and theoretical consistency has been rather weak in recent years. One reason for the dearth of research on mandatory rules may be the fact that modern legislation in the area of contract law, at least in Europe, has focused exclusively on the relationship between businesses and consumers. As many scholars of general contract law tended to avoid the shady area of consumer protection, it was left to experts in this field, who developed the understanding that consumer law was a special area, detached from the traditional areas such as contract and tort law.

3.1. Common Law

This is particularly true for the common law. As far as England and Wales are concerned, articles discussing the distinction between mandatory rules and default rules are rare.[9] Many textbooks ignore the distinction between default rules and mandatory rules altogether,[10] while others simply point out that '[a] wide range of social policies might justify the imposition of compulsory obligations.'[11]

To this, some authors add concepts of economic theory by pointing out that mandatory rules are needed to compensate for market failures and externalities.[12] Reserving the insights of economic analysis for the next section, these arguments, taken in the abstract, do not contribute much to the legal analysis.

It seems that the category of mandatory rules remained somewhat alien to the common law of contract even outside of the United Kingdom. It is said that it was imported into US law by scholars like Karl Llewellyn who were familiar with German pandectist theory and its affiliation with the classical distinction

[9] cf B Rudden, 'Ius Cogens, Ius Dispositivum' (1980) 11 *Cambrian Law Review* 87; M Freedland, 'Ius Cogens, Ius Dispositivum, and Personal Work Contracts' in P Birks and A Pretto (eds), *Themes in Comparative Law — In Honour of Bernard Rudden* (2002) 164. Another exception, in book form, is A Ogus, *Costs and Cautionary Tales* (2006) 83 ff.

[10] cf H Beale, *Chitty on Contracts*, Vol I, 30th edn (2008) Chs 15 and 16, dealing with unfair terms and public policy but ignoring mandatory rules.

[11] H Collins, *The Law of Contract*, 4th edn (2003) 248, 251.

[12] ibid 248.

between *ius cogens* and *ius dispositivum*, which were translated as 'iron rules' and 'yielding rules'.[13]

3.2. Civil Law

Turning to the pandectist literature of the late-nineteenth century Germany gives rise to another disappointment. While it is true that the prominent authors of this age all note the distinction between default rules and rules of a mandatory nature, most writers are content to leave it at that.[14] The normative reasons underlying the choice between these two types of rules are not examined. Therefore, this literature is not very helpful in analysing and evaluating the modern law of contract, especially in the area of consumer protection.

Within the European theatre, it seems that the French legal system is the most fertile tree in the garden of mandatory law. Treatment of the subject is centred on Article 6 of the *Code civil*, which famously provides that

> On ne peut déroger, par des conventions particulières, aux lois qui intéressent l'ordre public et les bonnes meures.

Even though the German Civil Code contains a similar provision (§ 134 BGB), Article 6 of the *Code civil* serves as a statutory anchor for a discussion of mandatory rules in private law generally. In contrast, the scholarly discourse in Germany always remained focused on public law statutes, whether from the criminal or the administrative law branches.[15] The mandatory rules of private law are not deemed to fall within the subject matter of § 134 BGB, as they are self-enforcing — in the sense that they invalidate agreements of their own accord.

French legal doctrine distinguishes between two categories of the *ordre public*, termed *ordre public classique* and *ordre public économique*.[16] The former category refers to the statutory provisions protecting the public interest in the narrow sense of the various branches of government, foreign policy, questions of diplomacy, defence, and the like. The *ordre public économique*, in contrast, is the modern version of public policy that aims at protecting certain classes of parties that are thought to be in a weaker position in comparison to their counterparts.

[13] A Schwarz, 'Karl Llewellyn and the Origins of Contract Theory' in JS Kraus and SD Walt (eds), *The Jurisprudential Foundations of Corporate and Commercial Law* (2000) 12, 15 ff; I Ayres, 'Response: Valuing Modern Contract Scholarship' (2003) 112 *Yale Law Journal* 881, 885ff; JH Langbein, 'Mandatory Rules in the Law of Trust' (2004) 98 *Northwestern University Law Review* 1105, 1106, fn 3.

[14] B Windscheid 'Lehrbuch des Pandektenrechts', Vol I, 7th edn (1891) § 30, 69; cf also H Dernburg, Pandekten, Vol I, 4th edn (1894)) § 31, 69.

[15] For an overview, see Armbrüster, in *Münchener Kommentar zum* BGB, 5th edn (2006) § 134, para 50ff

[16] F Chabas, *Lessons de droit civil, Obligations, Théorie générale*, 9th edn (1998) para 118ff; J Flour, J-L Aubert and E Savaux 'Droit civil, Les obligations', Vol I: L'acte juridique, 11th edn (2004) paras 282, 292; Terré, Simler and Lequette, *Droit civil*, Les *obligations*, 9th edn (2005) paras 377, 382; cf also Bénabent, *Droit civil*, Les *obligations*, 10th edn (2005) para 160.

The domain of the *ordre public économique* is the playground of today's lawmakers and contains such topics as the law of landlord and tenant, insurance law, labour law, and consumer law.[17]

3.3. The Draft Common Frame of Reference (DCFR)

The framers of the DCFR based their work on the four principles of freedom, security, justice, and efficiency.[18] No reasonable person would call these principles into question, but the problems only begin here as the four values may point in opposite directions. However, with respect to the relationship between contractual freedom and mandatory law, the solution is unequivocal — freedom of contract takes priority, since it serves as the 'starting point':

> As a rule, natural and legal persons should be free to decide whether or not to contract and with whom to contract. They should also be free to agree on the terms of their contract.[19]

For the purposes of this article, the second sentence is the crucial one: the default rule is that the parties are free to agree whatever terms best fit their interests. The position expressed in the introduction to the DCFR is affirmed by the operative part of the DCFR itself. The general provisions in Book II on 'Contracts and other juridical acts' include an article affirming the priority of party autonomy. Article II.–1:102 DCFR was modelled on Article 1:102 Principles of European Contract Law (PECL) and Articles 1.1 and 1.5 of the UNIDROIT Principles of International Commercial Contracts and reads as follows:

1. 'Parties are free to make a contract or other juridical act and to determine its contents, subject to any applicable mandatory rules.
2. Parties may exclude the application of any of the following rules relating to contracts or other juridical acts, or the rights and obligations arising from them, or derogate from or vary their effects, except as otherwise provided.
3. A provision to the effect that parties may not exclude the application of a rule or derogate from or vary its effects does not prevent a party from waiving a right which has already arisen and of which that party is aware.'

Paragraphs 1 and 2 of Article II.–1:102 DCFR make it clear that mandatory rules that place limits on the freedom of contract are the exception, not the rule. The 'ordinary' provisions of the DCFR are only of a default nature and have to step aside where the parties have provided otherwise. Article II.–1:102 (3) DCFR adds the qualification that even mandatory rules do not exclude the authority of the parties to waive any rights that have already accrued under such a scheme. This is

[17] Terré, Simler and Lequette, above n 16, para 384.

[18] C von Bar, E Clive and H Schulte-Nölke (eds), *Principles, Definitions and Model Rules of European Private Law: Draft Common Frame of Reference (DCFR)* (Outline Edition 2009) 60.

[19] ibid 62.

important, as the parties to a dispute that is governed by mandatory law would otherwise lack the authority to settle their dispute by any means other than litigation to the very end. As a settlement necessarily requires some measure of retreat by both parties, it involves a partial waiver of vested rights. Without Article II.–1:102 (3) DCFR, the parties would be unable to settle controversial cases.

4. ECONOMIC ANALYSIS

As has already been indicated, economic analysis has made major contributions in advancing the understanding of mandatory law.

4.1. The Economic Justification for Freedom of Contract

Before delving deeper into the topic of mandatory rules, it is important to outline and define what is in question. Even though economic theory does allow for mandatory rules, freedom of contract remains the overriding principle.[20] Within the neoclassical economic model, the market is the mechanism for making social decisions on the allocation of the means of production and the distribution of goods and services. The invisible hand of the market is thought to be superior to the conscious decisions on allocation and distribution made by a collective decision-maker such as a planning agency. The market is populated by parties who are strictly rational, in the sense that they strive to maximise their utility, given their preferences. The primary function of the law of contract is to enable the parties to go beyond spot-transactions and to agree on sequential performance.[21] Where one party performs unilaterally, it exposes itself to exploitation by the other side, which may renege on its promise and decide to run with the value delivered to it. Basically, the same problem arises in respect to contracts involving customised goods that still need to be produced by the seller. Again, the seller runs the risk of exploitation by an opportunistic buyer who may refuse to accept the goods and pay the price.[22]

By focusing on the organisation of efficient exchanges over time, economic analysis certainly captures an important function of contract law. However, it must not be overlooked that contract law has a role to play in spot-transactions too. Tellingly, the Roman law of sale was developed in regard to such spot-transactions, agreed on in the open market where foodstuffs, animals, and slaves were traded.[23] The ancient 'warranty law' was created by the Roman police who

[20] BE Hermalin, A Katz and R Craswell, 'Contract Law'. in AM Polinsky and S Shavell (eds), *Handbook of Law and Economics* Vol I (2007) 21ff.

[21] Ibid 9ff; Shavell, *Foundations of Economic Analysis of Law* (2004) 9ff.

[22] Hermalin, Katz and Craswell, above n 20, 10 ff.

[23] R Zimmermann, *The Law of Obligations* (1990) 311ff; M Kaser and R Knütel, *Römisches Privatrecht*, 19th edn (2008) § 41 para 1 ff.

monitored and controlled the activities on the open market, and settled disputes where they arose. Such transactions raised a range of problems, such as the passing of risk, the consequences of defects, and liability in damages for the consequences of such defects. This shows that there is a need for legal rules — a law of contract — even for spot-transactions. In the absence of an elaborate 'warranty law', the parties to a contract of sale would have to draft, negotiate, and agree the relevant rules themselves, at the price of considerable transaction costs.

4.2. The Economic Justification for Default Rules

The previous point highlights the economic justification for the parts of contract law, which operate by formulating default rules, from which the parties may derogate if they so wish. In theory, the parties could devise and agree such rules among themselves, rendering a law of contract, made by legislators or judges, seem unnecessary. The real function of default rules is to facilitate transactions by relieving the parties of the burden of drafting and negotiating their own 'law of contract'. Default rules reduce transaction costs and, therefore, increase the benefit of the bargain to be shared between the parties. In addition, they increase the amount of transactions that can be executed in any given economy. These desirable effects require the default rule in question to provide a solution that reflects what both parties would have agreed on, had they attempted to achieve a negotiated solution. Where the pool of parties is not homogenous, in the sense that one group would have agreed on rule X and another one on rule Y, lawmakers and judges should pick the rule that the majority of potential parties would have settled on had they negotiated the issue — the so-called 'majoritarian default rule.'[24] The costs of contracting around the default rule are relevant only where such costs differ between several groups of parties. Given these differences, the objective is to reduce the combined transaction costs incurred by all the parties concerned.[25]

In recent years, the economic analysis of default rules has developed far beyond the function of saving transaction costs. The theory of penalty default rules points out that there are default rules that do not reflect the intentions of the majority of potential parties, but are contrary to the parties' interests.[26] Their purpose is not to economise on transaction costs but to provide the better-informed party with incentives to share the information with the other side. Here, default rules work as a remedy to an asymmetrical distribution of information relevant to a certain transaction.

[24] R Cooter and T Ulen, *Law and Economics*, 5th edn (2008) 221; Shavell, above n 21, 299 ff.

[25] Hermalin, Katz and Craswell, above n 20, 87.

[26] Path-breaking: I Ayres and R Gertner, 'Filling Gaps in Incomplete Contracts: An Economic Theory of Default Rules' (1989) 99 *Yale Law Journal* 87; advocating a different opinion: E Posner, 'There are No Penalty Default Rules in Contract Law' (2006) 33 *Florida State University Law Review* 563.

Another strand of research on default rules questions the assumption that the parties will deviate and create their own rule when the solution supplied by the default rule contradicts their interests. In theory, a tailor-made solution will only be negotiated where the value added by this solution is greater than the transaction costs incurred by achieving it. In practice, it seems that parties fail to derogate from default rules even where transaction costs are relatively low. It seems therefore, that default rules may be much 'stickier' than suggested by models of contracting.[27]

4.3. The Economic Theory of Mandatory Law

Compared with default rules, mandatory rules within the law of contract have received less attention.

4.3.1. Internalisation of External Costs

A classic purpose of mandatory law is to prevent the parties from imposing costs on non-parties.[28] In the interest of social welfare, the parties to a transaction should consider not only its total benefit, but also the full costs. Where this objective requires the creation of legal rules that attribute external costs to the party whose activity caused them, it is self-evident that the application of such provisions cannot be excluded by mere agreement of the parties. If the parties were allowed to contract around a rule that aims to internalise external costs, they would certainly take advantage of this authority. If it were possible to validly agree on a contract to the detriment of a third party, the parties would do so. Therefore, provisions against externalisation of costs must necessarily be mandatory in nature.

4.3.2. Safeguarding Rational Decisions

Another function of mandatory law is to serve as a safeguard for the rules on contract formation, or at least for relevant parts of the law dealing with contract formation.[29] Every legal system includes provisions that are meant to protect those members of society that are unable to make rational decisions and to act accordingly. The classic example is the law of capacity, which invalidates promises

[27] R Korobkin, 'The Status Quo Bias and Contract Default Rules' (1998) 83 *Cornell Law Review* 608; *id* 'The Endowment Effect and Legal Analysis' (2003) 97 *Northwestern University Law Review* 1227; O Ben-Shahar and JAE Pottow, 'On the Stickiness of Default Rules' (2006) 33 *Florida State University Law Review* 651; L Bernstein, 'Social Norms and Default Rules Analysis' (1993) 3 *Southern California Interdisciplinary Law Journal* 59ff.

[28] Cooter and Ulen, above n 24, 226 ff; Hermalin, Katz and Craswell, above n 20, 30 ff; Shavell, above n 21, 320.

[29] Cooter and Ulen, above n 24, 225 ff; cf also Hermalin, Katz and Craswell, above n 20, 40 ff; T Kronmann, 'Contract Law and Distributive Justice' (1980) 89 *Yale Law Journal* 472 490ff.

made by minors and the mentally ill. These rules are supported by economic reasoning: individual decisions only lead to efficient outcomes if they are made by rational agents.[30] Even though adults are assumed to have such capacity, the ability to make reasonable choices may be absent or impaired in a particular situation. For this reason contracts concluded under the influence of fraud or duress do not qualify as a means of resource allocation.[31]

4.3.3. Compensation of Informational Asymmetries

Another domain of mandatory law are situations where information is asymmetrically distributed between the parties. As long as this asymmetry only has distributional consequences, it is of no concern to economics. For the purposes of allocative efficiency, it does not matter how the surplus is divided between the parties.

However, informational asymmetries may also distort the allocation of scarce resources. Akerlof's seminal work in this area was concerned with the market for used cars. The upshot of the analysis of a so-called 'lemons market' was that the uncertainty of buyers about the quality of the cars offered, resulted in a 'race-to-the-bottom' that drove quality and prices down to a level that did not reflect the interests of either party. The situation may be remedied by imposing a 'duty to inform' on the party with superior information towards the party lacking it. An alternative is to make that party liable for breach of an implied warranty of fitness for ordinary use.

From the perspective of paternalistic elements in contract law, another consequence of informational asymmetry is even more interesting, namely restrictions on signalling.[32] In essence, signals are devices that a party with private information may use in order to credibly transmit this information to the contracting partner. Signals are helpful where the private information is beneficial to the party with such information, because it suggests that the quality of the goods or services promised, or the probability of performance, will be above average. A seller offering high-quality commodities might offer long-term warranties in order to induce buyers to pay a higher price in exchange. A construction company may agree to high penalty clauses in case of late completion, in order to induce the owner to accept its bid, even if it comes at a higher price. But even for diligent sellers and construction companies, the use of such signals comes at a considerable cost, which may pose a significant risk. Even assuming a perfectly rational actor, it may be that owners and buyers will find it difficult to separate good-type sellers or construction companies from bad-type sellers or construction companies, triggering a process that leads to ever more intensive signalling.

30 Hermalin, Katz and Craswell, above n 20, 40 ff.

31 Shavell, above n 21, 329 ff.

32 P Aghion and BE Hermalin, 'Legal Restrictions on Private Contracts Can Enhance Efficiency' (1990) 6 *Journal of Law, Economics and Organization* 381; K Hermalin and Craswell, above n 20, 34 ff.

In the end, good-type sellers or construction companies might have an interest in offering clauses calling for excessive penalties, even though they would be better off with more moderate penalties. This effect has been identified even without introducing psychological dispositions, such as over-optimism, self-serving bias and underestimation of low-probability events, which may reinforce the tendency to 'signal' excessively. Mandatory restrictions on signalling may, therefore, be in the interest of both parties. A pertinent example is the authority of courts to take action against excessive penalty and liquidated damages clauses.

4.3.4. Monopolistic Markets

An obvious case for legal intervention by means of mandatory law is the presence of a monopoly.[33] However, the preservation of competitive markets is primarily within the remit of competition or antitrust law, not of the law of contract. Competition law itself operates through the use of mandatory law. Otherwise, cartel members would (of course) exclude the application of competition law by agreement, which would render the entire legal framework meaningless.

Outside the domain of hard-core cartels, the division of labour between competition law, on the one hand, and contract law, on the other, is less clear. Tellingly, Article 102 TFEU (formerly Art 82 EC) prohibits the abuse of a dominant position in the market and, in doing so, invalidates contractual provisions that grow out of such abuse.[34] Vice versa, beyond the scope of competition law, a whole range of 'small cases' remain where the market stays competitive, while the transaction in question is affected by monopoly power. The rules banning usury are a pertinent example of the reaction of a legal system to a case of 'situational monopoly'.[35] Here, one party exploits the distress of the other party in order to extract benefits that it would not be able to obtain outside the distressed situation.

5. PATERNALISM — AN ANTIDOTE TO ECONOMIC ANALYSIS?

How does paternalism relate to economic analysis, particularly in the area of contract law? It is widely believed that paternalism is in conflict with economic reasoning, or even acts as its antidote. In order to obtain a more nuanced perspective, the concept of paternalism needs some clarification. Adopting a definition suggested by Gerald Dworkin, paternalism means 'the interference with a person's liberty of action justified by reasons referring exclusively to the

[33] Cooter and Ulen, above n 24, 230 ff; Hermalin, Katz and Craswell, above n 20, 39 ff.

[34] This is not to say that Art 102 EC is limited to invalidating contracts; for an overview, see RJ van den Bergh and PD Camesasca, *European Competition Law and Economics: A Comparative Perspective* (2006) 247 ff.

[35] Cooter and Ulen, above n 24, 230 ff.

welfare of the person being coerced'.[36] As has been pointed out in the literature, the requirement of 'coercion' must not be understood too narrowly.[37] In order to qualify as paternalistic, the intervention may also take advantage of the unconsciousness of a person (eg conducting a blood transfusion on an individual who rejects such measures for religious reasons), or may remove an opportunity that a person would otherwise have used at a later point in time (eg the removal of drugs from the bedroom of a depressed person in order to prevent suicide).

Given this definition — interference with a person's liberty against her will for the purpose of furthering her own welfare — it seems obvious that paternalism is at odds with economic theory. As explained above, economic reasoning maintains that the satisfaction of individual preferences promotes the common good. The underlying assumption is that individuals know best what is good for them. Paternalism relies on the opposite view: that individuals are error-prone in regard to the promotion of their own well-being. Therefore, it seems incompatible with economic reasoning.

Matters are, in fact, more complicated than the incompatibility thesis suggests. This is because economics is not concerned with the matter-of-fact satisfaction of real preferences, but with rational decisions that lead to efficient outcomes.[38] If the objective of economics was the satisfaction of actual preferences of individuals — and nothing more — one would not have to be concerned with asymmetrical information and other obstacles to rational decision-making. As a normative discipline, economic analysis presupposes that decisions are made rationally, and on the basis of as much information as is available, given the costs of gathering and processing such information. Where the condition of full information is not given, it is believed that regulatory interference with market processes, in the name of economic efficiency, is justified.

However, the argument does not stop there. Even absent asymmetries of information, it is conceivable that there are individuals who are unable to make rational decisions; that is, to choose rationally between different options. In as much as reality does not correspond with this assumption, it is difficult to see why, from an economic point of view, the law should not intervene. Not surprisingly therefore, Kaplow and Shavell argue that 'proper welfare economic analysis takes these imperfections [ie, limitations on individual's decision-making] into account'.[39] Their conclusion is:

[36] G Dworkin, 'Paternalism' (1972) 56 *The Monist* 64, 65.

[37] J Kleinig, *Paternalism* (1984) 5 ff; Culver, B Gert and CM Culver, 'Paternalistic Behaviour' (1976) 6 *Philosophy and Public Affairs* 45 46ff, whose critique of Dworkin's definition seems overdrawn.

[38] For a detailed account, see E Zamir, 'The Efficiency of Paternalism' (1998) 84 *Virginia Law Review* 229, 241 ff.

[39] Kaplow and Shavell, above n 4, 410 ff.

> … that the empirical inquiry becomes more difficult when individuals' choices in the marketplace or in other settings are not reliable indicators of their actual well-being.[40]

In summary, economic theory operates on the basis of a stylised, ambitious concept of rational choice and does not take the actual choices made by individuals as a given. Therefore, standard textbooks on economic analysis of contract law do not criticise or even reject traditional legal concepts, such as capacity, fraud and duress, even though they serve to invalidate promises that were made in accordance with actual preferences.[41] In the textbook of Cooter and Ulen, the rule invalidating promises made by incompetent persons is explained as follows:

> A rational decision-maker can rank outcomes in order from least preferred to most preferred. In order to rank outcomes, the decision-maker must have stable preferences. If the decision-maker's preferences are unstable or disorderly, he or she cannot make competent judgements about his or her own interests. Such a person is legally incompetent. For example, children, the insane, and some mentally retarded adults are legally incompetent.[42]

No-one will dispute that the preferences of children must not be taken at face-value and that this justifies legal intervention. It should also be clear that this intervention is of a paternalistic nature. The actual preferences of minors, the mentally retarded and the insane are discounted in favour of decisions made by others — parents or guardians — in 'the best interest' of the child or adult. Even though the case for intervention is uncontroversial, the justification seems questionable. Is it really true that children under the age of majority and mentally disabled people are unable to form stable preferences? Imagine a mentally disabled billionaire who developed a habit of giving money away randomly, such as paying taxi-drivers a fortune for short journeys. The preference of making other people happy, by showering them with money may be stable, yet the law would intervene nonetheless. Of course, faithful economists might reject the intervention as unwarranted in the previous example, but it is hard to deny that there are other examples where even stable preferences will be set aside. If a twelve-year-old develops a stable preference for heroin, few economists would dispute that paternalistic intervention is justified.

If it is accepted that economic analysis is built on rational decision-making and not simply on maximising the actual preferences of the moment, which are formed on the basis of deficient information, then it is immediately clear that the problem is not black and white.

An adult person is certainly in a better position to form stable preferences and to act accordingly, than a child or mentally retarded person might be; but it is obvious that adults differ dramatically not only in their ability to make rational

40 ibid 413.

41 R Cooter and T Ulen, above n 24, 279 ff.

42 ibid 280.

decisions but also in their capacity to form preferences that satisfy the conditions of commensurability, transitivity, invariance, cancellation, and dominance.[43] Among those, the requirement of commensurability is by far the most important and complex. It requires that actors are able to identify the perceived consequences of all the options available in a given situation in advance, to measure the expected utilities, and to transform the result into numbers, in order to make a comparison and to pick the option that promises the most utility.[44] Particularly where outcomes are uncertain, a calculation such as this is complicated, even for academics with plenty of time, let alone ordinary people operating in real-life situations under considerable time pressure.

The next step in the analysis is to confront the question of whether it may even be legitimate to override the actual preferences of an individual in a given situation and to reshape them in the desired way. Whether this is done for the purpose of furthering some abstract notion of the 'common good' or the 'good life', goes beyond the scope of this article. However, the issue of paternalism arises where the intervention is justified by reference to the interests of the party whose preferences are to be realigned.[45] A pertinent example is the regulation or prohibition of smoking, even in areas where third parties are not affected at all or are only trivially affected.[46] As smoking harms the health of the smoker, such regulations are of a paternalistic nature: the smoker has the preference to smoke but must not indulge in this habit for the sake of his own health. By banning smoking, lawmakers may hope that the habit or addiction may subside in order for the smokers themselves to benefit in the long run. This line of reasoning raises a serious issue: whether the actual preferences of the individual at the time she wants to light a cigarette, may be set aside in light of her perceived preferences years later, when disease would set in.

It seems that there is nothing within the economic approach that stands in the way of a critical assessment of preferences. A purely paternalistic approach would measure the actual preferences of an individual against an 'objective', external yardstick in order to justify intervention, if the two do not match up. An individualistic approach would not subscribe to an external measure of well-being, but would rather rely on the articulated long-term preferences of the individual concerned, or even the future preferences of the individual as perceived by the scholar or policy-maker instead. There is no point denying that reliance on articulated — but not actuated — preferences, or even the construction of future preferences, remains problematic, since it opens the door to the imposition of external conceptions of 'rational preferences'. Therefore, lawmakers

[43] R Korobkin and T Ulen, 'Law and Behavioral Science: Removing the Rationality Assumption from Law and Economics' (2000) 88 *California Law Review* 1051, 1064.

[44] Kaplow and Shavell, above n 4, 18, fn 6.

[45] cf RH Thaler and CR Sunstein, *Nudge* (2008) 4ff.

[46] For a thorough analysis, see RE Goodin, 'The Ethics of Smoking' (1989) 99 *Ethics* 582ff; see also JD Hanson and KD Logue, 'The Costs of Cigarettes: The Economic Case for Ex Post Incentive-Based Regulation' (1998) 107 *Yale Law Journal* 1163 1203ff.

and judges would be well-advised to act with restraint when disregarding the actual preferences of the individual in favour of 'rational preferences'. Moreover, there is nothing that stands in the way of taking future preferences into account, even where they contradict the actual preferences of the individual at the present time.

6. CATEGORIES OF INTERVENTION

The next step in the analysis is to identify situations where the intervention of the law in the form of mandatory rules is warranted.

6.1. Protection of Self-Determination

6.1.1. Capacity, Fraud, and Duress

Significant parts of the law of contract aim at protecting the autonomy of the contracting parties in the sense of rational self-determination. The classic examples are the rules on capacity, which protect people who are incapable of acting rationally. It is self-evident that the legal rules protecting minors and the mentally ill are not themselves subject to derogation by party agreement. A person suffering from Alzheimer's disease cannot waive the protection accorded by the law.

The rules on capacity do not exhaust the basic problem that people may conclude contracts in situations where they cannot act rationally. Capacity is a borderline case, as it is not concerned with the particular situation in which a promise is made, but with the characteristics of the person making the promise. The traditional doctrines on fraud and duress go one step further, in that they do not react to the condition of the person making the promise but to the situation in which the promise is made. For promises made at gunpoint, the law rightly presumes that the person concerned was incapable of making a rational choice, even though the promisor was a healthy adult. Basically, the same considerations apply to cases of fraud. Here, the choice was influenced by error, and the error was caused intentionally by the other side. The reason why the contracting partner engaged in such a manoeuvre is his assumption that, without the misrepresentation, the promise would not have been made. Again, it is obvious that such circumstances are inimical to rational choice, to the effect that the promise may be set aside at the discretion of the promisor. The protection from fraud would be meaningless if it were possible to waive such protection by means of an act that is itself a product of fraud. The rules against fraud are mandatory for a good reason.

Whether the rules on capacity, insanity, fraud, and duress may be categorised as 'paternalistic' is subject to debate. As explained above, they are not only staples of Western legal systems but are also supported by economic analysis.[47] Nonetheless, it seems possible to argue that the 'natural' will and the real preferences of the person are set aside where the law intervenes to protect the young and mentally ill, as well as normal adults acting under the influence of fraud or duress. Likewise, the use of rational self-determination as a yardstick for measuring real-life transactions may be disparaged as camouflage for the exogenous preferences of the decision-maker. Those arguments do not carry much weight, however. It is simply implausible to celebrate the promises of minors and the mentally ill as acts of self-determination. Furthermore, while the law places the authority to make promises in the hands of parents or guardians where capacity is lacking, it does not authorise a third party to make choices on behalf of others in the case of fraud and duress. Here, it is simply wrong to label the intervention as paternalistic.

In current legal discourse, the traditional doctrines are beyond dispute. What moves the lawmakers and judges of today are not these classical exceptions to the principle of *pacta sunt servanda*, but the expansion of such rules into new areas, such as distance and doorstep selling, consumer credit, consumer sale, and consumer law in general. These are the instances that French legal doctrine has succinctly classified as touching upon the *ordre public économique*, which is to say, calling for the protection of the 'weaker party' within the contractual relationship.[48]

6.1.2. Doorstep Selling

Over the years, the European Union has created a body of law that aims to protect the consumer by introducing rights of withdrawal from contracts that were validly concluded. The starting point for this development was the Doorstep Selling Directive of 1985.[49] Pursuant to its Article 3, the Directive applies to contracts for the supply of goods or services by a trader to a consumer that are concluded away from business premises. Article 5 of the Directive confers upon the consumer a right to withdraw her promise within a specified time after receipt of a notice by the trader informing her of this right. Pursuant to Article 6 of the Directive, the consumer may not waive the rights conferred by the Directive. Article II.–5:101, Article II.–1:201 DCFR follow the same lines as the current Directive.

The purpose of the Doorstep Selling Directive is explained in Recital 5, which provides that the trader meets the consumer unprepared for contract negotiations and in a situation where she cannot compare the quality and price of the trader's offer with the offers of other traders. The rationale behind the right to withdraw is to enable the consumer to understand her obligations under the

[47] See section 3.3.2 above.
[48] See section 2.2 above.
[49] Council Directive 85/577/EEC, see above n 7.

contract and — additionally — to engage in some sort of cost-benefit analysis with respect to competing offers. The solicitation of a contract away from business premises therefore poses a serious threat to the rational self-determination of the consumer. However, the source of the most serious risk to the self-determination of consumers is not mentioned in the recitals, namely the fact that the seller (or rather his agent) intrudes into the privacy of the home of the potential buyer and thus forces a personal relationship on the buyer from which the latter may have difficulty escaping. The most striking case is the one where an agent visits the consumer at home, where the consumer may feel that the only way to make the sales agent leave is to sign the contract with which she is confronted. It is much easier to refuse a purchase in the anonymity of a public store than inside one's own home, sitting eye-to-eye with the seller or his agent.

In summary, the right of the consumer to withdraw a promise made on her doorstep is well-founded. The current Proposal for a Directive on Consumer Rights will do well to maintain it.[50] It is also obvious that the right of withdrawal cannot be waived by a transaction concluded on the doorstep of the consumer. Precisely because the self-determination of the consumer is at risk, the exclusion of the right of withdrawal from a contract contaminated by such risk must be ineffective. For this reason, the right of withdrawal must be mandatory.

6.1.3. Distance Contracts

Another situation where a consumer operating on the European market has a right to withdraw from a contract for the sale of goods or the provision of services involves distance contracts. Under Article 6(1) of Directive 97/7/EC, the consumer has to exercise this right within seven days of receiving the goods.[51] Similar provisions are to be found in Article II.–5:101, Article II.–1:201 (2) DCFR. Even though the legal tool remains the same, the right of withdrawal in cases of distance selling rests on a completely different foundation than the one granted in the case of doorstep sales. The latter is meant to allow the consumer to rethink and re-evaluate a deal struck in a situation inimical to rational decision-making. This concern is missing in cases of distance selling.

A consumer sitting at home in front of her computer is under no pressure whatsoever to enter into a transaction. She may freely decide to leave the website at any time, to compare offers of other sellers and come back whenever she wishes. The right of withdrawal is not a response to a situation where the rational self-determination of the consumer is put at risk. This does not mean, however, that the right of withdrawal in cases of distance selling lacks a normative foundation. Quite simply, it serves the purpose of allowing the consumer to physically investigate the goods before making a final decision to buy, or to reject them. As a consequence, the time limit for exercising the right of withdrawal

[50] Proposal for a Directive on Consumer Rights, see above n 8, Art 8ff
[51] Directive 97/7/EC, see above n 7.

does not run from the day of the conclusion of the contract but from the day when the consumer receives the goods in question, that is, the day of delivery.

Why is it important to identify the normative concerns underlying the different rights of withdrawal? The answer is that the normative justification of the right to withdraw is important in regard to the choice between their default or mandatory nature. As regards contracts concluded away from business premises, it has been pointed out that the legal regime protecting the consumer must be mandatory, because the protection would otherwise be worthless. This reasoning does not correspond to cases of distance selling, for the simple reason that the conclusion of the contract is not contaminated with a potential deficit of rational self-determination. Therefore, a waiver of the right to withdraw is not suspect per se, even if it is agreed at the time of contract. A consumer may rationally decide to waive the right of withdrawal in exchange for a better price. Intermediate solutions may also be devised. In particular, the contract could allow for a right of withdrawal but allocate the costs of withdrawal (for example the costs of sending the goods back and forth and repackaging them for another sale), entirely to the consumer. Under Article 6(1) of the current Directive on Distance Contracts, the only amount that may be charged to the consumer for exercising her right of withdrawal is the direct cost of returning the goods.

The argument for party autonomy outlined above may be criticised on grounds of commercial practices observed in markets for distance selling. In fact, most sellers that are active in this segment of the market offer rights of withdrawal voluntarily, and go even further than the Directive requires in taking the full costs of withdrawal upon themselves. The motive behind this practice is, of course, to entice the consumer to order the goods in the first place. If an internet shoe seller did not offer a withdrawal right, hardly anybody would order the goods, even if they were sold at low prices. The same consideration applies to clothes and other goods that must 'fit' in order to make sense for the buyer.

Even though it is doubtlessly true that, even without the Directive on Distance Contracts, rights of withdrawal would be offered and agreed on a voluntary basis, this does not establish a need to make the right of withdrawal mandatory. In a sense, the lawmakers in Brussels arrived at the same conclusion because they limited the scope of the Directive by means of an impressive set of exclusions. Pursuant to Article 6(3) of Directive 97/7/EC, the consumer may not exercise the right of withdrawal where any of the following transactions is involved:

— contracts for the provision of services if performance has begun, with the consumer's agreement, before the end of the time limit for withdrawal;
— contracts for the supply of goods or services the price of which is dependent on fluctuations in the financial market which cannot be controlled by the supplier;
— contracts for the supply of goods made to the consumer's specifications or clearly personalised or which, by reason of their nature, cannot be returned or are liable to deteriorate or expire rapidly;

- contracts for the supply of audio or video recordings or computer software which were unsealed by the consumer;
- contracts for the supply of newspapers, periodicals and magazines; and
- contracts for gaming and lottery services.

Interestingly, Article 6(3) of Directive 97/7/EC does not curtail the parties' freedom of contract, as the parties are free to agree a right of withdrawal if they wish to do so. It only abolishes the mandatory nature of such a right and also removes the corresponding default rule. Without going into the details of every category cited in Article 6(3) of Directive 97/7/EC, a first glance shows that there are valid reasons for their exclusion. If it were possible to withdraw from a contract for the supply of a newspaper some days after delivery, there would be a strong incentive to exercise that right after having read the paper. A similar form of moral hazard would exist if one were allowed to return unsealed audio CDs to the seller. In these situations, the creation of an unconditional right to withdraw would virtually destroy the distance selling markets in regard to the goods in question.

The current Proposal for a Directive on Consumer Rights intends to keep the mandatory withdrawal right but to expand the catalogue of exceptions further than Article 6(3) of Directive 97/7/EC. Article 19(1) of the Draft Directive would add contracts for the supply of wine, provided that the price was agreed at the time of the conclusion of the contract, and that delivery was arranged for more than 30 days later and that the price of the wine was subject to market fluctuations beyond the control of the seller (Art 19(1)(d) of the Draft Directive). Furthermore, under Article 19(1)(h) of the Draft Directive, contracts concluded at an auction shall be exempted from the mandatory right of withdrawal. The fact that the Commission has proposed expanding the catalogue of exceptions is telling. Again, it does not support the conclusion that withdrawal rights are dysfunctional in the case of distance selling. What it does show, however, is that the practice of contracting is very diverse, and that the interests of rational parties may differ from one situation to another, making it impossible to come up with a one-size-fits-all solution. It is highly unlikely that the catalogue of exceptions supplied by Article 19(1) of the Draft Directive exhausts the full range of cases, whereby a right of withdrawal is unwarranted as it does not correspond to the interests of the parties. This is immediately apparent with regard to future contracts, which are exempted if they call either for the supply of goods or services which are subject to price shifts in accordance with fluctuations in the financial market that cannot be controlled by the supplier, or for the delivery of wine at a later point in time. Quite obviously, there are many goods beside wine that may be sold under a forward contract, and the fluctuation of the market value of this good may be due to reasons other than fluctuations in the financial market. Other examples can be readily found, such as champagne, whiskey, or cognac. This critique is not meant to suggest that the catalogue of exemptions supplied by Article 19(1) of the Draft Directive should be expanded. It is a hopeless enterprise to try to draw up an exhaustive list of cases in which the right of withdrawal should not be available in advance. The lesson to be learnt from the Commission's efforts to rework the list is that the issue should best be left to party autonomy. The right of withdrawal should not be mandatory, but rather function as a default solution from which the parties should be allowed to derogate if they wish to do so.

The proposal to allow party agreements to exclude the right to withdraw is subject to objections turning on the prediction that sellers would immediately resort to this option if it were made available. This objection is without a sound basis for a number of reasons. Sellers engaged in distance selling have a strong incentive to offer an unconditional right to withdraw voluntarily. Even outside the area of distance selling, many shops are willing to grant their customers unconditional rights of return, which allow the buyer to return the goods in exchange for the purchase price within a fixed period of time. The reason why shop owners offer this privilege is not their altruism, but their interest in increasing the number of transactions. Obviously, consumers are more willing to buy products if they enjoy the option of returning them in case of remorse. The right to return works as an incentive to purchase. Therefore, it need not be made mandatory.

The second argument against the objection to party autonomy is based on Directive 93/13/EC on unfair terms in consumer contracts, which authorises the courts to intervene where the interests of consumers are harmed without just cause. The function and justification of this instrument will be explored in detail below. At this point of the analysis, it is important to point out that court control over consumer contracts, as established by Directive 93/13/EC, makes it impossible for sellers engaged in distance selling to exclude the right of withdrawal even where there is no valid reason to do so. A court would always be authorised to intervene if a seller of shoes or clothes excluded this right without a valid cause. The modern law of contract need not choose between unlimited party autonomy and mandatory rules but may opt for a third way, between the two extremes, namely court control over individual contracts where terms derogate from the default rules set by lawmakers. There is no evidence that this instrument would not work well in the area of distance selling and rights of withdrawal.

6.2. Court Control over Contract Terms

Directive 93/13/EEC on unfair terms in consumer contracts is a 'hybrid instrument' in several respects. It occupies the grey area between mandatory law and default rules. More precisely, it transforms the vast body of contractual default rules into semi-mandatory rules. The result of the transformation is not the full exclusion of party autonomy, because it is for the courts to decide, on a case-by-case basis, whether a contractual provision is unfair and thus not binding on the consumer (see Art 5(1) of Directive 93/13/EEC). The DCFR supplies a similar regime in Article II–9:401 ff. DCFR. Court control over individual cases substitutes the flat invalidation of contractual terms, which is the function of mandatory law. From a functional perspective, however, the legal regime of the Unfair Terms Directive also stands between the traditional positions. Given the current state of European contract law, and the framing of the problem of unfair terms as one of consumer protection, this function is difficult to discern. Its purpose is not to protect consumers as such, but to provide a remedy for situations in which the chance for rational choice is impaired. This is the case where, in the course of contract formation, one party is presented with a set of standard business terms that the other has taken time and care to develop. Where small stakes are involved, the party presented with such terms lacks any incentive to become active, ie to read the terms, to analyse them, and to engage in negotiations with the party that has drafted them. The stakes do not warrant the effort, so it is rational to remain apathetic. In itself, such rational apathy poses no problem as market forces drive the quality of goods and services traded in a competitive environment up to the efficient level. Nobody would argue with the baker about the composition of his bread, but this kind of ignorance and lack of interest remains innocent for product quality, because buyers will turn away from bakeries that offer sub-standard bread. With regard to contract terms, matters are different. Nobody cares about the fine print embodied in contract forms, because disputes are low-probability events that remain outside the focus of deliberate choice. As a consequence, sellers who offer high-quality terms cannot recoup the additional costs involved by charging a higher price, because buyers are not interested in the quality of contract terms and therefore unwilling to pay a higher price for a high-quality contract.

This process results in a 'market for lemons', as defined in the seminal article by Akerlof, in which the used car market serves as an example.[52] In a nutshell, the ignorance of the buyers about the quality of the cars put up for sale drives down the price they are willing to pay for a car, which in turn makes it rational for owners of high-quality cars to drop out. In the next round, the expectation of buyers is for even poorer cars, so that another group of sellers drops out, and so on. This process may continue until all potential parties have withdrawn from the market or, more realistically, when only bad cars (lemons) are offered for poor prices. Essentially, the same reasoning applies to the fine print of contract terms.[53] As pertains to contract terms, the market will never dry up completely,

[52] G Akerlof, 'The Market for 'Lemons': Qualitative Uncertainty and the Market Mechanism' (1970) 84 *Quarterly Journal of Economics* 488.

[53] The application of the 'lemons market' problem to standard contract terms is popular in German legal literature, less so with American writers: M Adams, 'Ökonomische Analyse des Gesetzes zur Regelung des Rechts der Allgemeinen Geschäftsbedingungen' in M Neumann (ed), *Ansprüche, Eigentums- und Verfügungsrechte* (1984) 655, 660 ff; H Kötz, *JuS* 2003, 209, 211 ff; HB Schäfer and C Ott, *Ökonomische Analyse des Zivilrechts*, 4th edn (2005) 513ff; G Wagner, *Prozeßverträge* (1998) 126ff; MI Meyerson, 'The Efficient Consumer Form Contract: Law and Economics Meets the Real World' (1990) 24 *Georgia Law Review* 594ff; but also Cooter and Ulen, above n 24, 302 ff; A Bebchuck and RA

because standard terms and conditions are not sufficiently important to influence the decision as to whether or not to execute the transaction. However, the inability of high-quality sellers to charge a price covering the additional costs results in a race-to-the-bottom where only the poorest terms are offered, ie those that are most detrimental to the interest of the buyer.

Put succinctly, the combination of rational apathy on the part of buyers and the ineffectiveness of market forces results in the degradation of contract terms. One remedy to this problem would be to transform the full set of default rules into mandatory law. However, in doing so, lawmakers would go overboard. The fact that the contract mechanism fails in the situation described above does not imply that the solution provided by a particular default rule is always first-best, ie that it always serves the legitimate interests of the parties in an optimal way. For the sake of party autonomy and contractual efficiency, it must remain possible to adapt the rules of contract law to specific situations by derogating from the off-the-rack solution embodied in a particular provision. The alternative to making contract law mandatory in its entirety is to address the problem more specifically by targeting the remedy on standard terms, and by abandoning the mechanism of mandatory law, in favour of court control over individual contracts. In essence, this is what the Unfair Terms Directive does.

The Proposal for a Directive on Consumer Rights follows the path of the Unfair Terms Directive in limiting court control to standard contracts with terms that were pre-formulated by the trader or a third party (Art 30(1) of the Draft Directive). In doing so, the Draft Directive inherits the shortcomings of the original scheme. Minor issues aside, the central point is that the problems standard contract terms raise for the functioning of the contract mechanism are not limited to B-to-C relations. Rather, it seems plausible that the same toxic combination of rational apathy and failure of competitive forces also affects transactions between businesses. In the business world too, it is rational, and therefore common, not to over-invest in contract negotiations. The fine print often goes unnoticed and unanalysed, even in transactions involving more than small stakes. It is certainly true that businesses are in a better position to protect themselves from oppressive terms, since they can draw up their own standard business terms and use them as a shield against a contract partner aiming to infringe on its interests. Furthermore, it is evident that high stakes often trigger serious efforts in negotiating a scheme of remedies for low-probability events such as breach of contract. However, these considerations suggest that standard business terms must not be judged by the same standard when used in B-to-B relations but also that they should remain within the remit of the control of a

Posner, 'One-Sided Contracts in Competitive Consumer Markets' (2007) 104 *Michigan Law Review* 827, 833, who argue on the basis of the assumption that 'a term [beneficial to the consumer] will be included if the average benefit exceeds the average cost' — which is the question.

court. This is why German law also authorises courts to exercise control over contract terms in B-to-B transactions.[54]

6.3. Regulating the Substance of Contracts: Consumer Sales

Within the European Union, the law of the sale of goods — as opposed to property — is governed by Directive 1999/44/EC on certain aspects of the sale of consumer goods and associated guarantees.[55] This directive created a regime of remedies for breach of contract for which the UN sales law — the Convention on the International Sale of Goods (CISG) — served as a model. This is not the place to discuss whether the substantive provisions of the Directive reflect sound policy or whether they deserve criticism. By and large, the framework of the Directive certainly has its merits.

For present purposes, the critical provision of the Directive is Article 7. Under Article 7(1) of the Consumer Sales Directive, 'any contractual terms or agreements concluded with the seller before the lack of conformity is brought to the seller's attention which directly or indirectly waive or restrict the rights resulting from this Directive shall ... not be binding on the consumer'. Article 7(1) also excludes party autonomy with regard to large portions of the law of sales, and the same applies under Article IV.A.–4:101 DCFR. This is remarkable given that the sale of goods is the most common and important type of transaction within the law of contracts. Given that mandatory law is not the natural mode of legislation in the area of contract law, there should be sufficient justification to use it anyway.

The Consumer Sales Directive tries to provide a 'high level of consumer protection' in order to strengthen consumer confidence and entice consumers to shop abroad.[56] For these purposes, the Commission thought it necessary to ensure that the legal protection afforded by the Directive would not be thwarted by an agreement between the parties that restricts the rights of consumers.[57] This reasoning is based on the implicit assumption that benefits conferred on consumer-buyers come at the expense of sellers, so that the allocation of rights and duties is an exercise in balancing the conflicting interests of the parties. In reality, the consumer-buyers themselves have to pay for any rights they have under a contract of sale, because the total costs associated with the relevant scheme of remedies will be reflected in the contract price. The more expansive the remedies conferred on the consumer, the higher the price the seller will charge for the product in question. Of course, this argument does not imply that

[54] R Zimmermann, *The New German Law of Obligations* (2005) 175 ff; BS Markesinis, H Unberath and A Johnston, *The German Law of Contract*, 2nd edn (2006) 165; P Ranieri, *Europäisches Obligationenrecht*, 3rd edn (2009) 385ff.

[55] Directive 1999/44/EC, see above n 7.

[56] ibid, at Recs 1 and 5.

[57] ibid, at Rec 22.

it is in the interests of the consumer to be confined to the narrowest scheme of remedies conceivable. Rational consumers will be prepared to pay extra in exchange for some protection from the delivery of defective products. Where this is the case, the law must supply the appropriate remedies. The crucial question for lawmakers legislating in the area of contract law, is not black and white, ie a choice between protecting consumer-buyers either extensively or narrowly. It is also misguided to think of the task in terms of balancing conflicting interests. Rather, the guideline must be the interests of rational consumers, given that they have to cover the costs of any expansion in the scope of protection accorded to them by the law.

Within the context of this article, the analysis of what the scheme of remedies for breach of contract of sale should look like need not be continued any further. The following discussion will assume that an appropriate scheme of remedies has, in fact, been put into place. Even then, lawmakers are well advised not to cast the solutions they arrived at in stone, but to allow for flexibility. Mandatory law excludes the authority of the parties from adapting the statutory scheme of remedies to their particular needs and their interests in the transaction at hand. The full exclusion of party autonomy may be warranted where lawmakers are confident that rational parties will never want to deviate from the scheme of remedies provided. These conditions may indeed be satisfied in reality. In all legal systems, for example, liability on the part of the seller for the consequences of defects cannot be excluded by contractual agreement where the seller, at the time of contract formation, knew of the defect and of the fact that it would deprive the buyer of the benefit of the bargain.[58] No rational consumer-buyer, if he or she thought about it, would agree to waive liability for known defects, if only for the reason that it would destroy any incentives on the part of the seller to be honest regarding the description of the goods he intends to sell.

The scheme of remedies supplied by the Directive on Consumer Sales does not pass this test. It is not the case that a rational buyer would never want to deviate from the statutory scheme of remedies set up by the Directive. In the present context, it is impossible to survey all the relevant situations systematically where rational consumer-buyers would have a legitimate interest in modifying or deviating from the Directive. Instead, anecdotal evidence must suffice. One striking example is the question of the allocation of the right to choose between replacement and repair, where defective goods have been delivered. Article 3(3) of Directive 1999/44/EC initially allocates this right to the consumer-buyer, in order to release the seller from the remedy chosen by the buyer, either where it is impossible, or where the remedy chosen involves disproportionate effort. This solution is reversed in the Proposal for a Directive on Consumer Rights, because Article 26(2) of the Draft Directive allocates the right to the seller whether to

[58] Art 8:109 PECL; Art 7.1.6 of the UNIDROIT Principles of International Commercial Contracts; §§ 276(3) and 444 BGB; but cf also *Photo Productions Ltd v Securicor Ltd* [1980] AC 827, 850 ff (HL, per Lord Diplock).

choose repair or replacement as a remedy for lack of conformity. There are certainly valid arguments in favour of both options, so that rational people may disagree on what the preferable rule is. In this situation, lawmakers should allow the parties to make their own choice instead of forcing the outcome of the legislative deliberations and power struggles of interest groups on the parties.

Another example of the adverse effects of the petrification of the law of sale concerns the market for used cars.[59] The German Federal Supreme Court (*Bundesgerichtshof*— BGH) has always allowed the seller of a used car to exclude liability for hidden defects. This case law formed the basis for the development of two separate markets for used cars. Potential buyers could choose between purchasing cars from a licensed dealer with a warranty and purchasing cars from an unauthorised dealership (often located in an abandoned gas station) without a warranty. It was common knowledge among consumers that there were two markets, and it was well understood that licensed dealers charged higher prices than the other traders who bought and sold cars for bargain prices. Depending on the attitude of potential purchasers towards the risk of a defect and on their willingness to pay, one group of consumers settled on the licensed dealers while others turned to the bargain traders. Particularly among young people with little money, plenty of time and some mechanical skills, it was common to buy a car for a low price without a warranty. With the enactment of the Directive on Consumer Sales, this bifurcated structure has been seriously impaired, if not destroyed. It is no longer possible to buy a car from a trader without a warranty. As a point of clarification with regard to the sale of used goods, Article 7(2) of Directive 1999/44/EC authorises member states to allow the parties to contractually reduce the time for which the seller is liable from the regular two years (Art 5(1) of Directive 1999/44/EC) to one year, which the German lawmakers have done.[60] The parties must not undercut this and are not permitted to exclude the liability of the seller for hidden defects altogether. In contrast, throughout the time preceding the adoption of the Directive, the BGH held that, with regard to the sale of a used car, the exclusion of liability for hidden defects was a matter of 'commercial reasonableness' (*wirtschaftliche Vernunft*).[61] The reasoning behind this argument was that the trader was under no duty to search the car for hidden defects since the costs incurred in doing so would be borne by the buyer anyway. In addition, when a used car breaks down after sale, it is difficult to tell whether a defect that becomes apparent at this time had already existed at the time of delivery. Therefore, it was a sound policy to resort to the ancient principle of

[59] M Martinek, 'Unsystematische Überregulierung und kontraintentionale Effekte im Europäischen Verbraucherrecht oder: Weniger wäre mehr' in S Grundmann (ed), *Systembildung und Systemlücken in Kerngebieten des Europäischen Privatrechts* (2000) 511, 537 ff.

[60] § 475(2) BGB.

[61] BGHZ 74, 383, 386 = NJW 1979, 1886; BGH NJW 1966, 1070, 1071; BGH NJW 1970, 29, 31; BGH NJW 1978, 261; critical: F Peters, JZ 1991, 385, 386; Soergel-Huber, BGB, 12th edn (1991) § 459 para 306.

caveat emptor and to allow traders of used cars to exclude their liability for hidden defects.

Apart from this (anecdotal) evidence from the German used car market, it is remarkable that, from a historical point of view, full liability on the part of the seller for defects was the exception and not the rule.[62] In classical Roman law, the seller was not liable for defects of the good delivered, of which he had no knowledge, unless he had chosen otherwise and provided a warranty (*dicta et promissa*).[63] Up to the present day, the principle of *caveat emptor* has survived in important corners of the law of sales. One example is the sale of property, where liability for hidden defects is excluded as a matter of course in most jurisdictions.[64] Even though the sale of property lies beyond the scope of Directive 1999/44/EC, it remains telling that the parties and their legal advisers believe it to be in their own best interest to stick to the principle of *caveat emptor* when dealing with objects of particularly high value. Is it at all realistic to assume that the rule of no liability is appropriate only where the object of sale is an immovable? The answer to this question can only be negative.

The lawmakers in Brussels would have been well advised to allow the parties to derogate from the statutory scheme of remedies supplied by the Consumer Sales Directive. The risk involved would have been small. The Unfair Terms Directive would have, in any case, provided a tightly-knit safety net. Contractual deviations from the statutory scheme of remedies would have been subject to judicial control on a case-by-case basis. Consumers would have retained the right to appeal to a court, had they been deprived of the protection that is appropriate under the circumstances. Against the background of the Unfair Terms Directive, it is difficult to see a justification for mandatory law. Court control over contract terms that derogate from the default rules of contract law is a much more flexible instrument than the clumsy, black-or-white tool of mandatory law.

The Proposal for a Directive on Consumer Rights incorporates the provisions of Directive 1999/44/EC, albeit in a modified form. One important deviation has already been mentioned, namely that Article 26(2) of the Draft Directive allocates the right to choose between repair and replacement to the seller instead of the buyer. The major novelty of the Draft Directive, however, is to be found in its Article 27(2), which reads as follows:

> Without prejudice to the provisions of this Chapter, the consumer may claim damages for any loss not remedied in accordance with Article 26.

Whereas the right to damages was not touched upon by the Consumer Sales Directive, the Commission now wants to move forward and incorporate this remedy as well. The DCFR follows suit through a combination of Article III.–3:101 (1), Article III.–3:701 ff., and Article IV.A.–4:101 DCFR. From a general

[62] Zimmermann, above n 23, 307 ff.

[63] Kaser and Knütel, above n 23, § 41 at para 45; Zimmermann, above n 23, 308 ff.

[64] For the German perspective, see U Huber, (2009) 209 *Archiv für die civilistische Praxis* 143, 162.

point of view, a right to damages as a remedy for the delivery of defective goods is adequate. What is missing in the Draft Directive, however, is an equivalent to Article 79 CISG, Article 8:108 PECL, Article 7.1.7 of the UNIDROIT Principles of International Commercial Contracts and Article III.–3:104 DCFR. Under these provisions, the seller is released from liability where delivery of a product in conformity with the description in the contract failed due to an impediment beyond his control. If Article 27(2) of the Draft Directive were to be passed into law, the parties would not be able to remedy the situation themselves, namely by including a *force majeure* clause in the contract, because the right to damages is mandatory (Art 43 of the Draft Directive).

The combination of Article 27(2) and Article 43 of the Draft Directive deserves criticism not only for its failure to provide an exception in cases of *force majeure*, but also for other, more general reasons. In commercial practice, the right to damages is one of the preferred objects of party agreements. For a variety of transactions, it is common, if not to exclude, then at least to specify, and limit the scope of, any damages available in case of breach. Staple provisions of contract practice include limitations on the amounts of damages available (caps), on the amount of time a product is warranted and on the categories of damages recoverable (pecuniary v non-pecuniary loss). Article 27(2) of the Draft Directive stands in the way of such agreements. The seller is always liable for the full amount of damages, without an option to limit his exposure along the dimensions of time, quantum, and category. The DCFR remains subject to the same criticism.

It may seem unfair to sellers to impose full and unrestricted liability on them, regardless of the kind of good involved in the sale, and of the risks involved in the manufacture and transport of the particular item. However, it would be wrong to gauge the problem by weighing up the competing interests of buyers and sellers. Even though this may be true from an ex-post view, the ex-ante perspective is more relevant. From an ex-ante point of view, contractual limitations on the amount of damages owed in cases of breach serve two functions, namely to prevent cross-subsidisation and to solve the problem of excessive reliance. The latter is caused by the fact that the amount of damages incurred is a function of the reliance investment of the buyer before the time of breach.[65] If the buyer can be certain of either receiving perfect tender, or being compensated in full, she has no incentive to curb her investments and to take the probability of non-performance into account. While it is true that a general rule attenuating the incentives for excessive reliance has not been developed yet, the parties may rectify the problem in their contract, namely by agreeing liquidated damages that reflect the damages the buyer would have incurred had she invested in reliance

[65] cf Cooter and Ulen, above n 24, 269 ff; Shavell, above n 21, 357 ff.

optimally.[66] In making the full compensation rule mandatory, the Draft Directive takes this solution out of the parties' hands.

Secondly, the invalidation of limits on the liability of the seller will lead to cross-subsidisation of those buyers who stand to lose large amounts in case of breach — the 'large-loss-buyers' — by another group of buyers whose expected damages are small — the 'small-loss buyers'. Under a mandatory rule of full compensation, the seller will estimate the expected costs of liability and add them to the price charged for the product in question. Where sellers cannot discriminate on price, because they cannot tell the two groups of buyers apart, the only solution for them is to charge each buyer the average amount of extra funds needed to cover expected liabilities. This amount will be 'too high' for the small-loss buyers and 'too low' for the large-loss buyers. A common example from an area other than the law of sales is the transport of goods. Ordinarily, carriers charge a price for their services that also covers the costs of some level of protection for cases of loss or other breaches. Customers who need more protection because they stand to suffer large losses in the event of breach may contract for more, but then have to pay a higher price as compensation. Articles 27(2) and 43 of the Draft Directive exclude the limitation of liability and thus make it impossible for the seller to offer a different set of contracts to their customers. This does not cause detriment to sellers, but harms their customers, specifically the low-risk buyers. They are forced to cross-subsidise the high-risk buyers because the contractual instrument for separating the two groups is taken out of the sellers' hands.

The same criticism applies to the DCFR, as its framers have supplied a mirror image of these provisions of the Proposal for a Directive on Consumer Rights in Article IV.A.–2:309 and Article IV.A.–4:101 DCFR.

7. OTHER JUSTIFICATIONS FOR MANDATORY LAW

7.1. Full Harmonisation

One of the most controversial features of the Proposal for a Directive on Consumer Rights is its ambition to fully regulate all the subject areas it encompasses. Article 4 of the Draft Directive introduces the principle of full harmonisation, which removes the authority of the member states to maintain or create provisions in their national laws that deviate from the prerogatives of the Draft Directive. For the purposes of Article 4 of the Draft Directive, it is immaterial whether a rule of national law may improve the situation of the consumer above the standard of the Draft Directive, or whether it lowers the level of protection.

[66] Cooter and Ulen, above n 24, 273 ff; Hermalin, Katz and Craswell, above n 20, 108.

Whether or not this shift away from the policy of minimal harmonisation is justified is beyond the scope of this article.[67]

What matters in the present context is the relationship between full harmonisation and the choice of mandatory law. The Commission does not link the two issues explicitly but stresses the need for certainty and uniformity:

> These disparities [within the consumer *acquis* and its transformation into the laws of the various member states] create significant internal market barriers affecting business and consumers. They increase compliance costs to business wishing to engage in cross border sale of goods or provision of services. Fragmentation also undermines consumer confidence in the internal market …
>
> Full harmonisation of some key regulatory aspects will considerably increase legal certainty for both consumers and business. Both consumers and business will be able to rely on a single regulatory framework based on clearly defined legal concepts regulating certain aspects of business-to-consumer contracts across the Community.[68]

Even though this reasoning does not explicitly address the role of party autonomy, it may imply that the advantages of uniformity in terms of increased legal certainty, better consumer confidence, and savings in transaction costs, justify the decision not to let the parties derogate from the statutory framework.

In reality, however, such a conclusion seems to be misguided. Full harmonisation removes the sovereignty of the member states, while it is fully compatible with the autonomy of the parties. Contractual freedom of choice does not undermine the goals behind full harmonisation, because the parties will only agree to derogate from the statutory framework where, in their judgment, the benefits of doing so will exceed the costs in terms of increased transaction costs. If anything, the argument works the other way around: under a framework of a fully unified consumer law, there is more need for party autonomy than under a system of national consumer laws that allow for deviations. Party autonomy could balance out the inflexibility of a statutory scheme that subscribes to the principle of full harmonisation and ignores local preferences.[69] Therefore, it is particularly regrettable that the Commission combined full harmonisation with immutability instead of party autonomy.

[67] Critically: M Faure, 'Towards a Maximum Harmonization of Consumer Contract Law?!?' (2008) 15 *Maastricht Journal of European and Comparative Law* 433; H Micklitz and N Reich, 'Crónica de una Muerte Anunciada: The Commission Proposal for a 'Directive of Consumer Rights'' (2009) 46 *Common Market Law Review* 471; W van Boom, 'The Draft Directive on Consumer Rights: Choices Made and Arguments Used' (2009) 5 *Journal of Contemporary European Research* 452; JM Smits, 'Full Harmonization of Consumer Law? A Critique of the Draft Directive on Consumer Rights', TICOM Law Working Paper No. 2009/02.

[68] Proposal for a Directive on Consumer Rights, see above n 8, at Recs 7 and 8.

[69] G Wagner, 'The Economics of Harmonizing European Contract Law' (2002) 39 *Common Market Law Review* 995, 999 ff.

7.2. Weakness of Consumers

In legal and political discourse, it is often argued that consumers are 'weak', at least in comparison with businesses, and that this creates a need for protection.[70] In the case of consumer sales, this seems to have been one of the major justifications for transforming this part of the law of sales into a set of mandatory rules.[71] However, the assumption of weak consumers is untenable in several respects. To begin with, it is simply implausible to assume that the vast majority of the population (consumers) suffers from some congenital psychological 'weakness'. It is also unrealistic, since the causes as well as the presumed consequences of this weakness are not explained. Are consumers unable to understand the product and the contract terms they are offered? Are they incapable of forming a rational will and of expressing it properly? Or are consumers aware of what they want, but simply unable to get their way because they lack bargaining power?

Framed in such broad terms, consumer weakness is a poorly-reasoned artefact. This is not to deny that consumers employ the same cognitive shortcuts and suffer from the same psychological shortcomings as any other human beings. In fact, consumers do not form a distinct class of human beings at all, since the concept denotes a social role rather than a social group. In some regards, everyone is a consumer.[72]

If anything, the assumption that consumers lack the relevant bargaining power vis-a-vis businesses may have merit. If one focuses on a single transaction, it is certainly true that a consumer will have a hard time negotiating with a large enterprise or even with small businesses. For example, the attempt to negotiate with a local grocery store about the quality and price of baked beans will be futile. Even though this is true, it does not prove anything. The *bargaining power* that consumers have does not come in the currency of negotiating power, but manifests itself in the form of an option to walk away. In competitive markets, consumers are strong since they are free to turn down offers they do not like, and to turn to a competitor who offers better quality or lower prices.

Again, there is no point denying that perfectly competitive markets do not exist and that there are a number of factors that might prevent consumers from arriving at rational decisions. Some of the most critical situations have been analysed above. As this survey reveals, the law does react to the 'situational' weakness of consumers as human beings by providing customised remedies. These remedies range from the invalidation of contracts made by minors and mentally disabled persons, through rights of withdrawal, to judicial control over standard business terms. The critical difference between this approach and the

[70] The Scandinavian systems rely heavily on the theory that consumers need protection because of their 'weakness'; Ranieri, above n 54, 374 ff.

[71] See section 5.3 above.

[72] Zimmermann, above n 54, 161.

wholesale assumption of consumer weakness is its specificity: legal intervention is legitimate only where a specific failure of the bargain mechanism, or of the market as a means of efficient resource allocation, can be established. The reaction of the legal system must be tailored not to social roles, but to situations of impaired rational self-determination.

8. COMBINING FLEXIBILITY AND LEGAL CERTAINTY: OPTIONS

The critique levelled at the dominance of mandatory rules in European consumer law offers the alternative of a multi-tiered system of specific remedies over the flat solution of immutable statutory rules. In particular, it has been advocated that the consumer should be allowed to waive her right of withdrawal in distance selling contracts, and that the mandatory nature of the law of consumer sales should be abandoned, in favour of court control under the Unfair Terms Directive.[73]

One argument against this approach is that flexibility may look attractive in theory but that it works to the detriment of both businesses and consumers in practice. Its main disadvantage is that it decreases legal certainty and the foreseeability of legal outcomes. The parties will only learn ex post facto whether a particular clause in their contract has stood the test of fairness, or was deemed to be unfair and found to be thus by the competent court. The literature focusing on the distinction between *ius dispositivum* and *ius cogens* has overlooked the fact that mandatory law serves another respectable purpose, namely the function of standardisation. Mandatory rules not only restrict the freedom of the 'stronger' party to the benefit of the 'weaker' party — or, in my terminology, protect parties in situations where rational self-determination is at risk — they also simplify transactions by supplying an immutable scheme of contract terms.[74] Where a contract is subject to mandatory rules, like the contract for the sale of a consumer good in Europe, the parties must settle on a single set of rules. This certainly restricts their freedom to customise contract terms to their special needs and interests. On the other hand, it makes life easier. For example, it reduces the cost of transactions. There is no point adjusting the contract terms since they are unalterable anyway. Mandatory contract terms act as a safe haven but go beyond this, as they abolish the freedom of the parties altogether: the safe haven *must* be used. With regard to transactions between businesses, on the one hand, and consumers, on the other, it seems plausible to argue that the benefits of standardisation will be distributed asymmetrically between the parties. Given that the costs to consumers of analysing, understanding, and negotiating contract terms are prohibitive, standardisation clearly works to their benefit. This is not to say

[73] See section 5.1.3 above.

[74] C Engel, 'Zivilrecht als Fortsetzung des Wirtschaftsrechts mit anderen Mitteln' (1995) 50 *Juristenzeitung* 213, 214.

that the savings in transaction costs must necessarily outweigh the dead-weight loss caused by imposing terms on parties against their best interests, but it does suggest that mandatory rules do generate benefits by standardising legal transactions.

For a general theory of contract law, it would be highly attractive to develop a tool that would marry the virtues of mandatory law in terms of standardisation to the obvious advantages of default rules in terms of contractual efficiency. It would have to combine the provision of a safe haven with the flexibility of allowing the parties to use it. Such a tool does in fact exist, and is described as an 'optional scheme'.[75] An optional scheme is characterised by the fact that the parties retain the authority to choose between different legal schemes, or 'options', but that they must not derogate from the schemes supplied by the legal system. A framework of options combines the advantages afforded by standardisation and flexibility. It is not that a uniform legal solution is imposed upon the parties. On the other hand, the parties are not left to their own devices. Rather, the legal system supplies a range of norms from which the parties may pick the set that maximises the joint surplus from the transaction at hand. Within the area of contract law, the 'options approach' calls for the creation of a menu of sets of contract terms from which the parties may choose freely. Once they have chosen, however, the parties would be unable to derogate from the scheme that they have selected.

The case of distance selling may serve as an illustration.[76] If the right of withdrawal was open to party agreement, a variety of different schemes would develop. Some internet sellers would stipulate generously long time limits for exercising the right of return, others would settle on short time frames, and others still would come up with peculiar form requirements, such as requiring a registered letter to be sent before the right of withdrawal is validly exercised. But the imagination of sellers would not stop there: they would move on to define the requirements for repackaging the goods and sending them back. Finally, all sorts of cost-allocation rules would develop. Such niceties would, of course be buried in the fine print that every reasonable consumer-buyer would click away without reading.

In scenarios such as this, the celebration of party autonomy may appear like the proverbial 'shibboleth for some well-known writers'.[77] There is no point denying that the development of a diverse multitude of contractually designed withdrawal schemes would become a nightmare. This may be one of the reasons why the internet industry lobbied in favour of a mandatory right of withdrawal

[75] cf G Bachmann, 'Optionsmodelle im Privatrecht' (2008) 63 *Juristenzeitung* 11, 13ff, distinguishing between 'soft options' — default rules — and 'hard options' — the kind referred to in the present art.

[76] cf H Eidenmüller, 'Die Rechtfertigung von Widerrufsrechten' (2010) 210 *Archiv für die civilistische Praxis* 67, 77 ff.

[77] *Lochner v New York*, 198 US 45, 75 (1905, per Holmes, J).

during the drafting of the Directive on Distance Contracts. Instead of setting aside party autonomy, the options approach would downgrade the current framework of the right of withdrawal, as set out in the Directive on Distance Contracts, to the status of an option that the parties may either accept or reject. A consumer surfing the internet for bargains could decide whether to purchase the item right away without a right of withdrawal or to preserve such a right and thus to preserve the option of 'having second thoughts'. Presumably, the price of packaging the good and including a right of withdrawal would be higher than the price charged just for the naked good, but such price differentials would only reflect the additional costs incurred by including a right of withdrawal. Such a solution would put an end to the cross-subsidisation of negligent consumer-buyers, who order goods without prior reflection, and diligent consumer-buyers, who take care to avoid ordering goods that do not suit their tastes and are thus less likely to exercise the right of withdrawal. By offering two different kinds of contract — one including a right of withdrawal and another one excluding it — the sellers could force the buyers to separate into two different groups. One group could be labelled the 'high-cost buyers,' since the frequency of withdrawal will be high, whereas the other group could be labelled the 'low-cost buyers,' as their the frequency of withdrawal will be low. At the same time, by allowing a choice between a definite purchase and a purchase that is revocable by the consumer ex post facto, the options approach would preserve the core of party autonomy, namely the right to choose between two meaningful alternatives. The crucial difference between ordinary default rules and options lies within the terms and conditions of the right of withdrawal. Under the options approach, the parties would not be authorised to modify the statutory framework of the right of withdrawal or to draw up their own scheme for a right of withdrawal from scratch. Under such a system, consumers would be able to use a 'switch' — turning the right of withdrawal on or off as they wish. Whoever opts for such a right would be certain to receive a standardised product that is well defined in the law and, therefore, at once well-balanced and easy to manage.

9. CONCLUSION

The purpose of the present analysis was to dismantle the assumption, popular among scholars and lawmakers, that mandatory contract law is needed to compensate for the perceived 'weakness' of particular groups in society, such as workers, tenants, or consumers. However, the purpose was not to denounce the category of mandatory contract law as such, or to deny that there are situations that require regulatory intervention. These situations are not characterised by the fact that there is a 'weak' party involved, but rather that rational self-determination is impaired or at risk. The reason why this is so may be rooted either in the individual characteristics of a party, which may be that they are minors, disabled or incapacitated for some other reason, or in the particular situation in which the contract was formed, for example on the party's doorstep. The analysis of the Proposal for a Directive on Consumer Rights has revealed that a significant part of the current EU consumer law *acquis*, which employs the means of mandatory law, is in fact appropriate. Just as significantly, however, there appears to be no justification for resorting to the use of mandatory rules in other areas of consumer law.

Apart from remedying situations where rational self-determination is put at risk, mandatory law serves the additional purpose of standardisation. Standardisation of contract terms reduces transaction costs and is more resistant to cognitive failures by the parties. However, the same goals may be reached without sacrificing party autonomy altogether, through the means of an alternative approach, namely 'options'. Optional contract law allows the parties to choose from a range of legal frameworks without the possibility of modifying any of them. In this manner, options allow for individual choice without simultaneously causing a dramatic increase in the complexity of contract practice. In combining the virtues of standardisation and party autonomy, options may be the 'third way' that leads Europe into the future.

3

The Role of Information Deficiencies in Contract Enforcement

ANN-SOPHIE VANDENBERGHE*

ABSTRACT

Information deficiencies play an important role in contract enforcement. Courts frequently refuse to enforce contractual terms when one of the parties lacks information. The difficult question is where the line is drawn (or should be drawn) between information deficiencies of which the law will take account and those which it will disregard. This article sets out the economic framework for determining when it is appropriate to shift responsibility for information deficiencies from one contracting party to the other. The overriding objective from an economic perspective is to ensure that the party who can produce and reveal information at least cost produces the optimal amount of honest information in society. The economic duty-to-inform doctrine provides simple rules to achieve that purpose. Greater intervention on the basis of information deficiency is warranted in cases where a special relationship of trust exists between contracting parties. The reason for this is that an adviser (agent) in a trust relationship is contractually bound by a greater duty to inform the principal, including a duty to provide information and advice about the principal's needs. The economic theory on which judicial control and regulation of contract terms rests (and which also limits its scope of applicability) is that people tend to sign contracts without reading them.

1. INTRODUCTION

The premises of economics push in the direction of freedom of contract, and this current can be resisted only with difficulty. If parties are rational, they will enter contracts only when it is in their self-interest, and they will agree only to terms that make them better off. Courts that refused to enforce these terms would make it more

* Ann-Sophie Vandenberghe is Assistant Professor of Law and Economics, Rotterdam Institute of Law and Economics, Erasmus School of Law.

difficult for future parties to use contracts to enhance their joint well-being. Therefore, courts should enforce the terms of the contract.[1]

UNDER THE PRINCIPLE of freedom of contract, courts are required to enforce the contractual terms that are the result of a voluntary agreement between contracting parties. This rule is beneficial for society, because it protects individual autonomy and enhances welfare by facilitating the realisation of preferences through the use of contractual exchanges.

And yet, courts do not always enforce (the terms of) contracts. They often refuse to enforce terms that seem unfair, that is to say, terms that significantly disadvantage one of the parties. Widespread judicial scrutiny of transactions can interfere with freedom of contract and may be perceived as a form of paternalism, because it runs counter to the notion that people themselves know best what is in their own interests. How do courts justify interference with freedom of contract? Interference is commonly based on: (1) lack of information or (2) inequality of bargaining power.

Lack of information often plays a role in a court's decision not to enforce the contract. Courts sometimes decide that a contract is unfair because one party was improvident, ignorant, inexperienced or unsophisticated. Lack of information plays a role in all of these cases. Long-standing doctrines of fraud and mistake deal with information problems at the pre-contractual stage. Courts may invalidate a contract when one party was imperfectly informed or mistaken about a relevant aspect of the contractual exchange. Even the doctrine of incompetence deals with a particular type of information problem, namely that incompetent persons, like children, lack information about their own needs and preferences. Courts relieve parties of their contractual obligations to protect them against their own ignorance or lack of information. But, in doing so, the consequences of the mistake or ignorance of one contracting party are shifted to the other party who relied on the contract's validity.

Information deficiency plays an important role in contract enforcement, although it matters in some cases but not in others. Courts sometimes relieve individuals of the responsibility for their apparent choices, but in other cases they will not allow a person to avoid his contractual obligations because he was imperfectly informed. It is not always clear where the dividing line is to be drawn between information deficiencies of which the law will take account and those which it will disregard.

This chapter sets out the economic framework for determining when it is appropriate to shift responsibility for information deficiencies from one contracting party to the other.

Modern economic analysis does not presuppose that people are perfectly informed and that they make perfect decisions. Instead, it is recognised that

[1] E Posner, 'Economic Analysis of Contract Law After Three Decades: Success or Failure?' (2003) 112 *Yale Law Journal* 829, 842.

decision-making is costly and that acquiring and processing information (including information about one's own needs and preferences) may be costly. An overview of pre-contractual information costs appears in section 2. Moreover, market forces may not be strong enough to cure information problems. Legislative or judicial intervention may then be needed to solve these problems in order to avoid the resulting misallocation of resources. The legal duty to inform is an appropriate legal instrument for solving information problems.

The economic purpose of a legal duty to inform is to overcome information asymmetries by giving incentives to market actors to produce and reveal more — and more honest — information. The difficulty lies in determining the precise extent of the duty to inform. From an economic perspective, the question is how to ensure that the party who can produce and reveal information at least cost produces and conveys the optimal amount of honest information in society. The economic duty-to-inform doctrine, described in section 3, provides simple rules to achieve that purpose.

In many legal systems, courts are more willing to relieve a party from disadvantageous contractual obligations if the parties are in a special relationship of trust. In section 4, it is argued that greater intervention on the basis of information deficiency is warranted when parties are in such a special relationship. The reason is that an adviser (agent) in a trust relationship is contractually bound by a greater duty to inform. Various legal rules and doctrines may be understood as providing incentives to the adviser in a trust relationship to give more — and more honest — information, including information about the other party's (principal's) needs.

Lack of information is one reason for courts to interfere with freedom of contract; inequality of bargaining power is another one. Courts sometimes decide that a contract is unfair because of the unequal bargaining power of the seller and the buyer and that this inequality may justify avoidance of the contract. Nonetheless, economists typically argue that courts should not avoid contracts because of the unequal bargaining power of the parties. The reason is that inequality of bargaining power, which may exist in various forms, including contracts offered on a take-it-or-leave-it basis, could not account for the prevalence of harsh contract terms that are not desired by the parties. The unequal bargaining power argument for interference with freedom of contract and the counter-arguments given by economists are outlined in section 5.

The economic theory on which judicial control of contract terms rests is that people tend to sign contracts without reading them. The causes of the signing-without-reading problem, the inefficiencies resulting from it and its implications for the standard of judicial control, its scope of application and the applicable form of legislative action are the subject of section 6.

2. IMPERFECT INFORMATION AND THE FORMATION OF CONTRACTS

2.1. Introduction

In early economic analyses, a strong version of the rational choice model was used, according to which it is assumed that individuals are perfectly informed and make perfect decisions. However, in modern economic studies, weaker versions of the rational choice model are used. The weaker versions of the rational choice model do not presuppose zero costs of acquiring and processing information or zero decision costs.[2] In extreme cases, involving incompetence, information and decision costs may be so high that a person is no longer able to look after his own best interest.

In a world in which all information could be produced and made available at no cost, contracting parties would be perfectly informed. However, in the real world, producing and communicating information is costly. Section 2.2 provides an overview of the information costs at the pre-contractual stage. However, the fact that producing and communicating information is costly does not necessarily imply that an insufficient amount of information is available in markets. Market forces exist that remedy information problems. However, as shown in section 2.3, market forces are generally not strong enough to solve all information problems. Legal measures may be needed to ensure that the optimal amount of honest information is produced in society.

2.2. Pre-Contractual Information Costs

2.2.1. Information Production Costs and Communication Costs

When people contemplate the possibility of concluding a contract, they need information on many issues in order to be able to assess the value of the exchange. Producing information is costly. Moreover, because information is asymmetrically distributed, parties need to exchange information. Costs need to be incurred to convey and communicate information from one contracting party to the other. De Geest gives an overview of the pre-contractual information and communication costs:[3]

- search costs: people need information on potential contractual partners and on the products and services they supply;
- information on the characteristics or attributes of the product;
- information on the characteristics of the producer: this type of information is especially important for contracts *intuitu personae*;

[2] G Stigler, 'The Economics of Information' (1961) 69 *Journal of Political Economy* 213.

[3] G De Geest, 'Economische analyse van het contracten- en quasi-contractenrecht' ('Economic Analysis of Contract and Quasi-Contract Law') (1994) 82–8.

- information on the potential circumstances surrounding the contract: complete and perfect contracts require information about all future states of the world in order to allocate risks appropriately;
- information about one's own needs and preferences: a person's willingness to pay depends on his ability to pay, which includes information about his own financial situation and possibilities;
- information on the production costs: this information is needed by the producers in order to calculate the price, as well as by consumers, who need to know at what price they could produce the relevant products and/or services themselves;
- information about alternative contracting parties on the market: this includes information on the market price and the market demand curve;
- information on the applicable law: information about default rules, mandatory rules and rules of evidence; and
- information on the actual terms included in the contract.

2.2.2. Decision Costs

People have to make decision costs. In other words, they need to invest an amount of cognitive effort to think through the options and select the product that meets their needs and desires best. People often have to invest a significant amount of cognitive energy into making sure that they have thought through their options and selected a product that meets their needs and desires.

2.2.3. Lie Costs and Verification Costs

Market actors may invest a huge amount of effort to mislead other parties. They may try to 'hide' negative aspects of a product or 'inflate' its positive aspects. The costs of producing false information are 'lie costs'. These are a waste of resources because they create no value.[4]

The lie costs of some parties may lead to verification costs of other parties.[5] Because some parties do not reveal information in an honest manner, trust levels may decrease. People will spend resources on verifying whether the information given to them is correct and honest. Verification costs are a waste of resources because information will unnecessarily be duplicated when it turns out that the information originally provided was in fact correct.

It is not always possible to verify whether information given by one party is false or honest. A distinction must be made between verifiable and non-verifiable information.[6] Non-verifiable information consists of subjective opinions or statements about which there is no scientific consensus. For example, when a car

[4] R Posner, *Economic Analysis of Law* (Boston, 1992) 110.
[5] De Geest, above n 3, 87.
[6] ibid 86.

dealer declares that 'Toyota is the best', it is impossible for third parties to determine whether the costs involved in this statement are to be classified as information costs or as lie costs.

2.3. Market Forces to Remedy Information Problems

It is sometimes argued in the economic literature that competitive market forces are strong enough to provide the optimal amount of information, thereby removing the need to have legal rules to overcome information asymmetries. It is true that market forces may cure informational problems through voluntary disclosure of information, but it does not make legal rules unnecessary. In any case, it takes time for market forces to solve informational problems. Legal rules may speed up the process.

Moreover, market solutions may not be perfect. Take the example of warranties.[7] Competitive pressures make sellers offer warranties (enforceable guarantees) for particular characteristics of their products. A warranty is a guarantee of results and therefore an indirect statement on quality, but it is an imperfect solution. The reason for this is that a seller who provides a warranty also has to bear the losses resulting from events that he cannot know (external factors) and from the buyer's (non-verifiable) moral hazard. Signalling is another way in which markets may overcome informational problems.[8] However, signalling is also imperfect, because it may induce people to invest too much in signalling.

In addition, market forces only provide solutions under certain conditions. For example, sellers have incentives to provide information to otherwise uninformed buyers, but only when the benefits of doing so outweigh the costs of information disclosure. Voluntary disclosure can sometimes be expected, since it will be to the advantage of various sellers to point out that their product or service has attributes that are more advantageous to many consumers than the product or service of their competitors. The principal situation in which voluntary disclosure of information will not occur is where the revelation of information would tend to cause many consumers not to buy the product at all. No seller of the product will have an incentive to disclose that kind of information. Sellers will also not reveal information that makes a particular product more attractive than consumers expect if other sellers of such products would also gain from that information. Gabaix and Laibson[9] present a model of consumer myopia that explains why firms often shroud the negative attributes of their products, particularly high prices for complementary add-ons. They show that competition will not induce firms to reveal information that would improve market efficiency.

[7] SJ Grossman, 'The Informational Role of Warranties and Private Disclosure About Product Quality' (1981) 24 *Journal of Law and Economics* 461.

[8] A Spence, 'Job-Market Signaling' (1973) 87 *Quarterly Journal of Economics* 355.

[9] X Gabaix and D Laibson, 'Shrouded Attributes, Consumer Myopia, and Information Suppression in Competitive Markets' (2006) *The Quarterly Journal of Economics* 505.

Firms will not educate the public about the add-on market, even when unshrouding is free. The reason for this is a phenomenon that they call 'the curse of debiasing'. Debiasing improves consumer welfare, but no firm can capture or even partially share these benefits. Educating a consumer about competitors' add-on schemes effectively teaches that consumer how to profitably exploit those schemes, thereby making it impossible for the educating firm to profitably attract the newly educated consumers.

Finally, in some situations in which there is a good deal of voluntary disclosure, the information may not be stated in a standardised manner and therefore does not facilitate comparative shopping. Legislative intervention may be needed to ensure that information is presented in a standardised way.

In general, market forces are not strong enough to perfectly solve asymmetrical information problems. Regulation is required through legislation or in the form of general contract doctrines.

3. THE LEGAL DUTY TO INFORM

3.1. Introduction

The presumption that an exchange is value-maximising is valid only when there is no force, fraud, mistake or incompetence. For example, the fact that parties accept the offer is not evidence that the sale will increase value if one or both of the parties are mistaken or imperfectly informed about the object or terms of the exchange.

Cases in which one of the contracting parties is imperfectly informed about relevant aspects of the contract are addressed in law through the doctrines of mistake and fraud and through the legal duty to inform. When a person's consent has been vitiated by a mistake (or fraud), courts may invalidate the contract. In doing so, a person who has made a mistake is able to shift the consequences to the other party: the costs that the other party has incurred in relying upon the validity of the contract will be wasted and he will lose whatever benefit he expected to obtain from the contractual exchange. However, all legal systems agree that not every mistake entitles a promisor to evade the consequences of his promise. The difficulty with which legal systems must cope is where to draw the dividing line between mistakes of which the law will take account and those which it will disregard.

Under the will or autonomy-based theory of contract, legal enforcement of contracts is justified in order to respect the autonomous will of people. Consequently, there is no justification for giving legal force to contracts that do not reflect the true and free will of people. A party whose will or intention is vitiated by a mistake (or deceit or duress) can claim that the contract is void. However, it has also been recognised in law that, as a basis for contractual enforcement, the 'will theory' would create too much uncertainty in any transaction. A perfectly voluntary or free will is elusive. Legal systems therefore also take into account the other contracting party's reasonable reliance on the validity of the contract. Not every mistake entitles a promisor to evade the consequence of his promise.

Nevertheless, there is no simple test in law to tell us in which of these cases the contract can be avoided by the mistaken party and in which it cannot. However, based on the law and economics literature concerning information imperfections, De Geest and Kovac have developed an economic duty-to-inform doctrine that provides simple rules for cases involving mistake, fraud and information imperfections in general.[10]

3.2. The Economic Duty-to-Inform Doctrine

When one contracting party is mistaken or imperfectly informed about an aspect of the contract, including his own reasons for contracting, it can no longer be presumed that the contract is value-maximising. However, De Geest and Kovac start by saying that the mere fact that a party is imperfectly informed should not be a reason to invalidate the contract.[11] The reason for this is that parties never have perfect information at the time of contracting. They have always more information ex post than *ex ante*. In this sense, they are always mistaken. If every mistake were to constitute a valid reason to avoid the contract, no contract would ever be binding. The costs of opportunistic behaviour would increase if contracts could be set aside too easily: a party that has the right to avoid the contract could threaten to use this right in order to induce the other party to agree to a change in the terms of the original contract in favour of the threatening party. Moreover, the invalidation of a contract is costly. The transaction costs that were incurred for the conclusion of the invalidated contract are wasted, and additional transaction costs need to be incurred to contract for the transfer of the returned goods to another party. Sellers who know that part of the contracts they conclude could be avoided at the wish of buyers will seek compensation for these costs by charging higher product prices to consumers who are careful as well as those who are not. This may result in adverse selection. Some of the careful consumers will refrain from buying products because they are unwilling to pay extra for the right to avoid the contract.

From an economic perspective, rules should be designed to ensure that the party who can produce and reveal information at least cost produces the optimal amount of honest information in society.

[10] G De Geest and M Kovac, 'The Formation of Contracts in the Draft Common Frame of Reference' (2009) *European Review of Private Law* 113.

[11] ibid 120.

Economically optimal rules give incentives to the *least-cost information gatherer* to produce and communicate information.[12] In most cases, sellers are the least-cost information gatherer. The reason for this is that they often acquire information as a by-product of owning and using the product (eg sellers know that the house they are selling has latent defects), that they have economies of scale in producing information or that they are more likely to be professionals than buyers (eg an antique dealer knows whether the object he is selling is an authentic antique or a mere copy).[13] If a buyer is mistaken or imperfectly informed about an attribute of the exchanged object for which the seller is the least-cost information gatherer, the seller should be sanctioned for not having produced and revealed the pertinent information to the buyer. The sanction may consist of the invalidation of the contract or a price reduction.

While sellers are the least-cost information gatherer in most cases, they are not so in all cases. In nearly all cases, the buyer is the least-cost information gatherer about his own wants, needs and preferences.[14] Posner argues that there should be no duty for sellers to disclose when only the consumer has the requisite information. This is the case, for example, when the performance of the product depends on the consumer's tastes, which may not be known to the manufacturer: 'Only the consumer knows whether the sweater is soft enough, the cantaloupe ripe enough — for him.'[15] A person who is mistaken about his own needs, motives or reasons for contracting should not be entitled to invalidate the contract. Examples of this include a person who decides to make a particular purchase because of an error in his own calculations or a person who buys 100 bottles of water for a birthday party because he mistakenly thinks that his guests are teetotallers. This lack of intervention in contracts in cases where a buyer is mistaken about certain aspects on which he is the least-cost information gatherer, encourages people to act with prudence and to become optimally informed about their needs before contracting.

Hence, from an economic perspective, the question of liability for non-disclosure should turn on which of the parties to the transaction, seller or buyer, can produce, convey or obtain the pertinent information at the lowest cost.[16] However, there are cases in which neither party is able to produce the information at a reasonable cost.[17] In that case, analytically speaking, there is no longer an information problem but a problem of risk allocation.[18] Who should bear the

[12] A Kronman, 'Mistake, Disclosure, Information, and the Law of Contracts' (1978) *Journal of Legal Studies* 1.

[13] De Geest and Kovac, above n 10, 113–32.

[14] An exception exists for parties who are in a relationship of trust. Here, the seller (agent) is explicitly asked to give advice on the needs of the buyer (principal).

[15] Posner, above n 4, 112.

[16] ibid 111.

[17] The costs of producing information are not reasonable from an economic perspective when marginal information production costs are higher than marginal ignorance costs.

[18] De Geest and Kovac, above n 10, 120.

risk that something happens that makes performance more or less valuable to the buyer? For example, who should bear the risk that the purchase of a wedding dress in anticipation of a wedding becomes less valuable if the wedding is cancelled? From an economic point of view, the superior risk bearer should bear that risk. The superior risk bearer is the party who is in the best position to prevent the risk from materialising (precaution) or is better able to insure against the risk (superior insurer).

There are limitations on the duty to inform when viewed from an economic perspective.[19] The first limitation is that information should not be communicated if the other party already has or should have the information concerned (eg in the case of clearly visible defects). It would be a waste of resources if a party had to incur costs to communicate information that the other party already has in its possession. The second limitation is that information should not be communicated if the information production and communication costs exceed the value of the information to the other party. Third, there should be no duty to reveal entrepreneurial information. Entrepreneurial information is costly to produce, valuable to third parties and is not protected under intellectual property laws. The rule that a person may conceal entrepreneurial information preserves incentives to invest in the production of entrepreneurial information by allowing the investor to obtain returns on his investment. Fourth, there should be no duty to be honest about non-verifiable information. A subjective statement may reflect an honest opinion or it may be a lie. However, third parties, like courts, are unable to find out whether the person who made the subjective statement gave his honest opinion or told a lie.

3.3. Rules on Mistake in the Draft Common Frame of Reference

The previous paragraph describes the *economically* optimal doctrine. It does not describe existing laws and doctrines. It is not within the aim of this article to carry out a thorough analysis of existing national laws and doctrines with a view to determining whether they allocate liability for information deficiencies in similar ways as the economic duty-to-inform doctrine. However, in what follows, I will briefly investigate whether the general rules on mistake in the Draft Common Frame of Reference (DCFR) contain elements that may be considered relevant from an economic perspective in determining whether a duty to inform should exist, such as the relative costs of information. The Draft Common Frame of Reference provides principles, definitions and model rules of European private law. These model rules, with comments and notes, bring together rules derived from the legal systems of the EU member states and the overarching Community law.[20]

[19] ibid 123–24.

[20] C Von Bar and E Clive (eds), *Principles, Definitions and Model Rules of European Private Law: Draft Common Frame of Reference*, Vol I (2010) 1.

Article II.–7:201 DCFR on mistake 'seeks to set out principles which strike a fair balance between the voluntary nature of contract and protecting reasonable reliance by the other party. It does not purport to lay down rules which are "common principles" to be found in different laws, though it reflects what is found in many of them.'[21] The principle laid down in Article II.–7:201 DCFR is that a party may avoid a contract for mistake when the other party has not acted in good faith, has taken deliberate advantage or has behaved carelessly but that a party may not avoid a contract for mistake when the mistake was inexcusable in the circumstances. As such, the question of liability for mistake under the DCFR turns on which one of the parties is to blame for the mistake. The text of this article does not explicitly mention that the blameworthiness of the parties is a matter of their relative information costs, which is the determining factor according to the economic duty-to-inform doctrine.

Comment E on Article II.–7:201 DCFR specifies that 'a party should not normally be permitted to remain silent, with the deliberate intention of deceiving the other party, on some point which might influence the other party's decision on whether or not to enter the contract.'[22] The following illustration is given:

> A sells her house to B without revealing to B that A knows there is extensive rot under the floor of one room. She does not mention it because she assumes B will be aware of the risk of it from the fact that there are damp marks on the wall and will have the floor checked. B does not appreciate the risk and buys the house without having the floor checked. B may avoid the contract.[23]

The outcome of this case corresponds with that implied by economic analysis. Party A has at little or no costs acquired information that the other obviously does not have and which is crucial to the contract. To obtain this information herself, Party B would have to check the floor, most likely by hiring an expert, which involves substantial costs. In this case, Party A is the least-cost information gatherer, and the cheapest way in which Party B may become informed is to oblige Party A to reveal to Party B what Party A already knows, namely by imposing upon A a duty to inform that there is rot under the floor. The sanction for non-disclosure is that Party B may avoid the contract. Requiring Party B to be aware of potential defects and to incur costs to investigate the property would be a more costly and less efficient solution. The outcome of the case given as an illustration in Comment E corresponds to that implied by economic analysis, but in the comment the outcome is obtained through application of the general legal principle of good faith, not by applying economic reasoning.

Comment E further specifies that silence is incompatible with good faith unless there is a good reason for allowing the party to remain silent, for example 'when the knowledgable party has only gained the knowledge at considerable

[21] ibid 457.
[22] ibid 460.
[23] ibid 460.

expense, or in highly competitive commercial situations.'[24] This exception to the general rule corresponds with the exception for entrepreneurial information included in the economic duty-to-inform doctrine.

3.4. Implications of Behavioural Insights

Legal scholars are increasingly making use of existing scholarship in both cognitive psychology and behavioural economics, which suggests that human behaviour often deviates from rational choice in systematic and predictable ways, to explain legal phenomena and to argue for legal reforms.[25] Numerous tests done by psychologists and experimental economists have shown that people often do not exhibit the kind of reasoning ascribed to agents in rational choice models, particularly with regard to decisions made in the face of uncertainty and risk. Psychologists hypothesise that subjects make systematic errors by using decision 'heuristics', or rules of thumb, which fail to accommodate the full logic of a decision. These systematic errors are often referred to as 'biases', and this general topic often carries the label 'heuristics and biases'. The study of heuristics and biases tends to be dominated by attempts to expose systematic errors in human judgement and decision-making.[26]

For example, the principal concern with regard to credit borrowing is the cognitive bias for risk underestimation and irrational discounting (myopia). This is an acute problem in credit borrowing, because the repayment terms for typical debt products usually stretch out for years. Compounding this problem is a complex pricing structure, which often makes credit borrowing difficult to price.[27] Accordingly, one of the problems is that debtors often cannot appreciate what they are getting themselves into: unserviceable levels of debt. If debtors make systematic errors in judgement due to risk underestimation, myopia or some other psychological impediment, then they will make bad choices and do themselves harm, for example by taking out unaffordable credit, if left to their own devices. The problem is aggravated when sophisticated lenders strategically exploit the consumer's behavioural biases by designing and shaping contracts around the consumers' systematic deviations from perfect rationality. According

[24] ibid 460.

[25] C Jolls, CR Sunstein and R Thaler, 'A Behavioral Approach to Law and Economics' (1998) 50 *Stanford Law Review* 1471–550.

[26] P Slovic and S Lichtenstein, 'Comparison of Bayesian and Regression Approaches to the Study of Information Processing in Judgment' (1971) 6 *Organizational Behavior and Human Performance* 649–744; A Tversky and D Kahneman, 'Judgment Under Uncertainty: Heuristics and Biases' (1974) 185 *Science* 1124–31.

[27] One particular mistake that may lead to 'incorrect' pricing is called 'use-pattern mistake'. People often misperceive their future use of the product, eg they underestimate the likelihood of paying late on their credit card bills. See O Bar-Gill, 'Bundling and Consumer Misperception' (2006) 72 *University of Chicago Law Review* 33; O Bar-Gill, 'The Behavioral Economics of Consumer Contracts' (2008) 92 *Minnesota Law Review* 749.

to Bar-Gill, such biased contracting is not the consequence of imperfect competition. On the contrary, competitive forces compel sellers to take advantage of consumer's weaknesses.[28] In the borrowing context, lenders may adopt a particular business model, called the sweatbox model, which is a two-stage model that entices all borrowers at the outset with low rates but then cranks up the heat through late payment fees and penalty rates for the 'sweaters'. The way lenders lure debtors into their sweatbox is by preying upon their underestimation of risk and optimism biases.[29]

The behavioural account of consumer contracting, which is based on models of consumer markets in which sophisticated firms interact with boundedly rational consumers and consumers who may have psychological biases, may be used to explain specific legal rules. For example, under the EU Consumer Credit Directive, creditors bear the responsibility of individually checking the creditworthiness of the consumer.[30] This rule may be considered an exception to the general assumption that each person is in the best position to assess whether a particular purchase is affordable based on personal information regarding a person's ability to pay. For example, when an individual consumer buys a television set, it is generally the consumer who is better situated than the electronics store to know whether the purchase is affordable. This presumption may be reversed in the borrowing context when consumer biases are taken into account. Consumers (debtors) are thought to be worse decision-makers than lenders when it comes to borrowing money. Lenders are thought to have a better idea of how much money a given debtor can afford to pay on a monthly basis without suffering financial distress. The reason is that debtors suffer from psychological impediments that may be debiased in the professional lending setting by creditors with superior cognitive capacities. One could argue that lenders have an incentive to assess whether the debtor can afford the product even in the absence of a legal requirement to do so. However, it has been shown that business models exist under which it is profitable for lenders to extend credit to debtors who very likely cannot repay (ie to make 'reckless' loans), contrary to the conventional perspective of minimising risk and avoiding defaults.[31] Under such conditions, it makes sense to make lenders responsible for individually checking the creditworthiness of the consumer and to render unaffordable credit off-limits.

[28] O Bar-Gill, 'Seduction by Plastic' (2004) 98 *Northwestern University Law Review* 1373.

[29] JAE Pottow, 'Private Liability for Reckless Consumer Lending' (2007) *University of Illinois Law Review* 405, 416.

[30] Directive 2008/48/EC of 23 April 2008 on credit agreements for consumers, OJ 2008 L 133/66. According to Art 8 (Obligation to assess the creditworthiness of the consumer) of the Directive: 'Member States shall ensure that, before the conclusion of the credit agreement, the creditor assesses the consumer's creditworthiness on the basis of sufficient information, where appropriate obtained from the consumer, and, where necessary, on the basis of a consultation of the relevant database.'

[31] RJ Mann, 'Bankruptcy Reform and the "Sweat Box" of Credit Card Debt' (2007) *University of Illinois Law Review* 375.

The movement within legal scholarship, which is referred to as 'behavioural law and economics', builds on the core insights of law and economics scholarship but supplements it with a subtle view of how and why and when humans make mistakes in judgement.[32] Instead of a strict adherence to rational choice theory, the new movement adopts a more subtle and context-dependent view of how individuals behave for the purpose of legal analysis. Based on the relevant decision-making capacities of actors in a specific setting, it can be used to formulate specific normative policies.[33] For example, the finding that debtors are worse decision-makers than lenders in the borrowing context may be used to support specific rules that shift some of the responsibility for making appropriate borrowing decisions towards the lenders. The basic tenet of economic analysis, that the question of liability in cases of imperfect information should turn on which of the parties to the transaction can produce information and avoid mistakes at lower costs, remains unchallenged. A major contribution of behavioural analysis is to point out — based on improved accounts of how people actually behave in specific contexts — which one of the parties to a specific type of transaction is in the best position to produce correct information at the lowest cost to avoid costly mistakes in specific settings.

4. RELATIONSHIPS OF TRUST: GREATER DUTY TO INFORM

4.1. Introduction

In many legal systems, courts are more willing to relieve a party from disadvantageous contractual obligations if the parties are in a special relationship of trust. According to Article II.–7:207 (unfair exploitation) of the Draft Common Frame of Reference:[34] '[a] party may avoid a contract if, at the time of the conclusion of the contract: (a) the party … had a relationship of trust with the other party … and (b) the other party knew or could reasonably be expected to have known this and, given the circumstances and purpose of the contract, exploited the first party's situation by taking an excessive benefit or grossly unfair advantage.'

If the parties are in a special relationship of trust — a relationship such as exists between patient and doctor; or a client and a legal or other professional adviser — then any contract made between them that is disadvantageous to the weaker party is presumed to be due to the undue influence of the other party or to an abuse of the trust reposed in said party.

A strong asymmetry of information exists in trust relationships. One party is very well informed and the other is almost ignorant. However, this fact alone

[32] T Ulen, 'The Growing Pains of Behavioral Law and Economics' (1998) 51 *Vanderbilt Law Review* 1747–63.

[33] R Korobkin and T Ulen, 'Law and Behavioral Science: Removing the Rationality Assumption from Law and Economics' (2000) 88 *California Law Review* 1051–144.

[34] Von Bar and Clive, above n 20.

cannot justify the differential legal treatment of trust relationships. Information asymmetry between seller and buyer characterises almost all transactions. The difference with trust relationships is that in such relationships, the agent (adviser) is explicitly asked (and often paid) to give honest information. The other party (principal) is therefore entitled to look to the other for full and honest information and proper advice. The duty to inform in trust relationships is therefore much greater, and greater intervention on the basis of information deficiency is warranted (section 4.2 below).

The duty of care resulting from the good faith obligation in agency relationships (section 4.3), the suitability doctrine (section 4.4) and the duty imposed upon advisers to inform their customers about their compensation schemes (section 4.5) may be understood as legal rules that provide incentives to advisers in a trust relationship to give more — and more honest — information, including information about the needs of the other party (principal).

4.2. Greater Duty to Inform in Relationships of Trust and Confidence

Individuals often make decisions based on the advice or guidance provided by more informed professionals. When parties are in a special relationship of trust, the duty to inform should be much greater. The reason is that an adviser (agent) in a trust relationship is contractually bound by a greater duty to inform. In situations in which a person is quite helpless to protect himself, he may 'hire' someone with superior information to look out for his best interests. The person with superior knowledge (the agent) is explicitly asked (and often paid) to give advice on the needs of the other party (principal).

Given the circumstances and the purpose of the contract, the adviser (agent) should disclose entrepreneurial information, give his honest opinion even when the information is non-verifiable or controversial and provide information on the principal's needs. The agent in a trust relationship should determine and inform the principal about his needs, whether the contract provides benefits for which the principal is willing and able to pay and whether the principal is willing and able to bear the risk contained in the contract. An agent who fails to disclose this kind of information breaches his contractual obligations. Professional advisers are also bound by the rules of their deontological code to give honest information; it is not permitted to tell lies. This allows the principal to spend less time and money verifying the information given by the agent.

The implication of the greater duty to inform is that a greater intervention on the basis of information deficiencies is warranted when parties are in a trust relationship. In section 3.2 above, it was stated that, in general, each person is the least-cost information gatherer on his own needs. It follows that courts should enforce the contract when a person is mistaken about his own needs. This rule should be reversed when parties are in a trust relationship. A person who finds out that the contract he signed (through intervention of a person with whom he has a special relationship of trust) does not correspond with his wants and needs should be entitled to escape (part of) his contractual obligations. This rule sanctions the adviser (agent) in a trust relationship for failing to give information and advice about the needs of the other party (principal).

4.3. Good-Faith-Based Duty of Care in Agency Relationships

Financial service providers in the Netherlands have a duty of care towards their clients arising out of the general obligation of good faith in agency relationships. When financial institutions advise on which financial product to purchase, they have a duty to give honest information on the risk associated with the product, to warn customers that particular products may be too risky and to investigate whether the product that is recommended is within the customer's risk threshold.

In a recent Dutch case, the court in Alkmaar[35] found the defendant (a bank) liable for non-disclosure of information on the single premium insurances that were sold to the plaintiffs. The plaintiffs went to the bank for a loan of €50,000. In addition to the loan, the bank sold the plaintiffs five single premium insurance policies to cover the risk that the plaintiffs would not be able to repay the loan in case of death, disability or unemployment. The premiums for these policies, which amounted to €20,000 in total, had to be paid up front and at once and were financed by means of an additional loan. According to the court, a professional financial service provider, like the defendant, should have informed the plaintiffs of the disadvantage of having to pay extra interest when premiums are financed through an additional loan. The defendant should have informed the plaintiffs of possible alternatives that had no such disadvantages, like paying the premiums in monthly instalments. The defendant was therefore held liable for the losses suffered by the plaintiffs resulting from the defendant's non-disclosure of information.

4.4. Suitability Doctrine

Article 19(4) of the Markets in Financial Instruments Directive (MiFID)[36] provides as follows:

> When providing investment advice or portfolio management the investment firm shall obtain the necessary information regarding the client's or potential client's knowledge and experience in the investment field relevant to the specific type of product or service, his financial situation and his investment objectives so as to enable the firm to

[35] Rechtbank Alkmaar, 106424, 3 February 2010.

[36] Directive 2004/39/EC of 21 April 2004 on Markets in Financial instruments (MiFID), OJ 2004 L 145/1.

recommend to the client or potential client the investment services and financial instruments that are suitable for him.

The concept of suitability expresses a home truth about investing — investment decisions can be made only in light of the goals and needs of the person for whom they are made. Investors vary with respect to the degree of risk that they are able and willing to assume in their investments, and their portfolios should reflect their differing risk thresholds. Consequently, a security that is suitable for one investor may be unsuitable for another. Imposition of any suitability doctrine has a revolutionary flavour, because it shifts the responsibility for making inappropriate investment decisions from the customer to the broker-dealer.

When a broker-dealer recommends a security to a customer, he has a responsibility to determine that the security he recommended is within a particular customer's risk threshold. This implies that the broker-dealer must consider: (1) whether the security satisfies the individual customer's risk preferences or willingness to bear risk (ie investment objective); and (2) whether the risk is one which the investor has the capacity or ability to bear, notwithstanding customer preferences and desires.

With suitability being defined with respect to both the willingness and capacity of the customer to bear risk, the broker-dealer must obtain complete information about each customer's investment objective and financial background, including his other security investments, his home, savings account, job prospects and other significant non-security assets and liabilities.

According to Mundheim, the theory on which any doctrine of suitability must rest (and which limits its applicability) is that customers tend to rely on their broker-dealer: 'The broker-dealer community has made the investing public aware that it has the special skills needed to deal with such intricate merchandise as securities, and the public has been encouraged to — and has — relied on the superior skills of the broker-dealer community in its securities transactions.'[37]

It is not proposed that the law absolutely prohibits a broker from selling a security that would not be within the particular customer's risk threshold. If an investor persisted in requesting such a security, the broker is permitted to make the sale, provided that he first warns the investor that the purchase is dangerous and imprudent. Cohen states that the requirement to warn customers about purchases that would result in imprudent levels of risk would increase the flow of information available to the investor and protect against the hazards of high-pressure security salesmanship: 'Investment in securities can be fantastically complicated and technical for the lay investor, and brokers typically exert a great influence over customers' investment choices. Without a compulsory warning, a

[37] R Mundheim, 'Professional Responsibilities of Broker-Dealers: The Suitability Doctrine' (1965) *Duke Law Journal* 445, 450.

customer may be influenced by his broker to express a preference for a risk which he does not fully understand and which he is not really willing to undertake.'[38]

The recommendation of a particular security to a particular customer involves an exercise of judgement by the broker-dealer at the time of the sale. The suitability standard should not be a vehicle for second-guessing the judgements of broker-dealers. According to Mundheim, a broker-dealer should only be found to have violated his responsibility

> if no reasoning broker would have recommended the particular security to the particular customer in light of information about the customer which the broker-dealer knew or should have known. This review must be made in the light of the circumstances which existed at the time the recommendation was made. Price information of the security after it was purchased — whether favorable or unfavorable — should be irrelevant in determining whether the recommendation was suitable when made.[39]

The suitability doctrine would be an invitation for disappointed customers to benefit from the 'positive' risks associated with their investment but to shift 'negative' risks towards their broker-dealers, if price information on the security after it was purchased was relevant in determining whether the recommendation was suitable when made.

4.5. The Duty to Inform About Compensation Schemes

Article 26(b)(1) of Directive 2006/73/EC specifies that 'investment firms must disclose to the client the existence, nature and amount of the fee, commission or benefit paid or provided to or by a third party, in a manner that is comprehensive, accurate and understandable prior to the provision of the relevant investment or ancillary service.'[40] The Dutch legislator has mandated disclosure of the commission paid to all intermediaries who sell complex financial products (including insurance intermediaries and mortgage brokers).[41]

In general, the law does not require sellers to disclose information about their compensation scheme. Under the economic duty-to-inform doctrine, the same result would be obtained because such information is entrepreneurial or because the cost of communicating information about the compensation scheme is higher than the value of that information to the buyer. Buyers can usually make an informed choice when they have information on the price and quality of a product or service. How much a salesperson earns on the sale of the product is usually irrelevant to the quality of the buyer's purchase decision.

[38] S Cohen, 'The Suitability Rule and Economic Theory' (1971) 80 *Yale Law Journal* 1604, 1622.

[39] Mundheim, above n 37, 474–75.

[40] Commission Directive 2006/73/EC of 10 August 2006 implementing Directive 2004/39/EC of the European Parliament and of the Council as regards organisational requirements and operating conditions for investment firms and defined terms for the purposes of that Directive, OJ 2006 L 241/26.

[41] Besluit Gedragstoezicht financiële ondernemingen Wft.

How can a duty to inform about compensation schemes be justified? For cases in which buyers rely on the seller's superior information to give advice on the purchase decision, the seller's objectivity and independence are critical for the quality of the buyer's purchase decision. However, particular compensation schemes may cause pervasive conflicts of interest. In business involving an adviser-advisee relationship, conflicts of interest may compromise the adviser's objectivity and independence.

There are many different types of compensation system for intermediaries, but the great majority of advised products and services are sold on the basis of commission (ie *commission-based advice*). Commission can be defined as a payment to an intermediary conditional on the purchase of the product. The payments are usually made by the product provider to the intermediary. The consumer pays indirectly for the advice through higher prices (higher premiums in case of insurance or higher interest rates in case of loans) paid to the product provider. Moreover, consumers only pay for the advice when they effectively buy the product. A person who obtains advice but subsequently decides not to buy the product obtains the advice for free. However, there is no such thing as a 'free lunch'. Advisers receive compensation for the 'wasted' advice costs from those buyers who do buy the product, as they pay higher prices. An alternative compensation system is the *fee-based system*. Under this system, the buyer always pays for the advice, whether or not he subsequently decides to buy the product. The fee may be a fixed fee or an hourly fee for advice.

Whereas the fees paid directly by the customers do not affect the recommendations, commissions do affect recommendations. With commission-based advice, there is a risk of biased advice. Advice can be biased in three different ways.

The first type of bias is *product bias*. In advising across a range of product types, advisers recommend a product type that provides them with the highest commission even though the product type does not fit best with the needs of the customer. The second type of bias is *provider bias*. Within a particular product type, advisers recommend the provider that pays them the highest commission even though other providers' products offer better terms to the consumer. The third type of bias is *sales bias*. Commission provides incentives for intermediaries to sell a product, even when the 'best' advice might be not to purchase or to continue holding on to the product. This sales bias results from the intrinsic feature of commission-based advice that advisers are only paid for their advice when they actually sell the product. This may induce them to selectively disclose information (eg to hide bad information on the product) in order to effectuate the sale.

Safeguards to ensure the objectivity of advice may be needed to reduce biases in advice. One possible measure is to impose upon advisers a duty to inform their customers about their compensation schemes. Disclosure affords a forewarning of biased advice, and advisees may adjust for the bias. Some authors cast doubts on the effectiveness of disclosure in reducing adviser's bias.[42] Advisees may not adequately adjust for the bias. Additional safeguards to ensure the objectivity of advice, such as regulation of the way compensation schemes are structured, may therefore be needed.

5. JUDICIAL CONTROL OF CONTRACT TERMS: INEQUALITY OF BARGAINING POWER

5.1. Inequality of Bargaining Power

The notion of inequality of bargaining power in the market for contracts pervades discussions about the regulation of contract terms for reasons of fairness.[43] The question arises whether it is still right to treat freedom of contract as a central pillar of the legal system. Should it not be limited *ex lege* wherever the parties to a contract are unequal in bargaining power, 'parity of contract' is disturbed and the weaker party needs protection? Is it not time to replace or supplement the principle of freedom of contract with a principle of 'contractual justice'? Under such a principle, there should be equality in contracts as regards knowledge of the facts, in the exchange itself and in the subject matter of the contract for contracts to be valid and enforceable. Courts would be required to set aside contracts (or contractual terms) that were unequal or unfair.

A general legal requirement for the terms of a contract to be fair, so that they will be legally unenforceable if they are not, interferes with freedom of contract. The principle of freedom of contract rests on the assumption that each person is the best judge of what he wants and is willing and able to pay for. A person who enters on a voluntary basis into an agreement will surrender only as much as he is willing to give in order to obtain in exchange something he values more. It is assumed that people only agree to terms that leave them better off. If consent can be observed, it can be inferred that the contract enhances value. When a person who enters into a contract does so of his own free will and is capable of looking after his own interests, it is the responsibility of each person to act with prudence and to decide for himself on the price and other terms on which he is prepared to purchase. It is the agreement, as reached by two parties entering into a contract with a proper understanding of the bargain they are making, which then determines the price and the other terms of the exchange — and nothing else. If the meaning of a clause is clear, the principle of freedom of contract requires that it must be applied and that the courts have no power to relieve one party of its clearly expressed obligations. If a court declared void a particular contractual arrangement on the grounds that it was substantively unfair according to the

[42] D Cain, GF Loewenstein, and DA Moore, 'The Dirt on Coming Clean: Perverse Effects on Conflicts of Interest' (2005) 34 *Journal of Legal Studies* 1; D Schwarcz, 'Beyond Disclosure: The Case for Banning Contingent Commissions' (2006) 25 *Yale Law and Policy Review* 289.

[43] K Zweigert and H Kotz, *An Introduction to Comparative Law* (1998) 331.

fairness standard used, future parties for whom this particular arrangement is value-maximising would no longer be able to adopt it.

Moreover, widespread judicial scrutiny of contract terms may interfere with the principle of individual autonomy of which the freedom of contract principle is a manifestation. A rational person capable of determining his fate must be given the freedom to shape his life responsibly. He must be allowed to decide for himself whether or not to make a contract, towards whom he will undertake a legally recognised obligation and what the content must be. States, and by extension courts, should protect the freedom of the individual and safeguard his power of self-determination. The normative justification for courts to enforce contractual obligations is that they are 'willed' by the parties. Under judicial scrutiny, on the other hand, the court substitutes its judgment for that of the individuals involved.

In the case of inequality of bargaining power, however, courts and legislators express their doubts that the contract contains terms that the parties want and desire. In this case, it is presumed that the stronger party will force terms on parties that do not want them. From this point of view, the contract terms gain their effectiveness not from the private autonomy of the parties but from the submission of one party. Such terms must therefore be denied effectiveness if they contradict the principle of good faith and fairness. Contract terms are thought to be suspect and intervention is deemed to be necessary whenever terms are agreed without any negotiations at all and in cases where one of the parties does not have any influence on the terms of the deal. This is the way in which contracts are often concluded today. The need for judicial and regulatory control of standard form contracts became apparent when business organisations of all types, suppliers of goods, insurance companies and banks had developed standard contract conditions that deviate from the default rules and seriously disadvantage consumers. It was assumed, at least in consumer settings, that deviations from the legal default rules in standard form contracts are not based on the free will of the contracting parties but that they are the result of inequality of bargaining power. In a contract based on standard terms, there must therefore be some kind of justification for a departure from the legal default rules.

Economists, on the other hand, argue that inappropriate terms in standard form contracts are not the result of unequal bargaining power. Rather, inefficient contract clauses result from the failure of customers to read or understand the content of the contract.[44] The use of standard form contracts is typically characterised by imperfect information on the part of some of the parties to those contracts. The failure to read standard form contracts may be the result of a rational decision to save on transaction costs. However, the supplier of standard form contracts may exploit this fact by inserting inefficient clauses into the contract. The behavioural account of standard form contracts assumes that

[44] MJ Trebilcock, *The Limits of Freedom of Contract* (1993).

buyers, when confronted with standard form contracts, only compare a limited number of product and contract attributes when contemplating purchase, because they are boundedly rational rather than fully rational decision-makers.[45] As a result, competition between sellers will generate an efficient level of quality for the attributes that buyers consider ('salient attributes') but low levels of quality for 'non-salient' attributes. For all propositions (unequal bargaining power, failure to read or bounded rationality), the legal implications are much the same: courts should be cautious about enforcing standard form contracts.

5.2. An Economic View of the Unequal Bargaining Power Argument for Judicial Control

The notion of inequality of bargaining power is an intuitive idea, but one that deserves careful examination in order to assess whether it could account for the prevalence of unfair contract terms. Several variants of inequality of bargaining power exist, including: (1) monopoly power; (2) differences in wealth between the parties; and (3) standard contract terms offered on a take-it-or-leave-it basis.

Inequality of bargaining power may exist in a monopolistic market. When only one firm sells products in a particular market, it is called a monopolist. When trading partners are limited, bargains can be very one-sided. Faced with no alternatives, buyers have no choice but to accept the terms determined by the monopolist. Monopolists are able to charge higher prices, that is to say, monopoly prices, when no other suppliers are competing for customers. Inequality that stems from monopoly power would be a market failure, except that (a) firms are rarely monopolist and (b) even if they are, one cannot possibly account for the prevalence of unfair contract terms (ie harsh non-price terms) by reference to that monopoly power. The second point needs further clarification. A rational monopolist also has an incentive to offer the contract terms that parties desire, because in doing so it can maximise its profits.[46] The party with market power will offer terms if the other parties want them, but will not force terms on parties that do not want them. The reason that monopolists offer the terms that parties want is that they can charge a fee for it. The fee or price increase compensates the monopolists for the costs of offering the terms, and the customers accept the fee or price increase because the benefits of the terms are higher than the fee they have to pay for them. The inefficiency of a monopoly lies in the price, not in the quality of the products or the contract clauses. This theoretical claim has been supported by empirical evidence. Florencia Marotta-Wurgler has analysed software licence agreements drawn from many distinct

[45] R Korobkin, 'Bounded Rationality, Standard Form Contracts, and Unconscionability' (2003) 70 *University of Chicago Law Review* 1203.

[46] A Schwartz, 'A Reexamination of Nonsubstantive Unconscionability' (1977) 63 *Virginia Law Review* 1053, 1071–76.

segments of the software industry to empirically investigate the relationship between competitive conditions and the quality of standard form contracts. She has found little evidence for the concern that firms with market power, as measured by market concentration or market share, require consumers to accept particularly one-sided contract terms. In other words, firms in both concentrated and unconcentrated segments of the software market, and firms with large and small market shares, offer similar terms to consumers.[47]

Inequality of bargaining power may also be thought to exist when one contracting party is wealthier than the other contracting party. With their superior bargaining power, firms are able to 'outbid' customers for contract terms. Because customers need money more than firms, they may accept particular contract terms in return for a price decrease. For example, a debtor might be willing to accept a harsh remedial term in return for a lower interest rate. If this is the sense in which inequality of bargaining power is thought to exist between sellers and buyers, it demonstrates not market failure but market success. A market is successful when it moves resources from lower-valued to higher-valued uses. In order to increase wealth, parties must have different endowments, and this suggests that the parties to a contract generally will have unequal bargaining power.

Finally, inequality of bargaining power may be said to exist when the contract is from its inception an act of submission to a take-it-or-leave-it standard form contract with no possibility of negotiating its terms. Regulation of standard form contracts is based on the argument that standard contract terms — those offered on a take-it-or-leave-it basis with no opportunity for negotiation — are sufficiently suspect to satisfy the unequal bargaining proposition. In this respect, take-it-or-leave-it agreements are sometimes called 'contracts of adhesion' to reflect the lack of bargaining power.[48] Under a traditional law and economics analysis, however, the adhesive or standardised nature of the contract does not make it suspect. Standard form contracts are the equivalent of standardised products. Most products in modern markets are standardised. For example, all refrigerators are offered on a take-it-or-leave-it basis; you cannot ask the producer to design and produce a unique refrigerator, like a four-door refrigerator.[49] The take-it-or-leave-it characteristic does not make the consumer uninterested in information about the quality of the goods. The consumer may still decide whether to spend money on that product or on another one (either a similar product from a competitor or a different type of product). Consumers may equally decide whether to accept the standard terms of one supplier or those of

[47] F Marotta-Wurgler, 'Competition and the Quality of Standard Form Contracts: The Case of Software License Agreements' (2008) 5 *Journal of Empirical Legal Studies* 447.

[48] F Kessler, 'Contracts of Adhesion — Some Thoughts About Freedom of Contract' (1943) 43 *Columbia Law Review* 629; TD Rakoff, 'Contracts of Adhesion: An Essay in Reconstruction' (1983) 96 *Harvard Law Review* 1174.

[49] Schwartz, above n 46, 1069.

another one. If one supplier offers unattractive terms, a competing supplier wanting to attract customers, will offer more attractive terms.

Economists conclude that unequal bargaining power, in its different variants, cannot account for the prevalence of unfair contract terms. This is not to say that unfair contract terms do not exist. The claim made by economists is simply that they are not the result of unequal bargaining power. Their existence is the result of something else. That something else is the signing-without-reading problem, which is the subject of the next section.

6. JUDICIAL CONTROL OF CONTRACT TERMS: THE SIGNING-WITHOUT-READING PROBLEM

6.1. Introduction

Contract law provides a set of default rules that apply unless parties have agreed explicit terms to the contrary. While default terms may be efficient for the majority of contracting parties, a minority of parties may be better off adopting explicit terms that deviate from the default rule. Parties are free to decide on their own terms, and freedom of contract requires courts to enforce the explicit terms of the contract.

However, courts do not always enforce the explicit terms of the contract. They may refuse to enforce terms that seem unfair. For example, Article II.–9:403 DCFR states that 'in a contract between a business and a consumer, a term [which has not been individually negotiated] is unfair… if it is supplied by the business and if it significantly disadvantages the consumer, contrary to good faith and fair dealing.' An unfair term is not binding on the party that did not supply it (Article II.–9:409 DCFR). Under the DCFR, courts may set aside a contract term that significantly disadvantages the consumer in comparison with the default rule that would otherwise be applicable, unless it can be shown that the (disadvantageous) deviation from the default rule is justified and not contrary to good faith and fair dealing.[50] Judicial control is also possible in the case of contract terms between parties that are not businesses (Article II.–9:404 DCFR) and in the case of contract terms between businesses (Article II.–9:405 DCFR), but different fairness criteria apply than in the case of contracts between a business and a consumer.

The economic theory on which judicial control and regulation of contract terms rests is that people have a tendency to sign contracts without reading them. The following sections outline the causes of the signing-without-reading problem (section 6.2), the inefficiencies resulting from it (section 6.3) and its

[50] Von Bar and Clive, above n 20, at. 635. The rules on unfair terms in the DCFR are modelled on Directive 93/13 of 5 April 1993 on unfair terms in consumer contracts, OJ 1993 L 095.

implications for the standard of judicial control, the scope of its applicability and the form of legislative action (section 6.4).

6.2. The Signing-Without-Reading Problem

In an ideal world, people would read contracts before they sign them. In the real world, however, few people do so. And those that do read contracts often do not fully understand them. Not knowing the terms of the contract is a special form of information asymmetry. One party is not fully informed about the content of the contract, whereas the other party, usually the drafter of the contract, knows the exact terms of the contract.

At first sight, the solution to this type of information problem is simple. In most cases, misunderstandings can be avoided by reading the contract. The law could therefore insist that parties should read contracts before signing them and sanction parties that neglect to do so. The sanction could consist of acting as if they had read all the contract terms and had consented to them by signing the contract. This implies that courts would not invalidate contracts (or contract terms) when one party was not informed because of its failure to read the content. This sanction would create an incentive to read before signing.

In reality, the problem is more complex. Reading contracts costs time, and time (given the concept of opportunity costs) is money. Since rational parties balance the costs and benefits of reading documents, it can be rational not to read. However, if the drafters of the contract know that some parties will not read the document before signing it, they can abuse that fact and incorporate unfair clauses that benefit the drafters at the expense of the signers.[51]

6.3. Inefficiencies Resulting from the Signing-Without-Reading Problem

The signing-without-reading problem causes several inefficiencies.[52] First, inefficient clauses are adopted in the contract. An inefficient clause creates higher costs for one party (the signer) than it brings benefits to the other party (the drafter). Second, in the case of signing-without-reading, the same market failures may occur as in the case of asymmetrical information on the quality of the goods. Akerlof explains how asymmetrical information on the quality of goods may lead to adverse selection, meaning that good quality products may be driven from the market by bad quality products.[53] The same process may evolve when buyers

[51] G De Geest, 'The Signing-Without-Reading Problem: An Analysis of the European Directive on Unfair Contract Terms' in H Schäfer and J Lwowski (eds), *Konsequenzen Wirtschaftsrechtlicher Normen* (2002) 213, 214.

[52] ibid 217–8.

[53] G Akerlof, 'The Markets for 'Lemons': Qualitative Uncertainty and the Market Mechanism' (1970) 84 *Quarterly Journal of Economics* 488.

are not informed of the content of the contract. Goldberg argues that because the majority of consumers do not notice good contract clauses, harsh-term, low-price contracts will drive out efficient ones, even in competitive markets.[54] Finally, consumers who do not trust sellers may either stop buying goods because of the risk that inefficient terms are adopted in the contract or may spend too much effort on reading contracts to avoid being bound by inefficient contract terms.

Market forces are not strong enough to solve the signing-without-reading problem. Schwartz and Wilde[55] are optimistic that informed shoppers will be able to discipline the market. Consumers who lack information have incentives to acquire information. Some consumers will acquire information more easily than others; these are the people who read standard form contracts. However, the other consumers can free-ride on the efforts of the first group. If sellers cannot easily distinguish between informed and uninformed consumers, they cannot exploit the latter by including inefficient terms in their contract. However, Gazal has shown that we can only expect efficient standard form contracts in markets in very implausible situations.[56]

6.4. Solutions for the Signing-Without-Reading Problem

6.4.1. Judicial Control of Contractual Terms

Asymmetrical information on the terms included in the contract cannot be solved by increasing the amount of information obtained by consumers on the content of the contract. As noted above, information could be increased if consumers would read the contract, but a duty-to-read is too costly a solution. An entitlement to avoid the contract when a consumer can show that he was mistaken about the content of the contract due to signing without reading, similar to the doctrine of mistake, would also be difficult to implement. It is very difficult to prove a signing-without-reading problem in a direct way. Instead, substantive regulation of the content of contracts terms through judicial control is justified in this case as an implicit evidence rule. How can a signing-without-reading problem be inferred from the terms of the contract? The fact that the contract contains a term that informed and rational parties would never accept is implicit evidence that one of the contracting parties did not read or understand the contract.[57] What terms would informed and rational parties never accept?

[54] V Goldberg 'Institutional Change and the Quasi-Visible Hand' (1974) 17 *Journal of Law and Economics* 461.

[55] A Schwartz and L Wilde, 'Intervening in Markets on the Basis of Imperfect Information: A Legal and Economic Analysis?' (1979) 127 *University of Pennsylvania Law Review* 630.

[56] O Gazal, 'Economic Analysis of Unfair Terms in Standard Form Contracts', Erasmus Programme in Law And Economics Discussion Papers on Law and Economics No 100 (1999).

[57] De Geest, above n 51, 225.

These are terms that do not enhance the joint value of the contracting parties or inefficient terms. Examples include terms of which the costs to one party are much higher than the benefits they bring to the other party. In such cases, the value decrease to one party is larger than the value increase to the other party, resulting in a net reduction of total value. Under an efficiency approach to the standard for judicial control, courts would set aside contract terms that do not enhance the joint value of contracting parties.

6.4.2. *Which Terms Should Be Subjected to Judicial Control?*

The economic rationale for judicial control of contract terms is the signing-without-reading problem. It follows that such control should be confined to terms that people lack incentive to read or pay attention to. There is no need for judicial control of contract terms for which no signing-without-reading problem exists. It is difficult to prove the absence of a signing-without-reading problem, but its absence may be inferred on the basis of substantive or procedural evidence. Substantive evidence relates to the substance of clauses, whereas procedural evidence relates to the circumstances of contracting.

Procedural evidence of the absence of a signing-without-reading problem exists when the contract term was clearly individually negotiated. People obviously pay attention to the terms that they negotiate on an individual basis. However, even when terms are individually negotiated (in which case it may be assumed that people read the contract before signing), some people may not fully understand what they read. This is the signing-without-understanding problem. For example, people may not fully understand the legal consequences of a clause. Evidence of the absence of signing-of-understanding problems exists when the terms are drafted in plain and intelligible language.[58] Terms that have been drafted in advance (whether or not as part of a standard contract) are not individually negotiated. For such terms, signing-without-reading problems may be presumed, unless make-read techniques are so obviously attention-attracting (eg with very clear warnings) that the consumer must have been aware of the clause before signing.

Substantive evidence of the absence of a signing-without-reading problem exists for the subject matter of the contract and the price-related terms.[59] These are aspects that people take into account when buying a product or service. Finally, there is no need to check the fairness of terms that deviate from the default rules when the drafter's costs of the deviation from the default rule are higher than his costs under the default rule. In this case, the drafter will have to

[58] cp with Art II.–9:402(1) DCFR (duty of transparency in terms not individually negotiated): 'A person who supplies terms which have not been individually negotiated has a duty to ensure that they are drafted and communicated in plain, intelligible language.'

[59] cp with Art II.–9:406(2) DCFR (exclusions from unfairness test): 'For contract terms which are drafted in plain and intelligible language, the unfairness test extends neither to the definition of the main subject matter of the contract, nor to the adequacy of the price to be paid.'

charge a higher price than competitors who apply the default rule or deviate from the default rule in a way that is less costly to them. Uninformed consumers pay attention to prices (salient terms) but not to other terms (non-salient terms). Hence, uninformed consumers choose the contract with the lowest price. The fact that people choose the more expensive contract is substantive evidence that they are informed about the content of the contract, otherwise they would not choose it.[60] There is no signing-without-reading problem with respect to more expensive terms, which offer more protection to consumers than the default rules.

6.4.3. Legislative Action: Black Lists and Grey Lists

Legislators have developed lists of contract terms that may be regarded as unfair. There are two types of lists: black lists and grey lists.

Clauses that are put on the black list are considered unfair in all circumstances. They are always prohibited. From an economic perspective, it is appropriate to put contract terms that are inefficient in all circumstances on the black list. Examples of such terms include terms 'giving the seller or supplier the right to determine whether the goods or services supplied are in conformity with the contract, or giving him the exclusive right to interpret any term in the contract.' Such terms allow the supplier to play the role of judge. The supplier, however, is not a neutral judge. He has an incentive to change the terms in his own favour. Rational parties would never accept such clauses.[61]

When clauses are inefficient for one group of consumers and efficient for another group, determining the optimal policy is more complex. According to De Geest: 'Restricting contractual freedom, on the one hand, leads to social losses by not allowing a minority of consumers to adopt clauses that are efficient to them. Allowing contractual freedom, on the other hand, leads to social losses by introducing signing-without-reading problems.'[62] The best policy option according to De Geest is to adopt a *grey list* of suspicious clauses. These clauses are void in principle, unless there is evidence of true consent. Evidence of true consent may exist when the contract was clearly individually negotiated (and the terms are drafted in plain and intelligible language) or when the make-read techniques are so obviously attention-attracting (eg a very clear warning) that the consumer must have been aware of the clause before signing the contract.

An example of terms that may be put on the grey list are those 'inappropriately excluding or limiting the legal rights of the consumer *vis-à-vis* the seller or supplier or another party in the event of total or partial non-performance or inadequate performance by the seller or supplier of any of the contracting obligations.' Such terms are inefficient for most contracting parties because they

[60] De Geest, above n 51, 227.
[61] ibid 232–3.
[62] ibid 226.

give sub-optimal incentives to the supplier to perform his obligations, but may be efficient for some parties when, for some reason, the consumer is in the best position to bear the risks of the supplier's non-performance. To ensure that these terms are only part of the contract between parties for whom they are efficient, they should only be enforced when evidence of true consent exists in one of the ways mentioned above.

7. CONCLUSIONS

Information deficiencies play an important role in contract enforcement. Courts frequently refuse to enforce contracts when one of the parties lacks information. In that way, a person who lacks information is able to shift the consequences to the other party. When is it appropriate to shift responsibility for information deficiencies from one contracting party to the other?

From an economic perspective, it is appropriate to impose liability on the seller when he can produce, convey or obtain the pertinent information at lower cost, unless the information is entrepreneurial, non-verifiable, already known to the buyer or not valuable for the buyer. The buyer, on the other hand, should bear responsibility for information deficiencies related to his own needs, unless contracting parties are in a special relationship of trust. In most cases, people are in the best position to know what their own needs are. It is accordingly the responsibility of each person to act with prudence and invest a certain amount of cognitive effort to ensure that he has thought through his options and selected a product that best meets his needs and desires. In a relationship of trust, on the other hand, the adviser (agent) is contractually bound by a greater duty to inform, including a duty to give information and advice about the principal's needs. Greater intervention on the basis of information deficiencies is therefore warranted for trust relationships.

It is not within the aim of this article to conduct a thorough analysis of existing national laws and doctrines with a view to determining whether they allocate responsibilities for information deficiencies in similar ways as economically-inspired rules and doctrines would. Nevertheless, a preliminary analysis of the DCFR and European regulation on financial transactions reveals that they provide outcomes that largely correspond to those implied by economic analysis.

The economic theory of judicial or legal regulation of contract terms rests on the tendency of people to sign contracts without reading them. The implications of this theory are that courts should set aside (or legislators should prohibit) contract terms that rational, informed parties would never accept but that judicial control is unwarranted in cases where substantive or procedural evidence exists that there is no signing-without-reading problem.

4

Consumer Bankruptcy: A Third Way Between Autonomy and Paternalism in Private Law

NICK HULS*

ABSTRACT

The introduction of American ideas of consumer bankruptcy in European continental civil law systems appears to present an opportunity to resolve some of the paradoxes of paternalism analysed by Ogus.[1] Bankruptcy law for individuals in Europe has evolved from a neglected field of procedural civil law, in which creditor autonomy was the prevailing norm, into a blossoming field of social policy and consumer protection. This article sketches the history of 'bankruptcy waves' and reflects on the possibilities of a future regulatory wave in which the lessons of the credit crunch have been incorporated. It concludes with some thoughts on the theme of this volume.

1. INTRODUCTION

THE TENSION BETWEEN autonomy and paternalism in private law has a long history. In this article, I will present consumer bankruptcy as a hyper-modern private law institution in which a middle ground has been realised, at both national and European level.

I have never believed that private law institutions are politically neutral and have found it rewarding to explore the political dimensions of substantive and procedural regulations in the fields of debtor-creditor law. Unlike law and economics scholars, in the field of socio-legal studies we are not so much inclined to define contractual relations in individual, but in social, societal and sociological terms. Furthermore, unlike Margaret Thatcher, we believe that there is such a thing as society, and not only individuals.

* Professor of Socio-Legal Studies, Erasmus School of Law and Leiden Law School.

1 A Ogus, 'The Paradoxes of Legal Paternalism and How to Resolve Them' (2010) 30 *Legal Studies* 61–73.

I have deliberately chosen the include the phrase 'a third way' in the title of this chapter, because it refers to — and is an icon of — the discussions in the 1990s about the renewal of social-democratic political thought.[2] Third-way thinkers have tried to find an ideological middle way between the dynamics of market forces and societal innovation, on the one hand, and a leaner welfare state that is aimed at activating rather than pampering its citizens, on the other. This makes the concept relevant for the juxtaposition of autonomy and paternalism in contract law.

In 2011, we are facing the results of a big credit crunch after decades of unprecedented economic growth in the West, which has been financed to a large extent with borrowed money. Now that the financial system and the underlying markets have obviously failed to produce eternal prosperity, governments, businesses and consumers must repay the debts that they had previously accumulated.[3] One of the battlegrounds will be the bankruptcy of individuals, which makes this an ideal opportunity to test autonomous and paternalistic assumptions that constitute private law in action. Rich Western societies have to devise policies to distribute the damage between creditors, debtors and society at large in a fair and acceptable manner.

I have been a student of consumer credit contracts since I wrote my PhD dissertation in 1981[4] and was involved in drafting the Dutch Consumer Credit Act (1984–90). Substantive consumer credit contract law is a very timely subject these days, as we are facing pay-back time after the credit crunch. In credit law we can examine the strengths and weaknesses of both consensual and institutional approaches.

When a consumer signs a consumer credit contract, he uses his future earning power in the present. In the credit market, the person is a free and autonomous consumer, but for his future income he is usually dependent on his employer. Credit contracts constitute long-term relationships, and this means all kinds of events may interfere in the normal execution of the contract (eg divorce, unemployment, etc). If the debtor is unable to maintain his payments, he has a problem with his creditor. Because credit is so readily available nowadays, a debtor in default normally has many creditors. If a debtor cannot pay his debts, there will also be a fight between the creditors for the debtors' assets and future income. Here, procedural private law comes into play: collective debt enforcement often ends in bankruptcy.

In this article, I will examine the birth and development of the consumer bankruptcy model that Europe has modelled after the US Bankruptcy Code.

[2] A Giddens, *The Third Way: the Renewal of Social Democracy* (1998).

[3] See RA Posner, *A Failure of Capitalism: the Crisis of 2008 and the Descent into a Depression* (2009).

[4] N Huls 'Consumer Credit, Socio-Economic Considerations, Especially in Relation to Hire Purchase' (dissertation (in Dutch), Utrecht) (1981).

My starting point is a book that I published in 1994 — together with some colleagues — at the request of the European Commission.[5] The book was an academic attempt to promote the combination of existing informal social practices with a new legal impetus from the US Bankruptcy Code, at both EU and national level.

More recently, I have participated in the collective efforts of the Working Group on Consumer Bankruptcy of the Law and Society Association.[6]

2. A SHORT POLITICAL HISTORY OF DEBT ENFORCEMENT

Pacta sunt servanda is the ultimate incentive for the autonomous individual to take full responsibility for keeping the promises he has made. As such it is a rock-solid moral, legal and policy principle of human coexistence.[7] The binding power of agreements is also a vital element of our daily social life.

In pre-modern times, failure to pay debts was regarded as a punishable offence. Not honouring personal promises was considered a morally reprehensible deed. Non-payment of debt was primarily an offence against the contractual party, but it was also a social evil that lent itself well to a public response. Cruel practices (eg drawing and quartering or the stocks), forms of slavery (eg peonage or forced labour) and incarceration (debtors' prison) were the severe responses by which society and the legal system traditionally expressed their abhorrence.[8] Therefore, bankruptcy has a long and depressing[9] tradition of retribution.

A first breakthrough occurred when capitalism began to develop and industrial production methods became increasingly large-scale. Commercial transactions became larger and riskier, which meant that private entrepreneurs/owners were no longer willing to guarantee their companies' obligations. The legal answer to this need for restricting liability was the legal person (*rechtspersoon*). If an entrepreneur did not want to be liable in person, his company's debts were borne by a legal construct. The societal gain attached to the entrepreneurial spirit and risk-taking was considered to be greater than that of bearing personal liability for debts. The idea behind this legal construct was that society as a whole benefited from the legal protection of adventurous entrepreneurs. This limitation of the entrepreneur's liability was not considered to be paternalistic at all!

[5] N Huls *et al*, *Overindebtedness of Consumers in the EC Member States: Facts and Search for Solutions*, Collection Droit et Consommation No 29 (1994).

[6] J Niemi-Kiesliainen, WC Whitford and I Ramsay (eds) *Consumer Bankruptcy in Global Perspective* (2003); and J Niemi, I Ramsay and WC Whitford (eds), *Consumer Credit, Debt and Bankruptcy: Comparative and International Perspectives* (2009).

[7] H Arendt, *The Human Condition* (1958). See, in particular, the final sections of Part V.

[8] JH Dalhuisen '*Compositions in Bankruptcy: A Comparative Study of the Law of the EC Countries, England and the USA*'. PhD Dissertation (1968).

[9] 'Bankruptcy is a gloomy and depressing subject' is the famous opening phrase of Charles Warren's *History of Bankruptcy Law* (1935).

A second development was the need for bankruptcy as a collection tool against small entrepreneurs. This legal instrument is of particular importance in preventing individual creditors of a company in financial difficulties from jumping the queue and causing a damaging mutual struggle entailing significant social costs. Because bankruptcy is also a conflict between creditors *inter se*, the law traditionally recognises the figure of an independent administrator (trustee), who is responsible for the optimal and honest settlement of the claims, or an honest distribution of the losses, in order to prevent the bankruptcy degenerating into a situation in which the debtor is 'robbing Peter to pay Paul'. This is a classic collective action problem[10] that creditors themselves cannot resolve, given their conflicting individual interests. Government intervention in this multi-party constellation is necessary, without a need for paternalistic justification. Creditor autonomy does not do much good when the insolvent debtor has many creditors.

In contrast to the commercial world, bankruptcy law for individuals long remained an underdeveloped area. This legal field only really gained importance in the 1960s when Western economies developed into full-blown consumer societies, where credit began to play an increasing role. Credit was regarded as an important positive engine for economic growth. The moral objections to 'live now, pay later' faded into the background when big bona fide financial institutions began providing large-scale credit to broad swathes of the population. Initially the focus was on instalment payments, credit linked to specific purchases, but later loans and revolving credit came to prominence: credit the consumer could utilise freely.

Once consumer credit reached full maturity virtually everywhere in rich Western European countries, the interest in consumer bankruptcy along American lines arose of itself.[11] In America, the limited liability of the consumer in bankruptcy functioned as a social safety net for which the Europeans had welfare state provisions. American concepts like 'discharge of debts' and the 'fresh start' policy appealed to European policy-makers for various reasons. It fitted well in a period of deregulation and privatisation, where state interference was regarded, in the famous words of Ronald Reagan 'not as the solution, but as the problem'. European politicians wanted to slim down the bloated welfare state, and a debt clean-up law sat well within liberal thinking. It was after all a type of social policy for which the politicians could receive credit, while passing the bill to the creditors.

Furthermore, the American legal concepts fitted well in Europe's *Zeitgeist* of the 1990s. The over-indebted consumer was no longer regarded as a deviant who readily became dependent on the state but as someone who has taken too much risk on the financial markets. Entrepreneurial risk-taking was then part of the

[10] M Olson, *The Logic of Collective Action. Public Goods and the Theory of Goods* (1965).

[11] See G Hörmann (ed), *Consumer Credit and Consumer Insolvency: Perspectives for Legal Policy from Europe and the USA* (1986); M Balz, 'Insolvenzverfahren für Verbraucher?' (1986) *Zeitschrift für Rechtspolitik* 12 ff.

new ideal of citizenship in civil society. In that same period, the OECD criticised European governments[12] for the fact that their harsh bankruptcy laws made small entrepreneurs risk-averse to setting up new businesses, and they became a target group for the new bankruptcy legislation.

In sum, the political message of the 1990s was that protection of debtors against creditors yields big societal benefits, and the transformation of old-fashioned procedural private law is a good mechanism for gaining these benefits.

3. HISTORICAL AND COMPARATIVE ANALYSIS OF 'WAVES' OF BANKRUPTCY REGULATION[13]

Historically, there are four periods of more or less intense activity by legislators in developing bankruptcy law.

3.1. The First Wave: Fair Distribution of Property

The first regulations were derived from the French Commercial Code of 1806. The French regulated the distribution of the property of merchants in favour of their creditors through a form of creditor self-regulation. The French code mandated the *tribunal de commerce* (lay institutions) to proceed in bankruptcy cases.

The second step in the regulation of bankruptcy occurred at the end of the nineteenth century and took place not only in continental Europe but also in England and America. Bankruptcy had become particularly important against the background of the industrial revolution in continental Europe. In 1877, Germany passed a more general bankruptcy code that incorporated merchants and companies but, significantly, did not exclude individual debtors. Similar legislation was adopted elsewhere in Europe. The US Bankruptcy Act was passed by the US Congress in 1898.

This late-nineteenth-century law was based on the idea that bankruptcy should help creditors to recover as much as possible of the debt owed to them from the commercial debtor's assets. In fact, under the Greek, French and Belgian bankruptcy schemes, only merchants and companies can be declared bankrupt. Other schemes, like the Spanish, British and German ones, distinguish between companies and individuals. Although they do not expressly exclude the individual's debtor whose indebtedness does not arise from commercial activity, the design of these bankruptcy codes shows a clear leaning towards commercial debts.

At the heart of the bankruptcy procedures is the property of the debtor. Without property there is no bankruptcy. In most bankruptcy schemes, the

[12] eg, OECD, *Reviews of National Science and Technology Policies: the Netherlands* (1986).

[13] This paragraph is based on Udo Reifner's analysis in chapter 6 of Huls *et al*, above n 5.

interests of the creditors are paramount. The distribution of the debtor's property is consequently the main purpose of continental bankruptcy legislation. The discharge of debts and the protection of debtors is not its primary focus.

3.2. The Second Wave: Restructuring

The second wave of reforms in bankruptcy legislation came at a time when the world economic crisis of the 1920s and 1930s highlighted the problems of over-indebted companies and merchants whose economic survival was seen as valuable for the whole economy. Rescue plans and state support for weak enterprises in order to save jobs brought a whole new philosophy: that one should not only consider the interests of creditors in recovering outstanding debts but also give assistance and support to overcommitted debtors. The US Chandler Act of 1938 introduced bankruptcy procedures that were intended to provide an alternative settlement that would facilitate the survival of bankrupt enterprises. The rights of the creditors were not challenged, but measures intended to bring about an equitable settlement were proposed. These measures included the suspension of payments during the 'bankruptcy' procedure, which gave the debtors relief so that they could seek such settlements. The American division between chapters 7 and 13 of the Bankruptcy Code characterised the new dualism in bankruptcy law.

The suspension of payment rules required the consent of the creditors before they could be applied. This approach lacked some of the traditional stigma attached to bankruptcy, but the influence of the second wave in bankruptcy law on the real economy was not very large.

3.3. The Third Wave: Emergence of Debtor's Protection in Bankruptcy Law

While the second wave of reforms in bankruptcy law can be located quite precisely in time (the Great Crash of 1929), the development of exemption laws to protect the standards of living of the debtor (the third wave) were mostly introduced into civil codes as general principles of protection against garnishment of wages and seizure of property.

The primary objective was to guarantee the physical survival of the debtor, and thus to limit the social welfare spending of the state, on the one hand, while trying to ensure that the debtor was still able to earn a living, on the other. The law lists the items that are exempt from garnishment. Most bankruptcy laws make reference to these exemption laws.

3.4. The Fourth Wave: Reregulating Insolvency (1980s)

While bankruptcy laws increasingly regulated the ways in which the insolvency of the debtor was dealt with instead of simply enforcing the creditors' claims, a new breed of creditors, in particular the banks, devised new means of debt enforcement that rendered bankruptcy steadily less efficient. The banks developed their own forms of insolvency regulation through reservation of property, leasing, wage assignments and pre-authorised rights to auction real estate.

In the early 1960s, studies showed that bankruptcy procedures had become inefficient. As a result most practical insolvency measures had developed outside traditional legal procedures.

Coinciding with the demise of traditional bankruptcy philosophy, there was trade union pressure to rescue important industries. This pressure pushed the idea of general bankruptcy reform. In the 1980s, nearly all EEC countries worked on proposals to revise their regulations on the insolvency of debtors. The shift from bankruptcy to insolvency regulation was also visible in the new categories of debtors in the bankruptcy laws.

While the bankruptcy reforms in all countries reflected some shift in emphasis from protecting the creditors' interests to protecting the debtor, bankruptcy regulation still essentially remained a market-based solution. It was a response to problems that had arisen much earlier and an attempt to impose a legal framework on what was an economic development. The insight that debt problems and insolvency do not require the protection of creditors so much as that of debtors led to a paradigm shift that focused on making bankruptcy procedures fit for the idea of consumer protection. During this period, the consumer credit revolution was taking place.

Problems of new poverty, over-indebtedness and lifelong dependence on banks and other creditors made it obvious that social protection laws targeting seizure of property, wage garnishment and other forms of debt enforcement were no longer adequate in modern consumption societies.

The traditional bankruptcy schemes did not allow ordinary people access to a fresh start. The reasons were as follows:

- Insolvency procedures for merchants and companies were designed to be self-financing procedures. They presupposed some minimum level of assets owned by the debtor and therefore barred from insolvency procedures those people who had nothing to sell apart from their labour.
- Insolvency procedures for commercial organisations were intended to achieve the distribution of property to the creditors or the restructuring of the company's assets. Over-committed private debtors, however, did not generally have any seizable property.
- Bankruptcy legislation was much too complicated for consumer problems.

3.5. The Post-1990 Paradigm of Consumer Bankruptcy in Europe

The laws that were developed in this period have many common elements, namely:

- all countries agreed that their traditional bankruptcy legislation did not meet the needs of individual debtors;
- nearly all procedures restrict access for individuals in non-commercial activity, even though it is acknowledged that individual debtors may have old commercial debts;
- all procedures can only be instigated by the debtor;
- all procedures include the future earnings of the debtor;
- all procedures allow for discharge from those debts that are included in the plan and will not be paid off within their given time limit;
- all schemes make provision to exclude those who abuse the scheme;
- the procedures have little or no costs attached to them and are specially designed to allow access for poor people.

The intellectual underpinning of modern insolvency law was laid down in the Cork Report.[14] There are three parties: the debtor, the creditor and society. Society is concerned with relieving and protecting the individual insolvent from the harassment of creditors and enabling the individual to regain financial stability and have a new chance. It accords the insolvent this relief in return for contributions, not only from his (non-exempt) assets but also from his future earnings, as can reasonably be made by him without reducing him and his family to undue and socially unacceptable poverty and without depriving him of the incentive to succeed in this new chance.

This led to the following principles:

- To recognise that we are living in a society based on credit, which has brought us great prosperity. This requires, as a necessary result, proceedings to remedy the accidents of the credit society.
- To diagnose and treat imminent insolvency at an early stage rather than at a late stage.
- To protect the debtor and his family from undue demands and harassment by their creditors and, at the same time, to have regard for the rights of the creditor, whose position can also be threatened.
- To prevent conflicts between individual creditors through a fair distribution of the proceeds among all creditors.
- To sell the non-exempt assets of the insolvent, which should properly be taken to satisfy his debts, with the minimum of delay and expense.
- To establish and encourage professional and independent debt-counselling.

[14] Insolvency Law and Practice, Report of the Review Committee (HMSO, June 1982).

— To determine the causes of over-indebtedness and to take suitable measures if fraudulent behaviour is found.
— To guarantee the public interest that is at stake in cases of insolvency.
— To lower the unproductive costs of ineffective debt-collection.

4. WHERE AUTONOMY AND PATERNALISM MEET: US CONSUMER BANKRUPTCY

The US Bankruptcy Code makes it very easy for debtors in the most capitalistic and materialistic country on earth to free themselves of their debts. In the 1980s, the American 'fresh start' policy inspired many European countries to transform their bankruptcy laws from a collection mechanism serving creditors into a social policy instrument that offered debtors in financial difficulty the opportunity of a new perspective.

The US Bankruptcy Code has its own very typical American 'wild west' history: the struggle against bonded labour and peonage, the Supreme Court ruling in *Local Loan Company v Hunt* (1934), states that offer generous exemptions to become an attractive base for immigrants and, last but not least, the fact that bankruptcy is included in the Constitution, which gives the federal government the authority to act as a regulator in this private law area.[15]

What particular aspects of the Bankruptcy Reform Act of 1978 made it so attractive for European countries, which had completely different legal cultures, to remodel their laws?

I believe that the most inspiring aspect of the 'fresh start' policy is its future-oriented perspective. While traditional European bankruptcy laws put the emphasis on the blame of the debtor in the past, when he incurred his debt, US law looks to the future. How can the debtor be put back on his feet, how can he regain a perspective on life and, most pragmatically, how can he be turned once again into a productive taxpayer? In other words, how can his life be prevented from becoming 'a walking debtors prison' and how can he regain his autonomy?

Financial risk-taking and its associated entrepreneurial spirit is regarded positively in the US. The stories of successful entrepreneurs whose first companies went bankrupt are well known. A bankruptcy in the US is a chapter in someone's life that should be closed as quickly as possible, so that he can move on.

In the US, bankruptcy has the effect of a social safety net for a number of events in the lives of citizens that in Europe are covered by social welfare provisions: unemployment, illness, hospital admission and so forth. As a result of events beyond his control, a consumer can end up in financial difficulty. If he does not have the perspective of a better future, this could tempt him into

[15] From DT Stanley and M Girth, *Bankruptcy. Problems, Process, Reform* (1971) to E Warren, JL Westbrook and TA Sullivan, *The Fragile Middle Class: Americans in Debt* (2000).

dishonest behaviour, which is socially undesirable. In the US, this system is financed not by taxpayers' money but by creditors.

It also sits uncomfortably with American regulatory culture to have the government impose restrictions on credit provision. This is regarded as politically undesirable intervention in corporate decisions of the banks, on the one hand, and as an infringement of the freedom of the consumer, on the other. Credit was and continues to be regarded as a positive engine driving economic growth. Concepts such as improvident credit-granting and usury rates can count on little sympathy, because their effect is to exclude poor people from credit. There are, of course, some concerns about excessive credit-granting, but the problems that arise from this can best be resolved by the self-regulating powers of the market and liberal bankruptcy law.

It should not go unreported that the financial services industry has lobbied for years against some very liberal components of the BRA (Bankruptcy Reform Act). An important criticism was that the consumer's choice between chapter 7 (liquidation) and chapter 13 (the repayment plan) provokes strategic behaviour. For a debtor without income but with assets, it is very attractive to opt for chapter 13, while a debtor without assets and with a regular income gains by opting for chapter 7. In both cases, the debtor gets a cheap discharge of debts at the expense of his creditors. The financial services industry lobby has succeeded twice. In 1984, a substantial abuse clause restricting free choice between chapter 7 and chapter 13 was added to the law. In 2005, the financial services industry was again successful in its frontal attack on the misuse of the bankruptcy regulations by consumers, resulting in the Bankruptcy Abuse Protection and Consumer Protection Act (BAPCPA) 2005.

4.1. Differences and Similarities Between the US and Europe

There are considerable differences in the legal cultures of the US and the countries of north-western Europe. This has to do with the fact that countries adhering to the civil law tradition have something like an '*ordre public*',[16] a facet of a state that aspires towards what is good for the collective as a whole and a legal order that is perceived as 'just' by the people.

Another major difference is that when Americans hear the word 'solidarity', they quickly place their hands on their wallets, afraid as they are of tax increases. In Europe, it goes without saying that certain risks will be carried collectively and financed from the public purse, while in the US these risks are dealt with in the private insurance market.[17]

[16] See Ogus, above n 1, at 65 and Wagner in this volume. See also M Garcia Villega, 'Comparative Sociology of Law, Legal Fields, Legal Scholarship and Social Science in Europe and the United States' (2006) 31 *Law and Social Inquiry* 2, also published in French in (2009) *L'Année sociologique* 29–62, 50. Peter Gabel once observed that 'European lawyers always have the fog of the State in their heads'.

[17] See the contribution of Schwarcz to this volume.

However, there are similarities as well. Credit in Europe is now totally democratised: all segments of the population make intensive use of it. The expression 'living beyond one's means' has lost its pejorative connotation. In modern capitalism, extending credit to consumers has been depersonalised to a high degree. In other words, it is based on technologically advanced credit scoring and assessment techniques.

Boundaries were also shifted in the investment market. Investors without collateral were also able to benefit from the rising stock and house prices. One of the many innovations in the financial markets was investing with borrowed money.

Since the 1990s, the various financial markets in Europe are no longer separated. Politicians expressed their approval for the fact that banks and insurers merged and that financial institutions began operating in each others' turf. In a very short period, an integrated global market for financial services had come into being. Saving, investing, insuring, lending, asset management and payments were no longer separate markets but were melding into each other. The advent of the internet meant that distance and time differences very quickly ceased to play a role in international transactions. Huge sums of money flashed around the world in an instant, seeking the highest return. The financial vanguard consisted of gigantic multinationals and huge professional investors doing business worldwide. All manner of new and complex financial products were developed which also further transcended the traditional boundaries.

4.2. The Politics of Autonomy and Paternalism

Radical market thinking dominated political, economic and legal discussions in the 1990s. The 'system' provided unbroken economic growth, and because there had been no other ideological alternative since the fall of the Berlin Wall in 1989, free-market capitalism developed into the dominant global perspective.

The past few decades in Europe were characterised by the celebration of the autonomy and self-regulation by the market. Anyone arguing for protection of debtors, prudent banking or limits on risk acceptance by financial institutions was not only seen as paternalist but also demonstrated a lack of knowledge in terms of keeping up with the speed of financial innovation. The advanced mathematics of calculating and estimating risk margins (computational finance) created its own world, with its own mandarin language that was only comprehensible to very specifically trained insiders (quants).[18] The burden of proof for the usefulness or necessity of government intervention was on the paternalists.

In this period, critical questions about the desirability of teaser rates, payment protections insurance and stock trading with borrowed money in the consumer

[18] WH Buiter, '*Lessons from the Global Credit Crisis for Social Democrats*', Den Uyl Lecture (December 2008).

arena were all dismissed. In the period before 2007, pleas for consumer protection were regarded as hard paternalism: a wish to deny the common man the benefits which the free capital market or the stock market also holds in store for him. The consumer was considered to be perfectly capable of deciding for himself (autonomously) whether a transaction was too risky.

The rhetoric of the proponents of consumer bankruptcy emphasised the autonomous core: private law provides the consumer — the sovereign ruler of the market — with a mechanism to deal with his many selfish creditors. Because they grant credit so easily, it is fair that creditors are forced to share the burden of over-indebted consumers. Debt enforcement and its consequences are never left entirely to the autonomy and contract freedom of the parties involved. State involvement is necessary and desirable to achieve acceptable outcomes. In the modern credit society, consumer bankruptcy is not only a problem for the debtor-creditor relationship at the individual level but also for the relationships between the various creditors.

5. THE CONVENTIONAL WISDOM AFTER THE CREDIT CRUNCH

Nowadays, for the first time in ages, the American way of life, including living on credit, is regarded as a problem in an economic sense. Because of the high risks involved, lending to consumers who could not repay was an extremely profitable activity. The risky packages in which the subprime loans were cut up and securitised could be used in the short term to speculate on international stock markets.

When it became apparent in 2007 that many toxic financial products had been put on the market, because the value of the homes under the mortgages had decreased, the worldwide financial bastion collapsed. From that moment onwards, the issue was no longer how to share the profits but how to shift and recoup the losses. The happy consumer, who had sensed profit as an investor, became an angry debtor who felt betrayed when confronted with his losses. Suddenly, the success stories dried up and the search for (or pursuit of) scapegoats had begun. The anger of the public at large was directed at the bonuses of the bankers and the laxity of the regulators.

Because the various barriers that were intended to restrict financial market forces had been removed, a complicated global financial system, over which regulators had very little control, had come about in a fairly short time. The massive use of credit and debts in the corporate world was an important component of capitalism's success story in the 1980s and 1990s, because of the leverage effect. As long as economic growth persisted, the developments were characterised as the intended product of financial and technological innovation. When the financial system imploded, the excess leverage effect was fingered as one of the most important causes.

The financial crisis struck in 2007 in the US, when it appeared that the risks that the banks had taken using highly complicated financial constructions were ultimately insufficiently covered by the value of the properties on which mortgages had been issued and the repayment capacity of the debtors to whom the loans had been issued.

The government had to step in at this point, because some financial institutions were 'too big to fail'. The bankruptcy of big banks and insurance companies was not seen as a viable or acceptable political option, either in the US or in Europe. This was a clear example of market failure: big financial institutions could not take care of themselves but needed government help. The giants of financial capitalism were kept afloat with public money. The *masters of the universe*[19] needed the help of governments, which suddenly found themselves in the totally unexpected role of (temporary) owner of nationalised major banks.

A particular curiosity relating to the recent credit crisis is that some of the problems that, according to the law and economics literature, lead to dishonesty on the consumer side (eg information asymmetry and moral hazard) can now be identified just as clearly on the creditor side.

The financial industry has designed products that made the economic rationale of the transaction expressly misleading. Contracts were explicitly aimed at providing the consumer with insufficient information about its advantages and disadvantages. This is apparent from such terms as investment insurance, stock lease, repayment protection and so forth. The way in which costs are passed on to the consumer, for example with credit cards and usury policies, also excels in deliberately created vagueness. Because only the creditors have access to knowledge and information from the specialist whiz kids (quants), there is an information asymmetry in their favour. The financial industry cannot apportion responsibility for this to middlemen, regulators or consumers. Complexity and vagueness aimed at misleading and cheating consumers were at the core of the financial industry's earning model.

Another pillar of economic wisdom has also been devastated. We have always been taught that no rational banker would lend money to people who cannot repay their debts. The sub-prime market has shown that it is extremely profitable to sell financial products to poor people. Bankers seduced consumers with 'teaser' rates divided these high-risk loans in credit default swaps, etc, securitised them and sold them on the stock market. When the creditor eventually sold his part in these complex products in time, he obtained large profits. After a while, the losses were passed on to the creditors at the end of the transaction line and the debtors who faced high interest rates after the 'teaser' period had passed. The short and unhappy story of sub-prime market practices is an indication that unfettered market forces are profitable for some but ruinous for many others. We

[19] So well portrayed by Tom Wolfe in his novel *Bonfires of the Vanities* (1987).

can only hope that this experience will be in the minds of the lawmakers who are now designing policies to clean up the mess.

When some major financial institutions appeared to be 'too big to fail', ie too big for bankruptcy, the moral hazard problem was also brought clearly into focus.[20] Were the banks able to take such substantial risks because they knew that at the end of the day the state would come to their rescue? Whatever the case, the concept of prudent credit provision, in other words a bank that only lends money to those who can repay it, became an old-fashioned and outmoded idea.

Following the credit crunch and the election of Barack Obama as US president, liberals in America wonder whether, in the new political climate, the burden of proof may be shifted to the financial institutions, now that the consequences of the credit crisis are becoming clear and considerable damage has been inflicted. The costs and benefits have not been apportioned equitably between Wall Street and Main Street.

How will the damage that has been caused be settled? Does *casum sentit dominus* apply here, or will angry taxpayers force politicians to translate their rage into (collective) legal and financial claims?

Some people believed that the fall of the Berlin Wall in 1989 marked the end of Marxism; others wonder whether the credit crunch of 2007 signalled the end of ideological 'marketism'.

6. PATERNALISM WITH A FATHER

Once the largest consequences of the credit crunch are behind us, normal commercial credit provision will quickly manifest itself again. Not only the commercial entities selling products in the real economy but also the state will attempt to persuade citizens to borrow money as an alternative to collective subsidies (eg for education). This means that the number of creditors with which the consumer will enter into credit relationships will certainly not diminish drastically in the near future.

On the consumer side, too, the consequences of the credit crunch will soon become tangible. Some people will lose their jobs or part of their pension benefits; others will need to take on fresh debts in order to maintain their standard of living or refinance their loans.

For creditors, unsuccessful contracts are part of the cost of doing business in terms of granting consumer credit. Irrecoverable loans are sold on the commercial market to process servers or collection agencies, which in turn have a direct interest in dynamic collection. This sector is undergoing both increased professionalisation and significant hardening. The market is dominated by large commercial companies.

[20] See Buiter, above n 18, 17; and the Posner Becker blog at the website of the University of Chicago Law School.

Additionally, non-paying debtors are listed with the credit registration agency, causing difficulties for them when it comes to obtaining future credit. Credit reference in Europe was initially set up as a neutral instrument to combat excess credit, but the market for credit information has rapidly commercialised. Hopefully, some lessons may be drawn from the history of the credit rating agencies in the commercial financial markets.

All things considered, I expect financial stress for consumers to increase. More creditors will jostle consumers who can no longer meet their obligations. Various classic political questions accordingly arise: who gets what, when and how?[21] Commercial creditors try to circumvent bankruptcy via secured debts (mortgages!) and governmental bodies try to create privileged legal claims for themselves (eg taxation, social security and fines). On the other hand, there will (and must) always be exceptions to the possibility of granting the consumer a fresh start if he has not behaved in a morally responsible manner.

In the remaining part of this section, I will formulate some ideas for future regulation in the field of consumer credit and debt. My examples are taken from Dutch practice, but they may be of interest to foreign observers as well.

6.1. Strict Supervision

It has become clear that supervision in the financial world did not keep up with the developments in the market. This lack of equilibrium must be repaired. Professional financial institutions need a licence, which should form the basis of supervision by the state. Among other things, the law stipulates responsible credit provision. This can be linked to the norms that the bona fide sector has itself developed within the context of self-regulation. Apart from restrictions on abuse clauses in contracts[22] and advertising, a maximum interest rate is a good way to regulate responsible credit provision.

Because the financial markets (credit, insurance, savings, investment, etc) were steadily converging as a consequence of liberalisation and deregulation, the regulatory system needed an update. In the Netherlands, the Dutch Central Bank (DNB) was responsible for prudential supervision and the Financial Markets Authority (AFM) for the behaviour of financial institutions. It took quite a while before the two regulators became mutually attuned. For a long time, new products like stock leasing (a combined loan and an investment vehicle) were not monitored by either regulator. The credit crunch revealed that Dutch supervision of the financial markets was also not functioning properly. This lax supervision might aptly be called paternalism without a father.

What we need for the future is a supervisor who is present in the market and prevents banks from bringing toxic products onto the market again. In 1994,

[21] HD Laswell, *Politics: Who Gets What, When, How* (1936).

[22] Even in the US, see the CARD legislation (Credit Card Accountability, Responsibility and Disclosure Act) that came into effect on 22 February 2010.

Norbert Reich[23] had framed credit as an 'unsafe product' in order to find a legal basis for his Draft Consumer Financial Services Marketing Directive. The Commission was not at all enthusiastic about this approach to the problem.

In the US, Oren Bar-Gill and Elisabeth Warren[24] have argued for *ex ante* regulation of complicated financial products by a financial product safety commission. The Obama administration has translated their ideas into the Consumer Financial Protection Agency Act of 2009. The reception accorded to these proposals by the financial lobby shows how extremely politicised economic relations are in the US. The proposed interventions immediately conjured up the bogeyman of the all-powerful state that knows better than the citizens themselves. In this case, state intervention is not framed as paternalism but as maternalism: 'Big Nanny'.[25]

In this ideological context, the need for independent empirical research is obvious, because the creditors have an enormous informational advantage.[26]

I believe that credit is indeed a dangerous product if it is not regulated adequately. We should not base our policies on abstract economic and legal models alone, but focus more on concrete social human needs and societal processes. With a wise combination of pre-market approval of new products by a supervisor, combined with solid maximum interest rates, the state can regain some of its authority in this field.

6.2. Inclusion of Intermediaries

A second target group of regulation in the credit field are the intermediaries. It has long been known that intermediaries and sellers play a significant role in the creation of excess credit. Intermediaries are only interested in their own commission and can exercise considerable pressure on banks to accept poor credit risks, for example by offering them as part of a *package deal* with a number of good applicants.

In the past, the Dutch government has attempted to set upper limits on payments to intermediaries by credit providers and link them to consumer repayment, but these rules were circumvented to a considerable degree and were later withdrawn in the context of deregulation. This mistake should be addressed in the coming years.

[23] In Huls *et al*, above n 5, chapter 11.

[24] O Bar Gil and E Warren, 'Making Credit Safer' (2008) 157 *University of Pennsylvania Law Review* 101ff.

[25] DS Evans and JD Wright, 'The Effect of the Consumer Protection Agency Act of 2009 on Consumer Credit', George Mason University Law and Economics Research Paper Series No. 09–50.

[26] See E Warren, 'The Market for Data: The Changing Role of the Social Sciences in Shaping the Law' (2002) 1 *Wisconsin Law Review* 20–25.

7. NUDGING[27] COLLECTIVE MECHANISMS IN PRIVATE LAW

Supervision by the state is classic paternalistic intervention. However, the state can also nudge the consumer by means of indirect interventions that create more space for autonomous societal developments. Two Dutch practices in the context of modern consumer protection are worth mentioning here.

7.1 Collective Claims[28]

An important recent Dutch legal innovation is the Act on the Collective Settlement of Mass Claims (WCAM), on the basis of which a court can declare as binding a settlement that has come about following a collective action. The new law was first applied in an exceptionally large collective action in the Legio Lease affair. Some 400 000 consumers had bought shares with borrowed money, which turned out to be loss-making when share prices dropped after 1 January 2000 and interest tax deductions for consumer credit were halted. Dexia, a Franco-Belgian multinational, was forced into a settlement following a professionally constituted class action. This updating of Dutch tort law could contribute substantially to the (collective) autonomy of the consumer over a professional opponent who has offered hybrid financial products to inexperienced investors in a misleading, aggressive and non-transparent manner.

This initial campaign was developed and directed by two law firms in The Hague. They sought a professional collaboration with the mass media and the political world (spin doctors) and made inventive use of the opportunities offered by the internet to communicate with tens of thousands of clients simultaneously.

Just as employees are able to enforce certain improvements through unionisation, here we have an exceptionally powerful type of collectivisation in private law, which is able to develop a momentum to which huge and powerful financial institutions have to respond.

7.2. Collective Bargaining of Consumer Contracts

A second, more harmonious type of collectivisation is negotiation between consumer organisations and central business organisations about general legal provisions governing consumer transactions. Led by independent chairmen and under the auspices of the Social Economic Council (SER), the standard-bearer of

[27] See RH Thaler and C Sunstein, *Improving Decisions About Health, Wealth and Happiness* (2008).

[28] See WH van Boom, 'Collective Mass Claims in the Netherlands' in M Casper *et al* (eds), *Auf dem Weg zu Einer Europäischen Sammelklage?* (2009) 171–92.

the Dutch *polder model* (ie consociational politics),[29] general terms and conditions are being created in a number of important sectors and are being thoroughly tested by consumer organisations. The SER hallmark engenders confidence in consumers that the legal provisions in the contracts are in order. This mechanism has not yet been fully implemented in the field of credit and debt.

8. THE ETHICS OF CONSUMER BANKRUPTCY

How can we encourage all autonomous market participants to conduct themselves in a morally responsible fashion?

I think strict supervision is necessary to keep the financial world in good ethical shape. A robust combination of extensive truth in lending regulation and an aggressive fight against abusive practices is already on the political agenda. We need the law to tame the predators among the creditors and to put the interests of consumers first.[30]

However, there are also moral ambiguities on the consumer side. Hans Boutellier has carried out an interesting analysis of the mindset of the modern citizen.[31] He suggests that the modern citizen wants 'safe freedom'. Because of the increased vitality that is propagated in current culture, the modern citizen wants to explore the world, take risks and run his own life without borders. He hates being patronised by the state, particularly when it comes to his consumer freedom. The citizen wants as few rules as possible that might restrict his own behaviour. However, if another citizen or an organisation causes him loss or restricts his freedom, he invokes the help of the government, because he wants to claim damages and also wants the existing rules to be applied rigorously to the other party.

I believe Boutellier's analysis paints a keen picture of how the consumer behaves in the market for financial services. In times of economic prosperity and growth, and if interest rates are low and the prices of shares and houses rise, no-one needs a cautioning state that preaches restraint or sings the praises of saving. The sovereign consumer can decide this for himself and does not want to listen to warnings.[32]

However, if the economic tide turns, interest rates rise and the underlying asset values drop, and loans must be repaid, the citizen suddenly looks very critically towards the state. Why are the savers (the rich) protected by a deposit system

[29] A Lijphart, *Thinking About Democracy: Power Sharing and Majority Rule in Theory and Practice* (2008).

[30] See U Reifner and J Ford (eds), *Banking for People: Social Banking and New Poverty Consumer Debts and Unemployment* (1992); U Reifner, *Die Geldgesellschaft, Aus die Finanzkrise Lernen* (2010).

[31] H Boutellier, *The Safety Utopia: Contemporary Discontent and Desire as to Crime and Punishment* (2004).

[32] Posner, above n 3, 328: 'Cassandras rarely *receive a fair hearing*' (emphasis added).

while the borrowers are not? In these circumstances, the debtor-citizen wants protection and redress from the government and wants to be declared free of liability by those who recommended the uncomplicated loan to him. The consumer, cradled in his sovereignty and autonomy, then becomes furious with the rich bankers, who told him he could also become rich on the money and capital market, loses his trust in the government, which does not resolve this problem for him, and casts a vote for a populist political party.

It is clear that some key political tensions between autonomy and paternalism are neutralised in bankruptcy law. However, consumer protection in the modern credit world is both necessary and full of ambiguity on both sides.

9. CONCLUDING THOUGHTS ON THE AUTONOMY-PATERNALISM DEBATE: POWER, NUMBERS AND SOCIAL VALUES

We have seen that the juxtaposition of autonomy and paternalism is not a timeless issue and that societal forces have contributed much to its cyclical development. Over time, Western societies have looked for an optimal mix of harder and softer mechanisms to deal with debtors in distress. I consider consumer bankruptcy to be a modern human invention, an example of what Schumpeter calls 'creative destruction'.[33] Debts are repudiated — or forgiven –[34] in order to enable human individuals to go on with their lives. One might hope that this form of limited liability of consumers will also nudge commercial creditors to lend money more carefully.

9.1. Autonomy v Paternalism, or Autonomy v Heteronomy

Ideally, a contract aims at a win-win situation. Both contracting parties hope to benefit from signing the agreement. Although the death of the contract has repeatedy been predicted in the past, contracts are omnipresent and alive and kicking in the real world of 2011. Even in the public domain — traditionally the field of public law — all kinds of new contractual relations are developing.[35]

If a law and economics scholar or a civil law professor looks at a contract, he will normally focus on the preferences of the contracting parties. In the autonomous paradigm, parties can take care of themselves while carrying out the contract, whereas in the paternalistic paradigm one of them needs the help of the state (or the courts). As a socio-legal scholar, my interest lies in the societal relationship between the parties and the legal institutions that determine such relations. Contract law is socially embedded.

A contract establishes a relationship between two parties. Because there is often an unequal power balance in credit and debt relationships, it is also

[33] JA Schumpeter, *Capitalism, Socialism and Democracy* (1942).
[34] K Gross, *Failure and Forgiveness: Rebalancing the Bankruptcy System* (1997).
[35] I Harden, *The Contracting State* (1992).

worthwhile to look into the heteronomous dimensions of the contractual debtor-creditor relationship in its various stages.

The distribution of wealth and power in a given society is too important to ignore, and the ways of achieving a just distribution is an eternal topic of fierce political debates. Traditionally, labour law and tenant law have been fields of private law, where the concept of 'subordination' has been evolving, because the unequal bargaining power of the contracting parties was always obvious.[36]

Historically, we have seen a combination of the collectivisation of labour contracts via unions and state intervention, and many private labour scholars wonder if these fields of law still belong to private law or whether they now belong to welfare law.

Ironically, bankruptcy is also related to distribution — not primarily of wealth but of scarcity: the assets of a destitute debtor. Some powerful creditors are in a position to evade the effects of the bankruptcy of their clients; others may not be so autonomous. The power relationship between creditors should not be ignored in procedural private law if society wants to achieve a fair loss distribution.

9.2. Individual and Collective Arrangements

The concepts of autonomy and paternalism seem to date from the period when one-to-one contractual relationships prevailed in society. In our present mass consumer society, a big challenge for private law lies in the handling of the masses and multi-party relations. This is where the problems of the 'asymmetric society'[37] arise: information surplus on the creditor side, credit score techniques, credit reference innovation and commercialisation place the consumer in a dependent and unequal position. The repeat players dominate the one-shotters.[38]

On the other hand, lawyers have designed mechanisms that create countervailing forces that are able to direct masses of claims against big organisations. Mass is power, and creative lawyers can translate many individual claims of consumers into a language that big business understands and cannot ignore: money. So there is no reason to lament about powerless consumers. If they are many and they can organise themselves, we do not have to worry very much about their loss of autonomy.

However, numbers also matter on a smaller scale. Even in an average consumer bankruptcy, between 10 and 20 creditors are confronted with each other and share the problems of enforcing their claims. Talking about the autonomy of the creditor when he is part of a multi-party constellation does not deliver many

[36] L Nogler, The Concept of 'Subordination' in European and Comparative Law (2009).

[37] JS Coleman, *The Asymmetric Society* (1982).

[38] M Galanter, 'Why the 'Haves' Come Out Ahead: Speculation on the Limits of Social Change,' (1974) 9 *Law & Society Review* 95.

economic results. He is in a distributional game with other creditors, who all try to jump the queue.

9.3. Social Values in Substantive and Procedural Civil Law

Advocates of consumer protection have made many intellectual efforts to infuse substantive private law with social values. A lot of consumer protection was smuggled into the Dutch Civil Code of 1992, and EU Directives introduced protective elements into the national civil law systems.

In the field of credit and debt, Thomas Wilhelmsson has coined the concept of 'social force majeure' as part of the bigger project of importing 'welfarism in contract law'.[39]

Especially in the field of credit law, we see a perfect culture clash of market values and social values. In the market, the debtors that represent a high risk for their creditors have to pay high premiums. While tax law in the welfare state is based on the principle that 'the strongest shoulders carry the heaviest burdens', the market is guided by Caplovitz's law that the 'the poor pay more'.[40]

The European Coalition for Responsible Credit (ECRC) promotes 'productive credit' as the key concept for modern law.[41] In this context, the substantive credit contract itself must reflect its life-time character, so that many contractual concepts from one-spot commercial market transactions do not apply here. Under this approach to contract law, consumer bankruptcy (which is part of civil procedural law) comes too late and is critically characterised as a means of 'keeping substantive contract law free from social poison'.[42]

From my perspective, however, procedural law — which is generally considered to be a very dull field of civil law — is an exciting field to explore the autonomy-paternalism tension, because it constitutes a battleground for competing claims of all kinds of creditors, both among themselves and vis-a-vis their debtors. Bankruptcy is the litmus test of the strength and weaknesses of civil obligations and liabilities. All civil law, be it substantive or procedural, must have beneficial consequences for society.

[39] R Brownsword, G Howells and T Wilhelmsson (eds), *Welfarism in Contract Law* (1994).
[40] D Caplovitz, *The Poor Pay More: Consumer Practices of Low-Income Families* (1967).
[41] Niemi, Ramsay and Whitford (2009), above n 6, 109 ff.
[42] U Reifner in Niemi-Kiesliainen, Whitford and Ramsay (2003), above n 6, at 152.

5

Regulating Consumer Demand in Insurance Markets

DANIEL SCHWARCZ*

ABSTRACT

In recent years it has become increasingly clear that risk aversion cannot by itself explain how and why individuals purchase insurance. From the perspective of risk aversion, individuals tend to purchase insurance when they should not, refuse to purchase insurance when they should, prefer sub-optimal payouts, and allow irrelevant considerations to influence their insurance preferences. This chapter considers the normative implications of these 'insurance demand anomalies'. It argues that many observed deviations from traditional theory are likely the result of mistakes, in the sense that consumers would act differently if they possessed perfect information and cognitive resources. From this perspective, regulatory interventions designed to improve consumer decision-making about insurance are potentially desirable. At the same time, the chapter argues that some insurance demand anomalies may actually reflect sophisticated consumer behaviour. In some cases, seemingly puzzling insurance decisions may help consumers manage emotions such as anxiety, regret and loss aversion, while in other cases they may represent valuable commitment strategies. Because consumers' insurance decisions may reflect sophisticated rather than mistaken decision-making, regulatory interventions that limit consumer choice are normatively troubling. Given these conflicting explanations for risk aversion's failure as a descriptive theory of consumer demand in insurance markets, the chapter explores a spectrum of 'libertarian-paternalistic' regulatory interventions. It argues that regulatory strategies that aim to encourage presumptively welfare-maximising insurance decisions without restricting individual choice represent a promising and normatively defensible opportunity for improving consumer behaviour in insurance markets.

* Associate Professor of Law, University of Minnesota Law School. A version of this paper, titled Insurance Demand Anomalies and Regulation, was published in the Journal of Consumer Affairs. For helpful comments and suggestions, I thank Ken Abraham, Tom Baker, Oren Bar-Gill, Prentiss Cox, Brenda Cude, Kristin Hickman, Claire Hill, Bert Kritzer, Brett McDonnell, Amy Monahan, Francesco Parisi, Arden Rowell, Steven Schwarcz, Peter Siegelman and Paul Slovic. I also thank the participants in Erasmus Law School's conference on Juxtaposing Autonomy and Paternalism in Private Law, the University of Minnesota's seminar on Alternative Perspective on Law and Economics and the National Bureau of Economic Research's Insurance Project Workshop. Christina Alexander and Carl Engstrom provided excellent research assistance.

FOR ALMOST HALF a century, economists assumed, with little empirical foundation, that the purchase of insurance was explained entirely by risk aversion within Expected Utility Theory (EUT).[1] According to this theory, people who purchase insurance enjoy diminishing marginal utility as their wealth increases, meaning that each additional dollar improves their well-being less than the previous dollar.[2] As a result, people can maximise their expected utility by spending a small amount in the present to protect against the risk of a large monetary loss in the future, so long as the expected value of the future payment is roughly equivalent to the present payment.[3]

It has become increasingly clear in recent years that risk aversion alone cannot explain how and why individuals purchase insurance.[4] From the perspective of risk aversion, individuals tend to purchase insurance when they should not, refuse to purchase insurance when they should, strongly prefer sub-optimal insurance payout schemes and allow completely irrelevant considerations to dramatically influence their insurance purchasing preferences.[5] Although these deviations from EUT are often labelled 'anomalies', their number and persistency have come to belie this characterisation.[6]

Despite the wealth of empirical research documenting insurance demand anomalies, the normative implications of this consumer behaviour have received

[1] See generally J Von Neumann and O Morgenstern, *Theory of Games and Economic Behavior* (1964). Technically, EUT does not require any particular utility function. Recent behavioural work has sought to explain insurance decisions by including within the utility function unconventional variables, such as the prospect of regret or loss aversion. Such models do not explain insurance by reference to risk aversion, even if they do fall within the general domain of EUT. As such, references to 'traditional' or 'classic' EUT in the text should not be understood to encompass such recent behavioural innovations to EUT.

[2] See S Shavell, *Foundations of Economic Analysis of Law* (2004) 596.

[3] See J Mossin, 'Aspects of Rational Insurance Purchasing' (1968) 76 *Journal of Political Economy* 533.

[4] From a descriptive perspective, the failure of traditional EUT is not cabined to insurance decisions but applies to individual risk-based decisions more generally. The leading competing theory of individual decision-making under uncertainty is Prospect Theory. See generally D Kahneman and A Tversky, 'Prospect Theory: An Analysis of Decision Under Risk' (1979) 47 *Econometrica* 263, 263–70; A Tversky and D Kahneman, 'Advances in Prospect Theory: Cumulative Representations Under Uncertainty' (1992) 5 *Journal of Risk and Uncertainty* 297. For another interesting general theory of decision-making under uncertainty, see D Krantz and H Kunreuther, 'Goals and Plans in Decision Making' (2007) 2 *Judgment and Decision Making* 137. See also G Lowenstein *et al*, 'Risk as Feelings' (2001) 127 *Psychological Bulletin* 267, 267–71.

[5] See generally Part 1 below.

[6] In the words of two leading insurance economists, deviations from traditional EUT 'are not minor anomalies but reflect a systematic tendency for insurance in practice to differ from insurance in theory.' D Cutler and R Zeckhauser, 'Extending the Theory to Meet the Practice in Insurance', Brookings-Wharton Papers on Financial Services (2004) 3, available at: muse.jhu.edu/journals/brookings-wharton_papers_on_financial_services/v2004/2004.1cutler.html (last visited 15 March 2010). Matthew Rabin and Richard Thaler describe risk aversion-based explanations of insurance decisions as 'plainly wrong and frequently misleading'. See M Rabin and R Thaler, 'Anomalies: Risk Aversion' (2001) 15 *Journal of Economic Perspectives* 219, 230. They analogise economists' defences of traditional EUT to a Monty Python sketch in which a pet shop owner attempts to convince a disgruntled customer that the bird he recently purchased is not dead, despite the customer beating the dead parrot on the store counter. ibid, at 230.

only minimal attention from scholars and policymakers.[7] To be sure, some commentators suggest that deviations from traditional EUT raise regulatory concerns.[8] Underlying this sentiment is often the unarticulated notion that consumers who select insurance in ways that are inconsistent with standard theory are making a mistake, meaning that they would behave differently were it not for cognitive or informational limitations.[9] Other prominent commentators have suggested that consumer behaviour inconsistent with traditional EUT cannot always be dismissed as mere mistakes, but may actually reflect sophisticated and informed choice.[10] From the perspective of welfare economics, this conceptualisation of consumer demand for insurance raises thorny normative implications for the role of regulatory intervention.[11]

This chapter explores these competing theories of consumer demand for insurance. Part 1 begins with a review of empirical research documenting four observed insurance demand anomalies that potentially raise regulatory issues. First, consumer demand for catastrophe insurance is generally bimodal, with consumers tending either to exhibit surprisingly little interest in such insurance or seemingly excessive enthusiasm for it. Second, consumers routinely purchase insurance against small financial risks that imply preposterous levels of risk aversion. Third, consumers typically prefer excessively low deductibles from the perspective of standard theory. Finally, consumers occasionally (though infrequently) purchase non-pecuniary loss insurance in ways that cannot be convincingly explained by anticipated changes in their marginal utility of wealth.

Part 2 then offers two competing explanations for these deviations from standard EUT. First, it argues that most anomalous demand in insurance likely

[7] See, eg Cutler and Zeckhauser, above n 6, at 43 (stating that the normative relevance of consumer insurance anomalies 'is a task for future efforts'); Krantz and Kunreuther, above n 4, at 163 (briefly discussing the prescriptive implications of their theory of consumer demand anomalies from the standpoint of how consumers should purchase insurance, but noting that their 'framework … raises a host of difficult prescriptive questions [and] we provide a sampler here but note that most of the answers are beyond the scope of this paper and should be addressed by future research'); Rabin and Thaler, above n 6, at 230 (noting that traditional EUT is quite attractive as a normative theory of how to purchase insurance without exploring this issue). This is noteworthy given that the original developers of EUT, Von Neumann and Morgenstern, viewed it as a normative theory. See C Guthrie, 'Better Settle Than Sorry: The Regret Aversion Theory of Litigation Behavior' (1999) *University of Illinois Law Review* 43, 49.

[8] The commentator who has explored this issue most thoroughly is Howard Kunreuther. See generally nn 13, 16, 18, 68, 131.

[9] See, eg E Johnson *et al*, 'Framing, Probability Distortions, and Insurance Decisions' (1993) 7 *Journal of Risk and Uncertainty* 36 ('The recognition that consumer perceptions and decision processes are imperfect and manipulable could be used to support insurance regulation and prohibition of certain types of insurance.'). For further discussion of the definition of a mistake, see Part 2 below.

[10] Cutler and Zeckhauser, above n 6, at 43 ('Given the importance that [insurance] consumers attach to minimizing regret and anxiety, there is a strong argument that such concepts should be given a role in our normative theories.'); Krantz and Kunreuther, above n 4, at 141 ('When important and stable extra-financial goals motivate insurance purchase, one might regard the decision as *anomalous* from a financial decision, but quite rational from a broader perspective of multiple goals.').

[11] See Part 3 below for a more extensive discussion of this issue.

reflects consumers' ignorance about insurance and limited cognitive resources when it comes to making insurance purchasing decisions. Second, and perhaps more controversially, it claims that some component of this demand may reflect consumers' sophisticated management of their emotional needs. In particular, consumers deviating from the classical prescripts of EUT may be using insurance to provide themselves with 'peace of mind', reduce regret from uninsured losses and counteract the negative feelings associated with loss. In other cases, they may make seemingly irrational insurance decisions that offset the consequences of their limited self-control.

Part 3 concludes by considering various 'libertarian-paternalistic' approaches to improving insurance markets.[12] It argues that such regulatory strategies, which aim to improve consumer decision-making without limiting individual choice, are an appropriate response to Part 2's conflicting diagnoses of consumer decision-making in insurance markets. That is because they simultaneously reduce the likely incidence of consumer mistakes while allowing consumers that are not making mistakes to continue purchasing insurance according to their genuine preferences.

1. DEVIATIONS FROM TRADITIONAL EXPECTED UTILITY THEORY IN INSURANCE DEMAND

Over the last several decades, empirical research from both the laboratory and the real world has repeatedly shown that the traditional EUT explanation of risk aversion does a poor job of explaining consumers' actual insurance decisions. This part provides a brief overview of four deviations from standard theory in insurance markets: bimodal consumer demand for catastrophe insurance, enthusiasm for insurance against small financial risks, preferences for low deductibles and willingness to purchase non-pecuniary loss insurance.[13]

1.1. Bimodal Demand for Catastrophe Insurance

Traditional EUT fares poorly in its predictions about how individuals purchase insurance against low-probability, high-magnitude risks. According to standard theory, consumers should generally find insurance against such risks desirable, so

[12] See C Sunstein and R Thaler, 'Libertarian Paternalism Is Not an Oxymoron' (2003) 70 *University of Chicago Law Review* 1159; C Sunstein and R Thaler, *Nudge* (2008). For criticisms of and responses to libertarian paternalism, see E Glaeser, 'Paternalism and Psychology' (2007) 73 *University of Chicago Law Review* 133, 150; G Mitchell and J Klick, 'Government Regulation of Irrationality: Moral and Cognitive Hazards' (2006) 90 *Minnesota Law Review* 1620 at 1627–41; G Mitchell, 'Libertarian Paternalism Is an Oxymoron' (2005) 99 *Northwestern University Law Review* 1245; C Hill, 'Anti-Anti-Anti Paternalism' (2007) 2 *New York University Journal of Law and Liberty* 44.

[13] For a more complete description of seeming anomalies in individuals' purchasing decisions, see H Kunreuther and M Pauly, *Insurance Decision-Making and Market Behavior* (2005) 27–49; WH Van Boom, 'Insurance Law and Economics: An Empirical Perspective' in M Faure and F Stephen (eds), *Essays in the Law and Economics of Regulation* (2008).

long as premiums are actuarially reasonable.[14] This is because money should have a larger impact on individuals' overall utility after a large financial loss than it has prior to such a loss. Differences in consumers' willingness to purchase such insurance should be attributable either to different degrees of risk-aversion or levels of wealth.

Contrary to these predictions, individuals frequently display surprisingly little interest in purchasing catastrophe insurance.[15] For instance, researchers found that homeowners living in earthquake-prone areas of California had not invested even minimal effort to learn about available insurance options.[16] Individuals' apathy towards insurance was not a product of any expectation that they would receive post-disaster government aid.[17] This pattern persists even in markets where insurance premiums are state subsidised. For example, many property owners living in flood-prone areas do not purchase federal flood insurance, which is both highly subsidised and often legally required.[18]

At the same time, consumers do display substantial enthusiasm for some forms of catastrophe insurance, depending on how the underlying risks are framed or the salience of those risks.[19] Thus, consumers are sometimes strongly drawn to terrorism insurance and insurance against so-called 'dread diseases' such as cancer.[20] They also tend to display relative enthusiasm for the purchase of earthquake and flood insurance in the immediate aftermath of earthquakes and floods, respectively.[21]

This consumer interest in limited forms of insurance against low-probability, high-magnitude risks often defy explanatory factors based on traditional EUT, such as differences in the magnitude or probability of potential losses. One study

[14] Indeed, according to traditional EUT, risk-averse individuals should always purchase insurance that is fairly pricedSee L Eeckhoudt *et al*, *Economic and Financial Decisions Under Risk* (2005) 51 (describing Mossin's theorem).

[15] See generally G McClelland *et al*, 'Insurance for Low Probability Events: A Bimodal Response to Unlikely Events' (1993) 7 *Journal of Risk and Uncertainty* 95 95–6.

[16] See H Kunreuther *et al*, *Disaster Insurance Protection: Public Policy Lessons* (1978) 236–43. Recent evidence confirms these results: prior to the 1989 California earthquake, 34% of homeowners told surveyors that earthquake insurance was not necessary. See R Palm, *Earthquake Insurance: A Longitudinal Study of Homeowners Insurance in California* (1995). After the earthquake, only 5% of respondents said earthquake insurance was not necessary. ibid.

[17] See Kunreuther *et al*, above n 16.

[18] See ibid. See generally H Kunreuther and M Pauly, 'Neglecting Disaster: Why Don't People Insure Against Large Losses?' (2006) 20 *Journal of Risk and Uncertainty* 5, 6 (discussing consumers' tendency to not purchase insurance for low-probability, high-loss events).

[19] The relevance of framing to consumers' insurance decisions extends well beyond the context of low-probability insurance. For instance, consumers are much more willing to purchase any form of insurance if it is framed as 'insurance' rather than as payment to avoid a loss. See PJH Schoemaker and H Kunreuther, 'An Experimental Study of Insurance Decisions' (1979) 46 *Journal of Risk and Insurance* 603, 612; JC Herschey and PJH Shoemaker, 'Risk Taking and Problem Context in the Domain of Losses: An Expected Utility Analysis' (1980) 47 *Journal of Risk and Insurance* 111, 130.

[20] Johnson *et al*, above n 9, at 35. Individuals in the United States have demonstrated surprising enthusiasm for terrorism insurance, especially in the wake of 9/11. See Wharton Risk Center, *TRIA and Beyond: Terrorism Risk Financing in the United States* (2005).

[21] See P Slovic, *The Perception of Risk* (2000) 14.

documented that a group of subjects was willing to pay more than twice as much for flight insurance covering 'terrorism' and 'mechanical failure' than similar groups of subjects were willing to pay for flight insurance covering losses for 'any reason'. The study reported similar distortions in subjects' willingness to pay for general health insurance compared with health insurance for a specific, vivid ailment and for general trip insurance compared with travel terrorism insurance.[22]

1.2. Enthusiasm for Insurance against Small Financial Risks

Ironically, risk aversion also does not fare well at predicting individuals' willingness to purchase insurance against small financial risks. According to traditional EUT, such insurance should generally be undesirable. This is because low-magnitude losses do not meaningfully impact overall wealth levels, and hence the expected impact of an insurance payout on overall utility should not differ substantially from the impact on utility of paying insurance premiums.[23] If such insurance were actuarially fair, a risk-averse person might nonetheless be slightly inclined, or at least indifferent, to purchasing it. But, in practice, loading costs for insurance against small financial risks are generally high due to the frequency with which claims must be managed. As a result, the level of risk aversion necessary to explain the rational purchase of these forms of insurance is implausible.[24]

In contrast to these theoretical predictions, consumers routinely display substantial enthusiasm for insurance against small financial risks. One study documented that 57 per cent of households who were offered insurance against the risk of having to pay repair costs for their phone lines purchased it. The cost of such insurance was 45 cents per month, whereas its expected value was 26 cents per month.[25] A similar willingness to insure against low-magnitude losses is apparent in ordinary homeowners and automobile policies, which provide coverage for fallen tree removal, broken windshield repair and rental car fees.[26] Perhaps the most omnipresent example is the extended product warranty for

[22] Johnson *et al*, above n 9, at 35. Earlier research has similarly suggested that people pay significantly too much for flight insurance. See R Eisner and R Strotz, 'Flight Insurance and the Theory of Choice' (1961) 69 *Journal of Political Economy* 355. Some recent research suggests that risk preferences may not, in fact, be stable across contexts and that people exhibit greater risk aversion in their home deductibles than in their auto deductibles. See L Barseghyan et al, 'Are Risk Preferences Stable Across Contexts? Evidence from Insurance Data' (June 2009), available at: papers.ssrn.com/sol3/papers. cfm? abstract_id=1220663. This finding itself is inconsistent with traditional EUT.

[23] See M Rabin, 'Diminishing Marginal Utility of Wealth Cannot Explain Risk Aversion' in D Kahneman and A Tversky (eds), *Choices, Values and Frames* (2000) 202, 202–08.

[24] See ibid.

[25] C Cicchetti and JA Dubin, 'A Microeconomic Analysis of Risk Aversion and the Decision to Self-Insure' (1994) 102 *Journal of Political Economy* 169, 172.

[26] See D Schwarcz, 'A Products Liability Theory for the Judicial Regulation of Insurance' (2007) 48 William and Mary Law Review 1389, 1414.

consumer durables, which numerous stores successfully offer to customers at exorbitant rates.[27] Laboratory experiments have similarly documented the preference of subjects for insuring against high-probability, low-cost events.[28]

1.3. Preferences for Low Deductibles

According to traditional EUT, policyholders should generally favour coverage with large deductibles.[29] In part, the logic for this result mirrors the logic of policyholders not demanding insurance for small financial risks: because even large deductible levels are typically small relative to individuals' overall wealth, opting for such deductibles does not increase the risk of a large loss but does dramatically decrease loading costs. But large deductibles also disproportionately reduce the costs of insurance coverage in two ways. First, they reduce moral hazard by requiring the policyholder to pay the first dollars of any loss.[30] Second, they may limit the risk of adverse selection because low deductibles are disproportionately valuable to high-risk individuals.[31] These factors contribute to make the cost savings from high deductibles much greater, on the whole, than the benefit conferred by a low deductible.

Despite these potential savings, consumers routinely select surprisingly low deductibles. A recent study found that a substantial majority of consumers in both car and homeowners insurance markets select a deductible of $500 rather than $1000, even though the marginal cost of this additional coverage is approximately four times its expected value.[32] At least partially in response to these preferences, some personal lines insurers do not offer deductibles higher than $1000 for property coverage, and most such insurers do not offer deductibles at all for liability insurance.[33] Consumers' preferences for low deductibles also appear to be relatively intense. Thus, massive consumer outcry in the 1970s

[27] See Cutler and Zeckhauser, above n 6, 3, 25–28 ('[I]nsurance against small-cost consumer durables is among the most profitable items sold by commercial electronics stores', yet 'the purchase of this insurance seems hard to justify.').

[28] One well-known study simulated an insurance decision by having subjects choose a red or blue ball from an urnSee Slovic, above n 21, at 56–57. The blue ball represented a hazard against which study participants could insure. By varying the ratio of colored balls, experimenters could manipulate the probability of loss. Contrary to standard theory, subjects strongly preferred to insure against high-probability, low-cost events. See ibid. This result was consistent among different populations and was replicated across a number of different experimental designs. ibid, at 62–67.

[29] Mossin, above n 3, at 561–63.

[30] See K Abraham, *Distributing Risk* (1986) 15.

[31] See P Siegelman, 'Adverse Selection in Insurance Markets: An Exaggerated Threat' (2004) 113 *Yale Law Journal* 1223, 1265–66.

[32] See J Sydnor, '(Over)Insuring Modest Risks' (Draft, December 2009) 2–3 available at: wsomfaculty.case.edu/sydnor/deductibles.pdf last visited: 15 March 2010; see also Kunreuther and Pauly, above n 13, at 28.

[33] See Sydnor, above n 32, 7, 9–10; Kunreuther and Pauly, above n 13, 28.

forced the Pennsylvania Insurance Commissioner to withdraw a proposal to raise the minimum deductible for automobile policies from $50 to $100.[34]

1.4. Willingness to Purchase Insurance Against Non-Pecuniary Losses

Most forms of insurance do not compensate consumers for losses that neither directly nor indirectly decrease wealth levels.[35] For instance, homeowners insurance does not compensate policyholders for the emotional trauma that often accompanies the loss of one's home and personal possessions. Law and economics scholars often attribute the absence of such non-pecuniary loss insurance to consumer disinterest.[36] Increasingly, though, research suggests that supply-side problems may better explain the general absence of non-pecuniary loss insurance.[37] In fact, in at least two markets where non-pecuniary loss insurance is offered, consumers enthusiastically purchase it.[38]

Consider first the market for juvenile life insurance. According to the American Council of Life Insurers, approximately 15 per cent of people under 18 have some form of life insurance.[39] Another source reports that two million standalone juvenile life insurance policies were sold in 2004, with premiums averaging

[34] See JD Cummins and SN Weisbart, *The Impact of Consumer Services on Independent Agency Performance* (1978).

[35] For the purposes of this art, the term 'non-pecuniary loss' refers only to losses that neither directly nor indirectly impact wealth. As such, losses that do not directly impact wealth but which increase the need for wealth because they create the need for medical care or similar expenditures that are necessary to restore one's physical or emotional capacities are classified as pecuniary losses, cf S Shavell, *Economic Analysis of Accident Law* (1987) at 228–31 (defining non-pecuniary loss insurance).

[36] This claim if often made in connection with the desirability of emotional distress damages in tort law from the perspective of ideal insurance (rather than deterrence). See G Priest, 'The Current Insurance Crisis and Modern Tort Law' (1987) 96 *Yale Law Journal* 1521, 1547; Shavell, above n 35, 230–31.

[37] See J Hanson and S Croley, 'The Nonpecuniary Costs of Accidents' (1995) 108 *Harvard Law Review* 1785 (exploring the supply-side problems that insurers may face in providing such insurance). Two recent experiments provide direct support for consumers' willingness to purchase non-pecuniary loss insurance. One recent study found that a substantial majority of research subjects treated insurance against pecuniary and non-pecuniary losses exactly the same when presented with a set of hypothetical insurance transactions. See R Avraham, 'Should Pain-and-Suffering Damages Be Abolished from Tort Law? More Experimental Evidence' (2005) 55 *University of Toronto Law Journal* 941, 962. In a second study, subjects were given the option of purchasing an insurance policy that would pay the $200 purchase price of a vase if it broke in shipment. Half of the subjects were told that they 'fell in love with the vase at first sight' and it 'feels precious to you', while the other half was told, 'you don't have any special feeling for this vase'. C Hsee and H Kunreuther, 'The Affection Effect in Insurance Decisions' (2000) 20 *Journal of Risk and Uncertainty* 141,149. Subjects were willing to pay almost twice as much to insure the highly-valued vase, compared with the less-valued vase. Further experiments revealed that this effect could not be explained by subjects' perceived wealth differentials in the two treatments; the result replicated itself even when the item to be insured had zero market value. See ibid, 151–52.

[38] See generally Hanson and Croley, above n 37.

[39] See Cutler and Zeckhauser, above n 6, 40.

$213 per year and policies paying out an average death benefit of $35 310.[40] Of course, it is possible that this form of insurance protects policyholders against financial risk.[41] The death of a child may lead to funeral expenses, therapy costs and a temporary inability to work.[42] But these explanations are largely implausible. In fact, the death of a child generally results in a substantial increase in wealth because it relieves parents of child-rearing costs. Recent estimates place this cost at $9000 a year for families earning less than $57 000 annually, $12 000 a year for families earning between $57 000 and $98 500 annually and $21 000 a year for families with a yearly income above $98 500.[43] Moreover, the financial costs of a child's death are generally small: most health insurance plans cover mental health treatment expenses,[44] and federal law provides some measure of protection to employees who need to take bereavement leave.[45] Although the average funeral costs $6500, one can plan a modest funeral for substantially less.[46]

Another example of commonly purchased non-pecuniary loss insurance is Uninsured/Underinsured Motorists Coverage ('UIM' coverage).[47] In the event of an accident with an uninsured or underinsured motorist, UIM coverage pays the amount the insured would have been able to recover from a tortfeasor with

[40] See J Martin, 'Kids Life Insurance: A Pint-Sized Mistake' *Money* (September 28 2005). Life insurance for children is even more frequently sold as a rider to an adult's life insurance policy. ibid.

[41] In some cases, there may be other reasons to purchase juvenile life insurance. In particular, because many policies do not require medical tests, parents of a child with potential health problems may wish to purchase coverage to ensure that life insurance is available to the child in his or her adult years. This explanation, however, is clearly insufficient to explain the prevalence of juvenile life insurance.

[42] See V O'Connell, *Wall Street Journal* (January 30 1996) 12C (describing insurers' marketing of life insurance for children).

[43] M Lino, A Carlson, United States Department of Agriculture, Center for Nutrition Policy and Promotion, *Expenditure on Children by Families* 2009 (Pub No 1528–2008 2009) available at: www.cnpp.usda.gov/ExpendituresonChildrenbyFamilies.htm (last visited: 15 March 2010). These figures exclude college costs and other parental expenditures made for children after age 17. Admittedly, families without savings or any sources of financing might find it hard to pay for funeral expenses, but a quick internet search suggests that many funeral service providers offer financing to consumers.

[44] The Mental Health Parity and Addiction Act of 2008, which took effect on 1 January 2010, requires that employer-provided health insurance plans offer mental health benefits that are no more restrictive than those requirements placed on medical benefits. 29 USC § 1185a (2008). Additionally, many states have similar laws. See National Conference of State Legislatures, State Laws Mandating or Regulating Mental Health Benefits (February 2009) available at: www.ncsl.org/IssuesResearch/Health/StateLawsMandatingorRegulatingMentalHealthB/tabid/14352/Default.aspx (last visited: 15 March 2010).

[45] See, eg *Stubl v TA Systems, Inc*, 984 FSupp 1075 (ED Mich 1997) (holding that the Family Medical Leave Act ('FMLA') applies to parents suffering from depression due to the loss of a child). However, it is notable that the FMLA only provides leave to individuals whose grief rises to a significant level of clinical depression. See USC § 2601 et seq. Furthermore, the FMLA only provides for unpaid leave. ibid.

[46] See C Solomon, 'Plan a Funeral for $800 or Less', MSN Money, available at: articles.moneycentral.msn.com/RetirementandWills/PlanYourEstate/HowToPlanAFuneral.aspx.

[47] See Hanson and Croley, above n 37, 1862–63; Tom Baker, 'Insurance in Sociolegal Research' (working paper on file with the author).

sufficient liability insurance to pay for damages.[48] Because tort plaintiffs/claimants can recover emotional distress damages from defendants, policyholders with UIM coverage can also recover insurance proceeds for emotional distress (in addition to financial losses).[49] Admittedly, the relative percentage of UIM payouts that are compensation for non-pecuniary loss is not clear, as the average UIM payment is approximately the same as average economic loss.[50] But UIM coverage is designed so that there are certainly some, and perhaps many, cases where payments exceed economic loss.

Consumers' apparent demand for insurance against non-pecuniary losses is not necessarily incompatible with traditional EUT.[51] This is because it is possible that a non-pecuniary loss might increase an individual's marginal utility of wealth.[52] An emotional loss might make financial expenditures more desirable, as in the case of so-called 'retail therapy'. Similarly, a loss of physical capabilities might increase the marginal utility of wealth, for instance, by encouraging an avid athlete to substitute towards more expensive hobbies.[53]

However, these explanations for consumers' demand for juvenile life insurance and UIM insurance are largely implausible. In the case of juvenile life insurance, it is simply hard to imagine that a child's death increases the utility people derive from spending money.[54] This is particularly true given that a child's death generally increases overall wealth levels, which tends to reduce the marginal utility of wealth. In the case of UIM insurance, there may indeed be individual instances where a non-pecuniary loss will increase the marginal utility of wealth. But it seems telling that UIM insurance does not link insurance payments to factors that might plausibly track the subjective value of money. Such factors might include whether emotional distress is attributable to the temporary

48 See R Jerry, *Understanding Insurance Law*, 3rd edn (2001) 1034.

49 See ibid.

50 See Insurance Research Council, *Closed Claims Study* (2002) 72.

51 See PJ Cook and DA Graham, 'The Demand for Insurance and Protection: The Case of Irreplaceable Commodities' (1977) 91 *Quarterly Journal of Economics* 143.

52 See Shavell, above n 35, 228–31. As Shavell explains, '[i]f nonpecuniary losses will not result in a person valuing money more, then under the expected utility maximizing insurance policy he will not arrange for coverage against the nonpecuniary losses; coverage will be restricted to pecuniary losses, if any. Thus a person might not insure against the loss of his family portrait and might limit coverage against loss of a toe to medical expenses.' ibid, at 230. By contrast, '[i]f the value a person will place on money will increase as a result of a nonpecuniary loss, optimal insurance coverage will exceed pecuniary loss. Thus a person may purchase greater coverage against the possibility of being crippled than an amount equal only to the costs of medical treatment and forgone earnings.' ibid See also A Schwartz, 'Proposals for Products Liability Reform: A Theoretical Synthesis' (1988) 97 *Yale Law Journal* 353, 362–67; PM Danzon, 'Tort Reform and the Role of Government in Private Insurance Markets' (1984) 13 *Journal of Legal Studies* 517, 521.

53 See Shavell, above n 35, 228–31.

54 See G Priest, 'The Problematic Structure of the September 11th Victim Compensation Fund' (2003) 53 *DePaul Law Review* 527, 536–57 ('It makes no general sense for a parent to reduce the family's financial position while the child is alive in order to enhance its financial position after the child dies; indeed, the reverse. Thus, there is no economic reason to purchase life insurance on a child.').

experience of physical pain (which should not impact the marginal utility of wealth) or to partial or total disability (which might plausibly impact the marginal utility of wealth). Simply put, UIM's provision of full insurance for all forms of pain and suffering that are recoverable in tort law seems over-broad if consumers are merely trying to transfer wealth to states of the world where they enjoy a comparatively large marginal utility of wealth.

2. COMPETING EXPLANATIONS FOR OBSERVED INSURANCE DEMAND

Part 1 provides strong evidence that risk aversion within the traditional EUT framework poorly describes how individuals tend to make insurance decisions. These deviations from standard theory can be explained in two basic ways. The first, which can be labelled the *mistake hypothesis*, explains these insurance demand anomalies by reference to consumers' lack of complete information and/or their limited cognitive abilities.[55] According to the mistake hypothesis, consumer insurance decisions reflect the fact that time is scarce, cognitive resources are finite and information is limited.[56] If these obstacles could be overcome, consumer insurance decisions would better reflect the predictions of traditional EUT. In other words, according to the mistake hypothesis, classical EUT is perfectly defensible as a normative theory of insurance purchasing, even though it largely fails as a descriptive theory.

The second explanation for the anomalies canvassed in Part 1 is that they stem not from the limits of consumers but from the limits of traditional EUT itself. This explanation, which can be labelled the *incompleteness hypothesis*, is premised on the notion that classical EUT fails to fully capture the benefits of insurance. Consumer behaviour, from this perspective, is not the result of mistakes driven by limited information or cognition. Rather, even sophisticated consumers with full information would deviate from the prescripts of standard theory under the incompleteness hypothesis.

[55] See Sunstein and Thaler (2003), above n 12, 1162; see also C Jolls, C Sunstein and R Thaler, 'A Behavioral Approach to Law and Economics' (1998) 50 *Stanford Law Review* 1471 (outlining various mistakes that fit this definition). Sunstein and Thaler include in their definition of a mistake consumer decisions that people would change if they had unlimited self-control. This component of their definition is omitted based on the objection, articulated by C Hill, that it is impossible to characterise a lack of self control as a true mistake. See Hill, above n 12, 446–47. Hill's argument could be interpreted to extend further, to the proposition that it is usually impossible to characterise any decision as a mistake. This, in her view, is because preferences are constructed to such a degree that they do not exist outside of their informational and cognitive framing. See ibid, 447–48. Hill is surely correct that it is often difficult to say whether or not a particular decision is a result of a mistake, as identifying a mistake requires us to consider how a person would have decided in a parallel universe in which they had full information and unlimited cognitive resources. That this is difficult in individual cases, however, does not mean that the concept of a mistake is not normatively useful.

[56] See Kunreuther and Pauly, above n 18, at 9–16 (developing a model in which consumers rationally forego the process of thoroughly investigating their insurance options because of the search costs associated with doing so).

This part argues that the available evidence provides strong support for the mistake hypothesis. Much of the 'anomalous' insurance demand described in Part 1 appears to be driven by consumers' incomplete information or analytically-limited heuristics. Consumers generate systematically incorrect probability assessments and estimates of harm, invoke incorrect analytic constructs to measure the value of insurance and even make basic mathematical mistakes. Such errors, this part shows, could persist even in competitive insurance markets.

At the same time, this part argues that the incompleteness hypothesis is also a plausible explanation for some of the 'anomalous' consumer demand observed in real insurance markets. It argues that the insurance demand anomalies described in Part 1 can plausibly be explained as sophisticated consumer behaviour to manage emotions such as anxiety, regret and loss aversion. Moreover, the capacity of insurance to address these negative emotions is not necessarily an artefact of manipulative insurance sales or marketing.[57] Rather, it may be a sophisticated and informed strategy on the part of consumers to manage emotions that exist independently of insurers' (and their agents') sales efforts. Other sophisticated consumer strategies — such as committing to a forced-savings strategy — may also explain some seemingly irrational consumer behaviour.

2.1. Understanding Consumers' Bimodal Demand for Catastrophe Insurance

The mechanisms underlying consumers' bimodal demand for catastrophe insurance are relatively well understood in the decision-making literature. First, individuals' strategies for assessing probabilities produce systematic biases when it comes to low-probability events. Most people tend to assess probabilities based in part on the cognitive salience and availability of the underlying event being estimated. Although this heuristic serves them well with respect to high-probability events, it produces systematic errors with respect to low-frequency events.[58] In particular, it results in the overweighting of salient low-probability risks such as terrorism, as well as events that have recently occurred. At the same

[57] Of course, this is not to suggest that manipulative insurance sales or marketing could not lead one to purchase insurance in order to manage emotions. Indeed, insurers may frequently create anxiety where none previously existed by virtue of presenting the option of insurance in the first place. These scenarios may have important regulatory implications, particularly with respect to the regulation of insurers' marketing practices. See T Baker, Insurance Regulation and Behavioral Economics (June 4 2010) (draft on file with the author). But the point here is merely that insurance can be used to manage emotions that exist independently of any manipulative or unfair marketing or sales practices.

[58] See Slovic, above n 21, 13–14, 107; see generally W Kip Viscusi, *Fatal Tradeoffs: Public and Private Responsibilities for Risk* (1995) at 117–22. Various factors can contribute to the salience of a low-probability event, including recent instances of the event, media coverage of the event and the effect associated with the event. See Johnson *et al*, above n 9, at 38.

time, it leads to the underweighting of mundane low-probability risks such as dying in a car accident, as well as risks that have not transpired in recent memory.

Second, people tend to employ a sequential threshold approach to insurance decision-making. Under this approach, they refuse to consider the desirability of insurance when they perceive the probability of the underlying risk to be below a threshold level.[59] This threshold is different for different people and can itself be manipulated. Unless the likelihood of a loss is perceived to cross this threshold, the consumer will not even consider the desirability of insuring against it, regardless of its anticipated magnitude.[60]

These mechanisms for consumer decision-making about catastrophe insurance provide strong support for the mistake hypothesis. Indeed, consumers' biased estimates of low-probability risks are unambiguously mistakes. Simply put, probability assessments based on the cognitive availability and salience of a risk will produce objective and systematic errors when applied to low-probability risks. The sequential approach to insurance decision-making is similarly consistent with the mistake hypothesis. Although this heuristic likely saves time and energy, consumers with infinite time and cognitive resources would not ignore the desirability of insurance when they perceived the probability of a risk to fall below some arbitrary threshold. Doing so might result in the failure to purchase insurance whose expected benefit *exceeded* its expected cost, as might be the case when such insurance is governmentally subsidised.[61]

Although market forces might mitigate the impact of such mistakes, they would not eliminate them. In fact, insurers may even exploit consumers' biased estimates of the probability of salient risks to sell more coverage, as they do when they sell 'dread disease' insurance or flight insurance.[62] While insurers might conversely attempt to help consumers overcome mistakes that result in the purchase of too little insurance (as in the case of mundane risks), any such efforts would obviously not be fully effective. Perhaps even more importantly, private insurers often have little incentive to debias and inform consumers in this context, as supply-side problems limit the desirability of selling coverage for catastrophic risks.[63] As a result, most forms of catastrophic risk insurance — including flood and earthquake insurance — are largely supplied by the government, thereby muting market forces that might correct consumer mistakes.

While the mistake hypothesis likely explains a large percentage of consumers' bimodal demand for catastrophe insurance, at least some portion of this demand

[59] See generally Kunreuther *et al*, above n 16, at 241; Slovic, above n 21, 56–57.

[60] See Slovic, above n 21, 56–57.

[61] See section 1.1 above.

[62] See JD Hanson and DA Kysar, 'Taking Behavioralism Seriously: Some Evidence of Market Manipulation' (1999) 112 *Harvard Law Review* 1420.

[63] See D Jaffee and T Russell, 'Catastrophe Insurance, Capital Markets, and Uninsurable Risks' (1997) 64 *Journal of Risk and Insurance* 205 (explaining why insurers prefer not to insure against catastrophic risks).

may be better explained by the incompleteness hypothesis. In particular, consumers' sequential threshold approach to purchasing catastrophe insurance may actually reflect the sophisticated use of insurance to *reduce the anxiety associated with the prospect of a potential catastrophic loss.*[64] There is good evidence that insurance is valuable to consumers precisely because it provides 'peace of mind'.[65] Consider consumers' willingness to purchase 'probabilistic insurance', which, in the event of a covered loss, pays with some probability less than one.[66] Subjects find such insurance remarkably unattractive, demanding 'about a 30% reduction in the premium to compensate them for a 1% chance that their claim will not be paid'.[67] This distaste for probabilistic insurance can be explained by its failure to eliminate the anxiety that accompanies contemplating the prospect of a loss. Other studies support this interpretation, finding that subjects' reported concern that they might lose a valuable object better explained their willingness to purchase insurance against that risk than their probability assessments about that risk.[68]

To the extent that the value of insurance stems from anxiety reduction, consumers' sequential threshold approach to catastrophe insurance may reflect sophisticated and informed behaviour.[69] Consumers' refusal to investigate insurance against risks below threshold probability levels can be interpreted as a lack of interest in insurance against risks that do not induce anxiety.[70] For consumers who are not particularly risk-averse, such insurance would genuinely be undesirable under traditional EUT, so long as loading costs were non-negligible. By contrast, consumers' willingness to investigate insurance against risks whose perceived probability exceed threshold levels may reflect the fact that such risks generate anxiety that insurance could alleviate.

[64] See Krantz and Kunreuther, above n 4, 140–41 ('[P]urchasing flight insurance at the airport may, for some people, provide "peace of mind" and for the purpose of such anxiety reduction may be preferred to drinking alcohol at an airport bar.').

[65] This is consistent with insurers' marketing practices that associate the company with stability, comfort and family. See generally T Baker, 'Constructing the Insurance Relationship: Sales Stories, Claims Stories and Insurance Contract Damages' (1994) 72 *Texas Law Review* 1395, 1403–07 (surveying the various 'sales stories' that insurers use in their advertising, and noting the pervasiveness of themes such as promising, trust and security).

[66] P Wakker, R Thaler and A Tversky, 'Probabilistic Insurance' (1997) 15 *Journal of Risk and Uncertainty* 7, 9.

[67] ibid.

[68] C Schade, H Kunreuther and KP Kass, 'Probability Neglect and Concern in Insurance Decisions with Low Probabilities and High Stakes' (April 14, 2004) available at: opim.wharton.upenn.edu/risk/downloads/rain%20%20paper%20%20apr01.pdf last visited: 15 March 2010. See also P. Slovic, B Fischoff and S Lichtenstein, 'Informing the Public About the Risks From Ionizing Radiation' (1981) 41 *Health Physics* 589, 591 ('[P]eople often attempt to reduce the anxiety generated in the face of uncertainty by denying the uncertainty, thus making the risk seem so small that it can safely be ignored or so large that it clearly should be avoided.').

[69] For a related point in the administrative law context, see M Adler, 'Fear Assessment: Cost Benefit Analysis and the Pricing of Fear and Anxiety' (2004) 79 *Chicago-Kent Law Review* 977 (arguing that cost-benefit analysis in the regulatory context should include fear assessment).

[70] See Slovic, above n 21, 56–57.

Consider the example of earthquake insurance. Suppose that a consumer is not worried about earthquakes, perhaps because he perceives himself to live in an area where earthquakes are exceedingly unlikely. Even under traditional EUT, such a person may rationally decide not to purchase insurance with some loading cost.[71] Now consider how this person's behaviour might change in the wake of a salient earthquake. Even though he knows that an earthquake is no more likely now than it was before, he frequently worries about the effect an earthquake would have on his family, especially when he sees a news story about the recent earthquake.[72] From the perspective of standard theory, he should nonetheless be no more willing to purchase earthquake insurance now than he was prior to the recent earthquake. But from the perspective of reducing anxiety, such insurance may now be very valuable.

In sum, consumers' bimodal demand for catastrophe insurance can largely be attributed to informational or cognitive limitations. But the incompleteness hypothesis cannot be rejected based on the available evidence, at least for some consumers. Classical EUT fails to account for the anxiety-reducing value of insurance,[73] and this incompleteness may partially explain why it fails to predict bimodal consumer demand for insurance against low-probability, high-magnitude risks. To be sure, specific cases may be better explained by one hypothesis or the other: clearly the person who pays more for terrorism insurance than insurance against all risks is making a mistake. But, in the aggregate, some component of consumers' bimodal demand for catastrophe insurance may reflect sophisticated decision-making rather than systematic mistakes.

2.2. Understanding Consumer Demand for Insurance against Small Financial Risks

Consumers' enthusiasm for insurance against small financial risks is less well understood than their bimodal demand for catastrophe insurance. The most intuitive explanation for this phenomenon is that consumers overestimate the probability of loss in these situations and thus think they are getting a 'good deal'.[74] But this explanation does not withstand scrutiny. First, the extent to which

[71] See Eeckhoudt *et al*, above n 14, 5, 45–47. An alternative explanation, which is not strictly consistent with traditional EUT, is that individuals budget specific amounts for insurance purchases and consequently often believe that they cannot afford additional insurance. See Kunreuther and Pauly, above n 13, 19–20.

[72] Of course, one might object that people's worries are themselves irrational. But the point here is merely that the decision to purchase insurance as a means of managing these emotions is not itself a mistake. Whether or not the emotions one is seeking to manage are themselves somehow irrational does not impact on this narrower question.

[73] It is possible to amend classical EUT such that one's utility function incorporates the anxiety-reducing function of insurance.

[74] See BP Pashigan, L Schkade and G Menefee, 'The Selection of an Optimal Deductible for a Given Insurance Policy' (1966) 39 *Journal of Business* 35.

consumers would need to overestimate probabilities in order to believe they were breaking even by purchasing insurance is often quite large.[75] This is because consumers typically purchase insurance against small financial risks at the time of sale, as an add-on to a primary purchase. Competition to supply such insurance consequently tends to be minimal, producing large gaps between the cost of this insurance and its expected payouts.[76] Second, people actually tend to do a good job of estimating probabilities with respect to risks that occur frequently and can be observed.[77] Third, some consumers — though perhaps not many — presumably understand that companies would not offer insurance unless the cost of buying it exceeded the expected payout.[78]

A more plausible explanation is that consumers' demand for insurance against small financial risks stems from 'mental accounting'.[79] Mental accounting posits that individuals tend to evaluate risks in isolation, without appreciating the impact that external factors may have on those risk evaluations.[80] Consequently, a risk that is small in the context of one's overall wealth may appear large in isolation. Mental accounting also results in people tending to ignore the 'law of large numbers', which states that aggregating individual bets will tend to reduce the chances that actual outcomes deviate from predicted outcomes.[81] Individuals may therefore overweight the desirability of insuring against commonly-faced risks. For instance, although an individual may perceive risk when considering whether a newly purchased stereo will break, she ought to perceive little risk when considering the expected costs of all her consumer goods breaking in a particular year.

The mental accounting explanation supports the mistake hypothesis because it suggests that consumers' enthusiasm for insurance against small financial risks stems from their reliance on an imperfect heuristic. Mental accounting may be a valuable tool for cognitively limited people to make financially sensible decisions in daily life, but it produces systematic errors with respect to financial decisions that importantly depend on larger financial context.[82] Purchasing insurance

[75] Z Shapira and I Venezia, 'On the Preferences for Full-Coverage Policies: Why Do People Buy Too Much Insurance?' (2008) 29 *Journal of Economic Psychology* 747 (noting that people would need to believe that accidents were four times more probable than they are for overestimation to explain their preferences for low deductibles).

[76] See Cutler and Zeckhauser, above n 6, 5.

[77] See Sunstein and Thaler (2008), above n 12, 74–75; Slovic, above n 21, 6–7.

[78] See Cutler and Zeckhauser, above n 6, 45 ('People who ask why the store is willing to sell [durable goods] insurance will conclude that it is only because the warranty makes money.').

[79] See Rabin and Thaler, above n 6, 227.

[80] See R Thaler, 'Mental Accounting Matters' (1999) 12 *Journal of Behavioral Decision Making* 183.

[81] Slovic, above n 21, 11.

[82] Thus, Kunreuther and Krantz are clearly correct when they emphasise that mental accounting is not always irrational. See Kunreuther and Krantz, above n 4, at 159. Many heuristics are perfectly rational in the sense that they make decision-making easier and generally produce reliable beliefs, but they nonetheless systematically produce mistakes in the sense that people would change their mind were all informational and cognitive limitations eliminated.

against a small financial risk is precisely such a decision — whether or not a particular gamble is 'small' depends on broader context. Were consumers endowed with perfect information and cognitive resources, they would surely realise this.

Market forces do not undermine the mistake-based explanation for consumers' demand for insurance against small financial risks. No firm has an incentive to correct this type of mistake, because doing so would simply decrease consumers' willingness to purchase insurance against small financial risks. In addition, because this form of insurance is typically sold as a voluntary add-on to other products, a firm's attempt to capture market share by informing or debiasing consumers would not help that firm capture additional business. Rather, it would allow consumers to adjust behaviour and avoid the costs of such insurance without switching to the debiasing or informing firm.[83]

Mental accounting, however, is not the only explanation for consumers' surprising demand for insurance against small financial risks. Another, non-mutually exclusive, explanation is loss aversion.[84] Loss aversion posits that the pain individuals feel due to a loss substantially outweighs (usually by a factor of 2–1) the pleasure they feel from an equivalent gain.[85] From the perspective of loss aversion, insurance against high-probability, low-magnitude risks may help to reduce the potential for emotional unpleasantness stemming from losses.[86] This depends on whether insurance premiums are themselves experienced as a loss. But recent models suggest that many people do not experience insurance premiums as losses, in part because such premiums are within their control and are not 'surprise' events.[87]

[83] For an extended treatment of this argument, see X Gabaix and D Laibson, 'Shrouded Attributes, Consumer Myopia, and Information Suppression in Competitive Markets' (2006) 121 *Quarterly Journal of Economics* 505.

[84] Rabin and Thaler, above n 6, 226. To be sure, other explanations — some of which are canvassed in other parts of this paper — may also explain consumers' demand for insurance against high-probability, low-magnitude risks. For instance, consumers may purchase such insurance to reduce potential regret should a good they purchase break. See section 2.3 below. The normative implications of this explanation are particularly confounding, however, because regret may well be endogenous to the offer of insurance. In other words, consumers might not feel regret, or anticipate that they might feel regret, if they were never offered the option of purchasing insurance in the first place. The text of this paper seeks to avoid this endogeneity problem by discussing the management of emotions that are largely exogenous to the insurance decision.

[85] See Tversky and Kahneman, 'Loss Aversion in Riskless Choice: A Reference-Dependent Model' (1991) 106 *Quarterly Journal of Economics* 1039, 1053–4; Tversky and Kahneman, above n 4 (incorporating loss aversion into prospect theory). Whether a prospect is considered a potential 'loss' or 'gain' depends partly on how it is framed.

[86] Some studies suggest that consumers may purchase warranties in order to reduce the anxiety they feel about the prospect of a product breaking. See R Hogarth and H Kunreuther, 'Decision Making Under Ignorance: Arguing with Yourself' (1995) 10 *Journal of Risk and Uncertainty* 15; Lowenstein *et al*, above n 4.

[87] See B Koszegi and M Rabin, 'Reference Dependent Risk Attitudes' (2007) 97 *American Economics Review* 1047; Sydnor, above n 32, 4.

In contrast to mental accounting, loss aversion is more consistent with the incompleteness hypothesis than the mistake hypothesis. Knowing that even small losses can cause large amounts of emotional distress, consumers reasonably insure against them. By doing so they avoid the potential unpleasantness of paying for the removal of a fallen tree or purchasing a replacement iPod through the relatively painless process of purchasing insurance.[88]

2.3. Explaining Consumer Demand for Low Deductibles

A number of different explanations have been advanced for consumers' persistent preference for modest deductibles, most of which are consistent with the mistake hypothesis.[89] One recent theory suggests that consumers prefer moderate deductibles because they are simply miscalculating expected values by incorrectly 'anchoring' on the size of the deductible.[90] According to this theory, insurance consumers calculate the expected payout of a policy by first aggregating expected losses and then subtracting the deductible from this amount. This approach substantially exaggerates the value of a low deductible by failing to take into account its irrelevance if a loss does not occur.[91] The theory finds support in three different experiments, each of which found that subjects — students with a background in economics who were provided with an explanation of deductibles — consistently made this error in attempting to price policies in a simulated insurance market.[92]

A second explanation for consumers' preference for low deductibles is that consumers make an analytic mistake, rather than a numeric mistake, by reasoning that a low deductible increases their chances of 'getting something' if they

[88] Rabin and Thaler, above n 6, 224–26.

[89] One researcher directly asked subjects why they chose the deductibles they did. For those who chose $50 deductibles, answers included (i) 'it was the smallest possible,' (ii) 'it gave general protection,' (iii) 'it was the best deal,' and (iv) 'any accident I have will be less than $200 since I am a careful driver.' For those who chose $100 deductibles, explanations included (i) their agent or bank chose it, (ii) this option was cheaper, (iii) 'could always squeeze out $100,' (iv) 'makes for fewer claims and that's better,' and (v) 'never had any accidents where I had to pay'. See ML Murray, 'Empirical Utility Functions and Insurance Consumption Decisions' (1972) 39 *Journal of Risk and Insurance* 31. These explanations seem to provide more support for the mistake hypothesis than the incompleteness hypothesis, though they are obviously difficult to interpret.

[90] Shapira and Venezia, above n 75, 749, 754–56. One additional explanation, not considered in the text, is that consumers substantially overestimate the risk of loss. See Pashigan *et al*, above n 74. For similar reasons to those described above, this explanation seems unlikely, given the amount of overestimation that would be needed and the fact that people are relatively familiar with the risk of a car accident. See Shapira and Venezia, above n 75, 748 (noting that this explanation assumes that people anticipate two accidents a year, which is substantially greater than average).

[91] See Shapira and Venezia, above n 75, 749.

[92] In particular, they priced policies with deductibles at well below the rate necessary to make a profit, but priced policies without deductibles in a manner consistent with earning a reasonable return. See ibid.

suffer a loss. Consumers thus mistakenly think of insurance as 'an investment'.[93] This explanation is consistent with a number of other observed deviations from traditional EUT that this chapter does not focus on, such as consumer demand for 'tontines'[94] — which bundle insurance policies with a lottery — and consumers' willingness to simultaneously hold annuities and life insurance.[95]

These mistake-based explanations are consistent with a competitive marketplace. It is certainly conceivable that a competing insurer would find it worthwhile to inform or debias consumers who were mistakenly selecting excessively low deductibles.[96] But such market corrections are unlikely, because newly-sophisticated consumers could adjust their behaviour and avoid their deductible mistake without switching to the firm that invested in debiasing or informing them.[97] For example, a State Farm consumer who realised that he was making a mistake by maintaining a $500 deductible after watching an Allstate advertisement trumpeting the cost savings from high deductible plans could simply stick with State Farm but increase his deductible to $5000. Indeed, it is much more likely that a consumer would react in this way than switch to Allstate, as switching carriers involves transaction costs that staying with the same carrier does not.[98]

Once again, however, it is at least theoretically possible to explain consumers' preferences for low deductibles in a manner that supports the incompleteness hypothesis rather than the mistake hypothesis. Some theorists have speculated that consumers' preference for low deductibles represents a sophisticated strategy to reduce regret.[99] Regret in this context refers to the disutility that individuals experience when their decisions turn out to be incorrect from an ex post

[93] See Kunreuther and Pauly, above n 13, 28; Cutler and Zeckhauser, above n 6.

[94] See T Baker and P Siegelman, 'Enticing Low Risks into the Health Insurance Pool', University of Pennsylvania Institute for Law and Economics Research Paper No. 09–07 (July 28 2009) available at: www.ssrn.com/abstract=1350423 (last visited: 15 March 2010).

[95] See Cutler and Zeckhauser, above n 6, at 13 ('[L]ife insurance and annuities cater to mutually exclusive circumstances: living too long and living too short. One would not expect the same person to want bother instruments in force at the same time.').

[96] See, eg R Epstein, 'Human Errors and Market Corrections' (2006) 73 *University of Chicago Law Review* 111, 119–20 (discussing situations in which sellers in a market will invest to correct consumer misperceptions).

[97] See Gabaix and Laibson above n 83. An alternative explanation for why firms might not invest in informing consumers about the benefits of large deductibles is that they anticipate that doing so will result in other firms doing the same. In that event, the only benefits a firm can derive from informing consumers in this way stem from their position as a first-mover, which may not be large enough to offset the costs of such an information campaign. See O Bar-Gill, 'The Behavioral Economics of Consumer Contracts' (2008) 92 *Minnesota Law Review* 749, 760.

[98] See Bar-Gill, above n 97. It is also possible that the hypothetical consumer might pay lower premiums by staying with State Farm than switching. Because a lower percentage of State Farm customers than Allstate customers would understand the benefits of low deductibles, given Allstate's advertising campaign, the profits generated by State Farm's larger cadre of unsophisticated consumers might partially cross-subsidise sophisticated consumers. See ibid

[99] See M Braun and A Muermann, 'The Impact of Regret on the Demand for Insurance' (2004) 71 *Journal of Risk and Insurance* 737. For another attempt to reconcile consumers' deductible choices with rational behaviour, see A Cohen and L Einav, 'Estimating Risk Preferences from Deductible Choice' (2007) 97 *American Economic Review* 779–81.

perspective. For instance, a person who decides not to purchase an extended warranty (perhaps after having read this chapter) might nonetheless regret that decision if the product she purchases breaks shortly after purchase. There is modest direct evidence that avoiding regret influences various decisions about risk, most notably decisions regarding whether to receive a vaccination.[100]

Hypothesising that consumers seek to avoid regret explains a variety of observed insurance decisions, including the preference for a relatively low deductible.[101] A regret-averse person would experience disutility from having purchased a high-deductible policy if he does indeed suffer a loss. As a result, one can formally show that, under certain relatively uncontroversial assumptions, perfectly sophisticated individuals whose utility functions incorporate regret-minimisation would 'hedge their bets' when loading costs are sufficiently high, purchasing a lower deductible than they otherwise might in order to mitigate the prospect of regret.[102] Such actors are not making a mistake in the sense that they would alter their decisions with better information or more cognitive resources.

Another explanation for consumers' preferences for low deductibles that supports the incompleteness hypothesis is that such deductible choices represent a rational forced-savings strategy.[103] It is well known that consumers often have trouble saving funds for a rainy day and, in some cases, tend to exhaust lines of credit because they have difficulty resisting spending.[104] For such consumers, purchasing low deductibles may be a rational strategy to ensure that they have the financial capacity to make important repairs when they need to do so. Unlike a more conventional savings strategy, the benefit of low deductibles is that they involve a single, up-front, investment that is relatively hard to undo in the face of temptation. The insurance contract essentially ensures consumers that they can only 'withdraw' funds in the event of a genuinely serious loss.[105]

[100] See Braun and Muermann, above n 99, 743 (discussing T Conolly and J Reb, 'Omission Bias in Vaccination Decisions' (2003) 91 *Organizational Behavior and Human Decisions Processes* 186).

[101] Others have attempted to use regret to explain the simultaneous preference for insurance and lotteries. See, eg DE Bell, 'Regret in Decision Making Under Uncertainty' (1982) 30 *Operations Research* 961.

[102] See Muermann and Braun, above n 99, 739.

[103] This is not dissimilar to sophisticated hyperbolic discounters who make rational purchasing decisions given their awareness of their susceptibility to hyperbolic discounting, See S DellaVigna and U Malmendier, 'Contract Design and Self-Control: Theory and Evidence' (2004) 119 *Quarterly Journal of Economics* 353.

[104] See, eg A Littwin, Beyond Usury: A Study of Credit Card Use and Preference Among Low-Income Consumers' (2008) 86 *Texas Law Review* 451, 466–78.

[105] In that sense, low deductibles may be similar to one recent set of proposals that would encourage 'self-directed cards that would equip consumers to resist more effectively the temptation of credit cards', for instance by allowing consumers to set effective credit limits and other pre-commitment devices. ibid, 455, 478–500.

2.4. Explaining Demand for Insurance Against Non-Pecuniary Losses

Recall that consumer demand for insurance against non-pecuniary loss is both theoretically consistent with traditional EUT and often (wrongly) claimed not to exist in practice. For both reasons, few scholars have given much thought to what, other than changes in the marginal utility of wealth, might explain demand for non-pecuniary loss insurance where it does exist.[106] As above, however, explanations consistent with both the mistake hypothesis and the incompleteness hypothesis are plausible.

It is entirely possible that people who demand non-pecuniary loss insurance are simply making mistakes. For instance, people may overestimate the extent to which a non-pecuniary loss will increase their need for wealth. Thus, those who purchase juvenile life insurance may overestimate the likelihood that they will need to (or want to) take an extended period of time off work or need extensive therapy in the event of a child's death. Indeed, there is strong evidence that people exaggerate the duration of losses that involve high affect (often labelled 'durability bias').[107] Alternatively, people may analyse the need for insurance against a potential risk without distinguishing between pecuniary and non-pecuniary losses at all. This prospect is supported by evidence that financial decisions are often reflexive and thus impacted simultaneously by logical processes (which might dictate the purchase of insurance for pecuniary risks) and emotional processes (which might conflate pecuniary and non-pecuniary risks given that such losses are often felt simultaneously).[108] It is also consistent with experimental evidence demonstrating that consumers are equally willing to purchase insurance against pecuniary and non-pecuniary risks.[109] For similar reasons to those canvassed earlier, such mistakes might persist even in a competitive marketplace.[110]

At the same time, there are at least two potential explanations for consumer demand for non-pecuniary loss insurance that are consistent with the incompleteness hypothesis. First, people may view insurance as a form of 'consolation' against the risk of loss. On this account, insurance not only pays money in the

[106] See Part 1 above.

[107] See DT Gilbert *et al*, 'Durability Bias in Affective Forecasting' in T Gilovich *et al* (eds), *Heuristics and Biases: the Psychology of Intuitive Judgment* (2002).

[108] See, eg P Bossaerts, 'What Decision Neuroscience Teaches Us About Financial Decision Making' (2009) 1 *Annual Review of Financial Economics* 383 (summarising modern literature on the subject); H Tzieropoulos *et al*, 'The Rationale Behind Irrational Decisions', Frontiers in Behavioural Neuroscience, Conference Abstract: 41st European Brain and Behaviour Society Meeting 2009; AW Lo and DV Repin, 'The Psychophysiology of Real-Time Financial Risk Processing' (2002) 14 *Journal of Cognitive Neuroscience* 323.

[109] See Avraham, above n 37, 946–50.

[110] In particular, it is possible that no firm would have any incentive to limit consumers' overestimation of the financial consequences of non-pecuniary losses or emphasise the distinction between pecuniary and non-pecuniary losses. This is because it is unclear how doing so would enhance the business of the firm that invested in informing/debiasing such consumers, given that these consumers would not need to switch to the other firm in order to benefit from this advice.

event of a loss but also provides a form of emotional support through 'symbolic value' or 'redemption for the lost object'.[111] This interpretation explains both peoples' willingness to pay more for insurance against emotionally-valuable items and their related willingness to incur comparatively high expenses to recover insurance proceeds in the event of a loss to such items.[112] By contrast, it is hard to explain peoples' increased willingness to incur collection costs as resulting from some error about the magnitude or probability of the underlying loss.

Alternatively, it is possible that individuals desire non-pecuniary loss insurance due to a desire to distribute resources from a high-utility state of the world to a low-utility state of the world. From this perspective, individuals care not just about maximising expected utility but also about equalising their overall utility levels across different states of the world. In other words, they are risk-averse with respect to bets concerning overall utility levels rather than simply with respect to bets involving wealth. Such risk aversion stems not from the decreasing marginal utility of wealth but rather from a corollary to the Rawlsian notion that it is preferable to distribute goods equally behind a veil of ignorance unless departing from that strategy increases the welfare of the worst-off individual.[113]

3. LIBERTARIAN PATERNALISM AND REGULATING INSURANCE DEMAND

Part 2 raises competing implications for assessing the optimal role of government in response to deviations from the traditional EUT framework in insurance markets.[114] On the one hand, the mistake hypothesis appears to explain most of the observed insurance demand anomalies better than the incompleteness hypothesis. To the extent that this is so, aggressive regulatory intervention designed to correct these mistakes and foreclose their exploitation by firms may be warranted.[115] The desirability of such intervention would turn primarily on practical factors such as the potential effectiveness of regulation, its direct and indirect costs and the harm to consumers in the absence of regulation.

On the other hand, the incompleteness hypothesis provides a theoretically plausible explanation for understanding a subset of each consumer demand anomaly identified in Part 1. Deviations from standard theory may consequently represent, to some degree, sophisticated consumer behaviour. This account vastly

[111] See Hsee and Kunreuther, above n 37, 146–47.

[112] See ibid 149–50 (explaining why the market value hypothesis cannot explain the ex post willingness to incur costs to collect claims but can theoretically explain ex ante willingness to do so).

[113] See Hanson and Croley, above n 37, 1812–34. As Hanson and Croley show, while Rawls' argument applies to how to distribute goods across multiple individuals, it can be extended to the decision about how to distribute goods across time with respect to a single individual. See generally ibid.

[114] See Cutler and Zeckhauser, above n 6, 20 (noting that 'behavioral explanations' for deviations from classical EUT 'make normative analysis difficult', while adding that '[f]ortunately for us, our analysis has a descriptive, not a normative, purpose').

[115] On the tendency of firms to exploit consumer errors, see generally Hanson and Kysar, above n 62.

complicates the normative case for regulatory interventions that would limit consumer choice, as it requires pitting the interests of some sophisticated consumers against the interests of other consumers who are (unknowingly) making mistakes.[116] To be sure, one can legitimately question the extent to which government regulation should always respect the preferences of sophisticated consumers, particularly where these preferences stem from the desire to manage emotions such as anxiety, regret and loss aversion.[117] But interventions designed to manipulate genuine consumer preferences for the benefit of those consumers are more troubling than interventions designed to correct consumer mistakes, because they undermine the premise of welfare economics and the related concept of consumer sovereignty.[118] Rather than confronting the propriety of such regulations directly, this part simply assumes that such regulation is less justifiable than regulation designed to correct genuine consumer error.[119]

Given these competing forces, this part considers various libertarian-paternalistic responses to consumer deviations from traditional EUT in insurance markets.[120] The basic premise of libertarian paternalism is that government interventions can simultaneously preserve choice while nudging consumers towards welfare-enhancing decisions. The range of such interventions is vast and exists along something of a spectrum between libertarianism and paternalism. For instance, product disclosure requirements are closer to the libertarian side of the spectrum: because disclosure requirements merely inform consumers about objective facts, they are highly consistent with libertarian principles. Similarly, selecting presumptively desirable defaults when defaults are impossible to avoid is likely unobjectionable to many libertarians.[121] Closer to the paternalistic side of

[116] Of course, it might well be justifiable to limit consumer choice even if that would foreclose genuinely attractive options for some consumers. But it is undeniable that identifying when this is the case is complicated, turning on the relative effectiveness of alternative regulatory strategies, the harm to consumers whose choices were limited, the benefits to consumers whose mistakes were prevented and numerous other factors.

[117] But cp Adler, above n 69 (arguing that regulatory policy ought to take into account the fear associated with death, illness and injury, in addition to the actual risks of these events transpiring).

[118] See L Kaplow and S Shavell, *Fairness Versus Welfare* (2006). According to the standard welfarist account, normative analysis ought to predict the consequences of policies, evaluate their impact on the welfare of all relevant persons and then aggregate these welfare impacts. This approach defines welfare as the satisfaction of preferences. Welfare economics does allow for the possibility that consumers will make mistakes. See ibid, 411–12. But it rejects the notion that preferences that are not mistakes should be manipulated by government actors for consumers' 'own good'. 'To trump preferences is, in essence, to redefine individuals' well-being in a manner that substitutes some other preferences – ones that are cleansed, so to speak – for individuals' actual preferences.... But such an approach is troubling from the perspective of welfare economics because the moral force and appeal of welfare economics lies in promoting the actual well-being of people, not in advancing some hypothetical notion of satisfaction that is distinct from that of the individuals who are the objects of our concern.' See ibid, 419–20.

[119] For a compelling critique of welfare economics, see D Farber, 'What, If Anything, Can Economics Say About Equity?' (2003) 101 *Michigan Law Review* 1791.

[120] See Sunstein and Thaler (2003), above n 12.

[121] See Glaeser, above n 12, 149–56 (discussing changes in default rules and other forms of soft paternalism).

the spectrum are interventions that seek to take advantage of behavioural tendencies, such as status quo bias and framing effects, to 'nudge' people towards presumptively welfare-promoting decisions and/or 'debias' them.[122]

Although all forms of libertarian paternalism maintain choice, more aggressive forms of such regulation are often objectionable to ardent libertarians because they require the government to determine presumptively welfare-maximising choices and attempt to 'manipulate' consumers into making those choices.[123] Additionally, aggressive forms of libertarian paternalism may impose a 'psychic tax' on consumers who seek to exercise choices inconsistent with encouraged decisions, causing them to experience emotional displeasure because they feel as if they acted badly or inappropriately.[124] In cases where the presumptively welfare-maximising decision merely decreases a risk rather than eliminating it, this psychic tax may also harm people who make the encouraged choices, causing them anxiety over the underlying risk.

This part considers a variety of libertarian-paternalistic responses to each of the four insurance demand anomalies emphasised in this chapter, including more aggressive forms of libertarian paternalism.[125] This approach is sensible for several reasons. First, as Part 2 suggests, the mistake hypothesis likely explains a much higher proportion of the deviations from traditional EUT than the incompleteness hypothesis. Comparatively intrusive forms of regulation may therefore be sensible. Second, as explored more fully below, disclosure-based responses are limited in their capacity to correct the consumer errors described in Part 2, which often do not stem from a lack of information in the first place. Finally, designing effective disclosures is notoriously difficult, especially under conditions of risk and uncertainty.[126]

[122] See generally Sunstein and Thaler (2008), above n 12. See also C Sunstein and C Jolls, 'Debiasing Through the Law' (2006) 35 *Journal of Legal Studies* 199.

[123] See generally Glaeser, above n 12, 150; Mitchell and Klick, above n 12. Nor are these the only criticisms of more aggressive forms of libertarian paternalism. Mitchell and Klick argue that soft paternalism can create a cognitive hazard by decreasing people's incentives to take care and debias themselves. But this does not seem like a compelling point in the present context, given the apparent problems that consumers experience in the status quo even without such interventions. Additionally, it seems implausible that consumers would choose to take less care in their insurance decisions given the interventions described herein. Most of these interventions would not appear to the consumer as government interventions, but would simply alter the way that information was presented to them in their market interactions.

[124] See Glaeser, above n 12, 150.

[125] cp Krantz and Kunreuther, above n 4, 164 ('In the preceding, we have emphasized consumer education partly in the spirit of libertarian paternalism and partly in the pragmatic belief that the issues involved here are too diverse and changeable to permit effective regulation.' (citation omitted)).

[126] See Slovic, above n 21, 166 (Although 'better information about risk is crucial to making better personal decisions… it may be quite difficult to create effective informational programs. Doing an adequate job means finding cogent ways of presenting complex, technical material that is clouded by uncertainty and subject to distortion by the listener's preconceptions — or misconceptions — about the hazard and its consequences.'). O Ben-Shahar and C Schneider, *The Failure of Mandated Disclosure* (Draft, March 2010) available at: papers.ssrn.com/sol3/papers.cfm?abstract_id=1567284 (last visited July 14 2010).

In considering relatively aggressive libertarian-paternalistic interventions, this part nonetheless seeks to remain cognisant of the downsides of such regulation, particularly the prospect that aggressive forms of libertarian paternalism may impose a psychic tax.[127] This potential side effect of libertarian paternalism is especially concerning given that a key reason for attempting to avoid paternalism with respect to consumers' insurance decisions is that these decisions may be motivated by reasonable emotional, or psychic, considerations.

3.1. Libertarian Paternalism and Catastrophe Insurance

As explained in Part 2, many consumers apparently make mistakes in failing to purchase insurance against catastrophes such as earthquakes, floods and hurricanes. These mistakes are particularly troubling because they can increase government costs in the wake of a catastrophe.[128] They may also create additional, related mistakes. Without insurance, individuals often fail to take protective measures against catastrophic risk, such as weather-proofing their homes, because the cost of doing so is immediate but the benefit is speculative and hard to assess. Insurance coverage can concretise the expected benefits of such precautions by impacting insurance premiums. In sum, there are particularly strong justifications for government policies that attempt to limit consumer mistakes about disaster insurance, and regulation should conceivably encourage all consumers to purchase such insurance in order to limit potential externalities.[129]

Although better disclosure could potentially limit consumer mistakes in this domain, the potential of such disclosure is ultimately limited. The most obvious form of improved disclosure would communicate the actual likelihood of a disaster to counteract consumers' tendency to underestimate risks that are not salient or cognitively available.[130] Unfortunately, mere numeric disclosures are unlikely to be particularly effective. Research suggests that more affect-laden approaches are often necessary to trigger consumers' willingness to consider the purchase of insurance in the sequential model of insurance.[131] Yet disclosures that sought to 'scare' people into purchasing insurance would impose a large psychic tax upon both those that chose not to purchase insurance and those that capitulated.

[127] See Glaeser, above n 12, 150.

[128] This includes both direct disaster insurance and increased use of more general elements of the social safety net, such as Medicaid and unemployment insurance.

[129] For these reasons, this section focuses on regulatory responses to this component of the bimodal demand for high-probability, low-magnitude insurance rather than the inverse potential problem that people purchase too much such insurance in certain circumstances.

[130] See Kunreuther and Pauly, above n 18, 14–15 (proposing better disclosure about loss probabilities and loading costs as one response to consumers' tendency not to insure against large losses).

[131] See Sunstein and Jolls, above n 122, 207–16.

One promising libertarian-paternalistic approach would encourage insurers to offer (in addition to any existing options) bundled disaster coverage for several different low-probability risks, such as floods and earthquakes.[132] Even if consumers underestimated the probability of each events individually, the combined probability of any event occurring might be sufficient to overcome the threshold level of probability that inhibits even the consideration of insurance in the sequential model of choice.[133] The key limitation of this proposal is that few consumers face even a small probability of exposure to both earthquakes and floods, so consumers are likely to consider such bundled insurance only in terms of the peril to which they are actually exposed.

To overcome this limitation, a related proposal would encourage insurers to offer (in addition to any existing options) disaster coverage for contract periods longer than a year, such as five or even 10 years. As with insurance that bundled different types of risks, such a policy might overcome errors generated by the sequential model of insurance by raising a risk above the requisite threshold for consumers to consider insuring against it. As one prominent commentator explains, 'instead of describing the chances of a 100-year flood as 0.01 per year, one could note that an individual living in a particular house for 25 years faces a 0.22 chance of suffering 100-year damage at least once'.[134] This approach would be more likely than the bundling of different types of disaster coverage to overcome threshold probabilities, as most risks do not differ substantially intertemporally.[135]

An alternative approach is to permit insurers to bundle disaster insurance with other forms of insurance that consumers tend to purchase too much of relative to

[132] See Kunreuther and Pauly, above n 18, 16. A more paternalistic intervention would be to require that insurers bundle such insurance with homeowners insurance. See H Kunreuther and M Pauly, 'Rules Rather Than Discretion: Lessons from Hurricane Katrina' (2006) 33 *Journal of Risk and Uncertainty* 101; H Kunreuther, 'Has the Time Come for Comprehensive National Disaster Insurance?' in RJ Daniels, DF Kettl and H Kunreuther (eds), *On Risk and Disaster: Lessons from Hurricane Katrina* (2006) 175, 175–203. This option would deprive consumers of the choice to purchase ordinary homeowners insurance without disaster insurance. Given the analysis in Part 2 suggesting that consumers may be making defensible choices in deciding not to purchase disaster insurance, such paternalism is harder to justify than the interventions suggested here. However, to the extent that libertarian paternalism does not effectively induce the purchase of disaster insurance, such interventions may, in fact, be justified, especially given the potential externalities associated with the purchase of disaster insurance.

[133] See Kunreuther and Pauly, above n 18, at 16. One might sensibly object that there is no need for regulatory intervention on this ground, as insurers would already be using this bundling strategy to increase sales to the extent that it were effective. But this objection ignores the point, made earlier, that insurers have various supply-side reasons why they may not want to sell disaster insurance. See section 2.1 above. Additionally, bundled insurance policies would transfer to the insurer the risk of new information surfacing during the coverage period that changes the probability or magnitude of the threat. This seems most likely for hurricane insurance, where global climate change does appear to be shifting our understanding of the underlying risk.

[134] See Slovic, above n 21, 71.

[135] This is not true of all risks, particularly those that may be impacted by global warming.

traditional EUT.[136] Consider one recent proposal designed to increase the purchase of health insurance among overly optimistic youths. It would permit — and perhaps even encourage — insurers to offer 'tontines', which are essentially potential lottery rewards that become available if the insured low-probability event does not transpire.[137] This strategy seeks to counteract under-insurance against catastrophic risks by exploiting consumers' seeming excess enthusiasm for tontines. It also helps counteract the prospect that consumers may not be drawn to catastrophe insurance because they incorrectly view it as an investment that tends not to pay out.[138] This approach has the benefit of almost completely avoiding psychic costs.

3.2 Libertarian Paternalism and Insurance Against Small Risks

Disclosure strategies represent one potentially promising approach to limiting consumer mistakes with respect to the purchase of insurance against high-probability, low-magnitude risks. One sensible strategy to decrease consumer errors would be to require disclosure of the percentage of consumers who actually use the warranties they purchase.[139] Alternatively, firms could be required to disclose the loss ratio — the percentage of premiums that are actually used for payouts — of this insurance.[140] Both approaches would better inform consumers about the expected value of this insurance and would, at the very least, help them realise that it is not a good 'investment'.[141]

In addition to improved product disclosure, consumer mistakes could also be limited by individual-use disclosure, which provides consumers with specific information about their own product use patterns.[142] Recall that a primary mistake that consumers may make when they purchase insurance against small financial risks is mental accounting, in which small risks are not considered in a larger context. These errors could be limited through strategic use of the

[136] See Slovic, above n 21, 71.

[137] See Baker and Siegelman, above n 94, 5–10.

[138] See section 2.1.

[139] See B Nalebuff and I Aires, *Why Not?* (2003) 181 (proposing that firms that sell consumer warranties inform consumers about the prospect that they will make a claim on those warranties); J Sovern, 'Toward a New Model of Consumer Protection' (2006) 47 *William and Mary Law Review* 1635, 1635–44, 1703 (similar proposal in rebate context).

[140] See O Bar-Gill, 'Informing Consumers About Themselves'. in *NYU Law and Economics Research Paper No. 07–44* (August 2007) 33, 53–57, available at: papers.ssrn.com/sol3/papers.cfm?abstract_id=1056381 (last visited April 8 2010).

[141] In order to be effective, the number of disclosures must be limited to a small number of truly important pieces of information. See generally R Craswell, 'Taking Information Seriously: Misrepresentation and Nondisclosure in Contract Law and Elsewhere' (2006) 92 *Virginia Law Review* 565.

[142] See Bar-Gill, above n 140, 37, 43–60 (exploring the distinction between product characteristic disclosures and consumer use-pattern disclosures).

disclosures that credit and debit card companies provide to consumers.[143] Many card providers already provide consumers with an annual summary of purchases in different categories.[144] One such category is 'consumer goods', though this category is frequently not broken down any further. Credit and debit card companies could be required to separately account for 'consumer warranties' and merchants could be required to report to the card company any repairs they actually provide under such warranties. With these mechanisms in place, consumers could receive an annual and five-year summary of the costs and benefits of consumer warranties they purchased. With some further coordination, these reports could conceivably be aggregated across a consumer's different credit and debit cards.

This particularised form of disclosure would help consumers overcome some of the limitations associated with mental accounting by framing the purchase of consumer insurance policies in larger context. Consumers who routinely purchase this form of insurance could see the law of large numbers in action. Although such a disclosure regime would be unlikely to change behaviour quickly, over time it would allow consumers to assess the value of these types of insurance products for themselves. Moreover, given advances in information technology, this form of regulation may not be particularly expensive to implement.[145] Even if the start-up costs of this disclosure regime were significant, they might be appropriate given the amount of money that consumers currently spend on product warranties.[146]

3.3. Libertarian Paternalism and Deductibles

To the extent that consumers are making mistakes by selecting excessively low deductibles, traditional disclosure-oriented strategies are not likely to prove effective. The basic problem is that the reason why people should prefer high deductibles is hard to explain briefly and simply: it implicates moral hazard,

[143] This proposal is only a slight variant of the RECAP disclosure proposals that Sunstein and Thaler describe in *Nudge*. See Sunstein and Thaler (2008), above n 12, 93–94.

[144] See Sunstein and Thaler (2008), above n 12, 143.

[145] At present, much of the relevant information is already sorted and presented to consumers by credit card companies. It would certainly not be difficult to require these companies to separately break down payments for warranties. However, it might well be costly to require card companies that do not already provide an annual summary to do so. Perhaps even more importantly, it might be costly to create a system whereby merchants kept track of which cards consumers used to make purchases and reported back any repairs associated with those warranties. Many merchants currently do store the card information of consumers for purposes of data analysis and facilitating returns, but it is unclear how difficult it would be to require them to report repair expenses back to the card company.

[146] See T Chen *et al*, 'Why Do Consumers Buy Extended Service Contracts?' (2009) 36 *Journal of Consumer Research* 611 (stating that consumers spent approximately $15 billion dollars on extended service contracts in 2005 and that consumers spent $8.3 billion dollars on warranties for computers, computer electronics and major appliances alone in 2007).

adverse selection and the nature of risk aversion. Rather than a straight-forward disclosure, however, government regulation could seek to nudge consumers towards purchasing higher deductibles through framing effects and forced choice.

First, insurers could be required to state deductibles in terms of a percentage of overall policy limits, in addition to absolute dollars.[147] Thus, a homeowners insurance policy that provides $250 000 of coverage for a dwelling would be framed as providing a deductible of 0.2 per cent of the policy limit, or $500. This framing should communicate to policyholders the small amount of risk they currently hold on to and encourage them to think about whether they could reasonably retain a larger amount of risk. It should also focus them on the analytically-relevant question from the perspective of risk aversion: how much risk do they want to retain, and how much do they want to transfer to the insurer?

Second, insurers could be required to offer any deductible up to at least 5 per cent of policy limits and to provide consumers with an initial set of prices for deductibles of 0.5 per cent, 1 per cent and 2 per cent.[148] Doing so would obviously increase consumer choice. More importantly, though, it would increase consumer awareness regarding the potential cost savings associated with higher deductibles — most consumer insurance markets are quite competitive on price,[149] so insurers would likely be forced to pass on to consumers the lower costs of high-deductible policies. Additionally, decision-making research has found that people often tend to select 'middle' options when they are given multiple options arrayed along a spectrum.[150] Forcing insurers to increase the number of choices at the upper range of plausible deductible values should consequently increase the percentage of consumers who select a higher deductible.

Third, and finally, insurers could be required to disclose the percentage of consumers who take advantage of small deductibles in the event of small claims. Research suggests that many consumers choose not to make a claim when their loss is not substantially larger than their deductible, because they worry that

[147] See OR Holsti, *Public Opinion and American Foreign Policy* (1995) (noting that survey respondents often believe that foreign aid is too high when told of the absolute number, but think that it is too low when told of the percentage of GDP that went to foreign aid).

[148] Yet another option is to require that insurers disclose the percentage of consumers choosing each deductible optionSee I Ayres *et al*, 'Evidence from Two Large Field Experiments That Peer Comparison Feedback Can Reduce Residential Energy Usage', National Bureau of Economic Research Working Paper No 15386 (September 2009). Of course, this is only a sensible idea if other reforms begin to encourage consumers to choose larger deductibles.

[149] See S Harrington, 'Effects of Prior Approval Rate Regulation in Auto Insurance' in JD Cummins (ed), *Deregulating Property-Liability Insurance* (2002) 285; S D'Arcy, 'Insurance Price Deregulation: The Illinois Experience'. in JD Cummins (ed), *Deregulating Property-Liability Insurance* (2002) 248.

[150] See, eg E Shafir *et al*, 'Reason-Based Choice' in WM Goldstein and RM Hogarth (eds), *Research on Judgment and Decision Making: Currents, Connections And Controversies* (1997) 69, 83.

doing so will increase future premiums.[151] If insurers were forced to disclose an estimate of how frequently this occurred, many consumers would presumably realise that the true cost of a low deductible is not just in the additional premium that is paid upfront but also in the additional premium that will be paid in the future as a result of taking advantage of this low deductible when small claims occur.

These strategies should be relatively cost-free to adopt and encourage people towards decisions that are more consistent with standard theory. At the same time, this approach should produce virtually no psychic tax and does not prevent sophisticated consumers from continuing to opt for low deductibles.

3.4. Libertarian Paternalism and Non-Pecuniary Loss Insurance

Libertarian-paternalistic interventions can also limit mistakes concerning non-pecuniary loss insurance. In the juvenile life insurance market, improved disclosure is the most obvious intervention.[152] Insurers could be required to disclose the projected decreased costs associated with the death of a child, especially for families saving for college expenses. Perhaps less controversially, insurers could be required to disclose the legal protections afforded to grieving parents, including the possibility of Family and Medical Leave Act (FMLA) leave in the event of depression and the requirement of mental health parity in many health insurance policies. To the extent that demand for this form of insurance stems from consumers' confusion as to emotional and financial loss, insurers might be required to disclose how policyholders typically use their insurance proceeds after a child's death.

Unfortunately, these disclosure strategies pose a potentially large risk of creating a psychic tax. Asking people to imagine the relative value of money in the event of their child's death may itself generate unpleasant emotions. This is true irrespective of whether the disclosure dissuades them from purchasing such insurance. It is also possible, though perhaps unlikely, that this approach would signal that insurance is somehow an inappropriate form of consolation, thereby undermining the potential value that some people genuinely experience when they receive insurance proceeds after a non-financial loss. Finally, disclosure strategies of this type might have the incidental effect of discouraging the purchase of other forms of insurance — such as ordinary life insurance — that are sold by the same agents, even when government policy ought to nudge people towards purchasing more, rather than less, of such coverage.

Less affect-laden contexts are more amenable to effective libertarian-paternalistic interventions that reduce consumer errors regarding non-pecuniary

[151] See Kunreuther and Pauly, above n 13, 29.

[152] As before, the effectiveness of such disclosure regulation hinges on the avoidance of excessive disclosure. See n 141.

loss insurance without imposing psychic taxes. Consider the purchase of Uninsured/Underinsured Motorists insurance. Here, insurers could be required to offer consumers the option of less extensive UIM insurance that covers only pecuniary tort damages but not pain and suffering damages. Additionally, regulators could insist that consumers who wish to purchase complete UIM coverage, which would include emotional distress damages, do so through an endorsement. That structure — which has already been tried in New Jersey[153] — effectively sets the default as limited UIM insurance that covers only pecuniary losses and requires consumers seeking non-pecuniary loss insurance to opt out of this default. Because consumers often do not opt out of defaults (referred to as 'status quo bias'), this approach might discourage consumers from paying for non-pecuniary loss insurance while simultaneously preserving their freedom to do so.[154] In New Jersey, only 20 per cent of drivers opted out of the default to full UIM coverage. Compare this to Pennsylvania, where consumers who did not want full UIM coverage were required to select an endorsement in exchange for a partial refund. Required to opt out in order to select the more limited coverage, 75 per cent of consumers stuck with the default of full UIM insurance.[155]

4. CONCLUSION

Decisions about insurance are among the most difficult that consumers face.[156] They require individualised predictions about the likelihood and magnitude of highly unlikely, and largely unfamiliar, future events. Faced with such complex decisions, it is hardly surprising that consumers frequently make mistakes. At the same time, insurance is a complicated and emotionally-laden product, and simplistic explanations of consumer behaviour seriously risk undermining some of the genuine value that insurance provides to consumers. Libertarian paternalism, which encourages presumptively reasonable insurance decisions while preserving choice, has an under-explored potential to navigate these competing interests.

[153] The New Jersey scheme did permit suit for non-economic damages in the case of a few statutorily defined serious injuries. For a more detailed overview of both the New Jersey and Pennsylvania schemes, see J Yeh and J SchmitAuto Insurance Claims in New Jersey' in EL Lascher and MR Powers (eds), *The Economics and Politics of Choice in No-Fault Insurance* (2001) 139–57.

[154] See Sunstein and Thaler (2008), above n 12, 8, 12–13.

[155] See Kunreuther and Krantz, above n 4, 160.

[156] See H Jackson, 'Regulation in a Multisectored Financial Services Industry: An Exploratory Essay' (1999) 77 *Washington University Law Quarterly* 319, 330–31.

6

Contracts and Capabilities: An Evolutionary Perspective on the Autonomy-Paternalism Debate

SIMON DEAKIN*

ABSTRACT

An evolutionary conception of contract law is suggested as a basis for assessing claims made in the autonomy-paternalism debate. Paternalism forms one part — although by no means the whole — of a discriminating approach to contract enforcement. Selective enforcement is a long-standing feature of contract law systems, which have developed alongside the emergence of market-based economies in liberal democratic societies. Contractual regulation of this kind can be justified in normative terms by reference to capability theory. Markets are significant capability-enhancing institutions, but their effect depends on complementary regulatory mechanisms, including some of those commonly (if not always accurately) termed 'paternalistic'.

1. INTRODUCTION

LEGAL PATERNALISM HAS been defined as an approach in which 'the law seeks to override individual choice on the ground that the individual or individuals in question might not exercise that choice wisely, with consequential harm to themselves'.[1] Paternalism, so defined, appears to involve the rejection of individual autonomy. It also seems to run counter to deep-rooted principles of private law, such as freedom of contract. Yet, paternalism is also widespread: 'legal systems of western liberal democracies contain innumerable paternalistic rules and doctrines.'[2] This poses the twin questions of how to

* Centre for Business Research and Faculty of Law, University of Cambridge. E-mail: s.deakin@cbr.cam.ac.uk.

[1] A Ogus, 'The Paradoxes of Legal Paternalism and How to Resolve Them' (2010) 30 *Legal Studies* 61, 62.

[2] W van Boom, 'Introduction', *Workshop on Juxtaposing Autonomy and Paternalism in Private Law* (Rotterdam, Erasmus University, 25 February 2010).

explain the prevalence of paternalism in modern, market-based economies and whether such intervention can be justified in normative terms.

This article will attempt to answer both questions by drawing on an evolutionary view of contract law. This is a perspective that sees contract law in functional terms as providing a framework for market-based exchange. Contract law performs this role, among other things, by taking a discriminating view of which contracts to enforce. Paternalistic justifications form a part, but only a part, of contract law's selective approach to enforcement. Selective enforcement has been a feature of all modern contract law systems, even at the height of nineteenth century 'laissez-faire'. The rules of contract law governing when and on what conditions contracts are enforced are the public expression of emergent solutions to coordination problems that have arisen in market settings of various kinds. Some of them can be found within private law doctrines (ranging from the narrowly defined 'incapacity' and 'public policy' to the more widely ranging 'good faith'), and some owe their existence to legislative intervention in specific contexts, such as worker or consumer protection. Whatever their origin, these rules of contract law express or encode norms of behaviour which, experience has shown, have the potential to contribute to market formation in various ways.

It is neither necessary nor desirable to conflate the set of paternalistic interventions with the wider set of regulatory interventions in contract law. Paternalism can be justified where parties need to be protected against the negative welfare implications of their own choices. This describes a narrow range of cases in which parties do not display rationality in contracting, that it so say, an ability to exercise choice in a consistent way. The contract law doctrines of incapacity and undue influence provide illustrations of this type of justification for non-enforcement. However, other doctrines giving rise to selective enforcement, such as most of the heads of public policy, and instances of contractual regulation of the kind that are widespread in employment law and consumer protection law cannot be explained in paternalistic terms. When parties enter into employment or consumer contracts on the basis of limited information or in situations of inequality of bargaining power, they may be making contracts that are based on mistaken beliefs or that are welfare-reducing in some way, but they are not acting 'irrationally' in the sense required for paternalistic intervention. The law intervenes here not to protect parties against themselves, but to overcome externalities and address information asymmetries in such as way as to extend the scope of the market and hence the division of labour, thereby promoting general societal well-being.

Selective enforcement is not a marginal addition to contract law, but is, rather, part of its core function in a market economy; it is also core to contract law in the internal legal sense of explaining some of its central doctrinal features. Two normative objections are commonly made against selective enforcement. The first is that the effects of regulation are indeterminate. Emergent regulatory solutions are necessarily imperfect: they may be transplanted out of context or lose their effectiveness over time in a changing environment. How far this is the case cannot be resolved a priori, but only through applied empirical work. The second objection is more basic. Even if regulatory interventions enhance aggregate well-being, they do so by making certain market participants (the wealthy, the well-informed or the simply fortunate) worse off than they would otherwise be. They can therefore be viewed (and have been by courts from time to time) as equivalent to an unconstitutional interference with contract and property rights.[3]

The resolution of this second question requires more than an empirical analysis of how contract law operates, although this can help in clarifying the nature and extent of the effects involved. In addition, it requires a consideration of the meaning of the notion of 'private autonomy' in a market setting. It will be argued here that the law of contract should (and generally does) protect private autonomy in the sense of the capacity (or 'capability') of individuals to participate in market-based exchange, but that this is not the same thing as the right to conduct an exchange free of legal regulation. This argument will be developed through the use of examples drawn from the regulation of contracts in labour market settings.

2. EVOLUTIONARY PERSPECTIVES ON CONTRACT LAW

Gintis[4] has recently proposed a unified evolutionary account of the behavioural sciences consisting of five conceptual building blocks: gene-culture coevolution,[5] the socio-psychological theory of norms,[6] game theory, the rational actor model[7] and complexity (or systems) theory.[8] A unified evolutionary theory of law would

[3] Most significantly, and controversially, in the decision of the US Supreme Court in *Lochner v New York*, 198 US 45 (1905).

[4] H Gintis, *The Bounds of Reason: Game Theory and the Unification of the Behavioural Sciences* (Princeton, NJ, Princeton University Press, 2009) ch 12.

[5] Gene-culture coevolution, sometimes referred to as 'dual inheritance theory', is the idea that genetic evolution both influences and is influenced by aspects of the environment that are culturally transmitted across generations, that is to say, embodied in enduring practices and routines. See R Boyd and P Richerson, *Culture and the Evolutionary Process* (Chicago, IL, Chicago University Press, 1985); P Richerson and R Boyd, *Not by Genes Alone* (Chicago, IL, Chicago University Press, 2004).

[6] Sociological and psychological theories see norms not simply as external constraints on action but as internalised standards of behaviour: see Gintis, above n 4, 212–14.

[7] On the rational actor model as the foundation of game-theoretical models of strategic interaction, see Gintis, above n 4, at ch 3.

[8] Complexity theory and systems theory are not synonymous, but for present purposes it is sufficient to emphasise the elements they have in common, in particular the idea of systems as emergent orders with adaptive, that is to say, evolutionary properties. The properties of systems are 'emergent' in the sense that they arise from the interaction of the component parts of the system and cannot be reduced to these component parts. See H Morowitz, *The Emergence of Everything: How the World Became Complex* (Oxford, Oxford University Press, 2002). They are evolutionary or adaptive in the sense of being subject to evolutionary processes of inheritance (stabilisation on the basis of the persistence of the system's internal 'code'), variation (random mutation at the point of self-copying or self-reproduction of the system) and selection (selective survival of traits on the basis of a standard of environmental fitness). Luhmann's theory of social systems makes extensive use of the idea of adaptation, while insisting that evolutionary processes are 'internalised' at the level of each system.

also draw on these elements, although they are not all of equal importance in understanding contemporary legal phenomena. The nature of the link between human genetic evolution and modern-day legal institutions, in particular, remains poorly understood, and further work is required to demonstrate the relevance of models of gene-culture coevolution in this context. For the purposes of theorising contract law, the interplay between game-theoretical models of strategic action, which make use of the (boundedly) rational actor model, and the idea of society as consisting of a set of adaptive systems should be the focus of analysis. Game theory can take us part of the way in understanding the evolutionary dimensions of contractual behaviour, but, as Gintis emphasises, it cannot go the whole way, since the macro-level properties of adaptive systems cannot be deduced from micro-level modelling using game-theoretical axioms.[9] Gintis's focus is on the behavioural sciences, and he does not extend his analysis to include a normative theory of social institutions. The study of law is not, or is only partially, a behavioural social science, and an evolutionary theory of law should in principle embrace interpretive and normative elements. Capability theory[10] offers one way forward here.

From an evolutionary perspective, the 'market' consists of a set of linked practices or routines that govern decentralised exchange. When the market functions effectively, it operates to ensure that scarce resources are allocated to alternate uses in a way that reconciles individual autonomy with collective welfare. Market practices such as exchange, pricing and arbitrage can be understood as emerging through the repeated interactions of numerous individual agents. Having been stabilised through routinisation, these practices are essentially self-organising and self-reproducing.

The evolved or emergent nature of market behaviour is generally taken to be the antithesis of centralised direction, whether through law or otherwise.[11] However, viewing the market as a self-organising system, in itself, tells us very little about the role that contract law plays in relation to market outcomes. This is because to view the legal system as directing market outcomes through a form of hierarchical ordering is misleading. The legal system is itself an adaptive system, which possesses many of the features of self-organisation that evolutionary theory ascribes to the market. The issue becomes one of understanding the

See N Luhmann, *Law as a Social System*, trans K Ziegert, ed F Kastner, R Nobles, D Schiff and R Ziegert (Oxford, Oxford University Press, 2004) ch 6 ('The Evolution of Law').

[9] Gintis, above n 4, at 248: 'The traditional equilibrium concept in game theory, the Nash equilibrium, is implemented by rational actors only if they share beliefs as to how the game will be played ... [but] the rational actor model includes no principles entailing the communality of beliefs across individuals. For this reason, the complex Nash equilibria that arise in modelling the coordination of behaviour in groups do not emerge spontaneously from the interaction of rational agents.'

[10] As recently restated by A Sen, *The Idea of Justice* (London, Allen Lane, 2009) chs 11–14.

[11] FA Hayek, *Law, Legislation and Liberty: A New Statement of the Liberal Principles of Liberalism and Political Economy* (London, Routledge and Kegan Paul, 1980).

nature of the inter-systemic evolution, or 'coevolution', involved in the law-market relationship.[12]

The predominant approach within law and economics is to see legal rules as an expression of an underlying behavioural logic. In Becker's foundational account, the economic axioms of 'maximising behaviour, market equilibrium and stable preferences' are capable, if 'relentlessly and unflinchingly applied', of explaining all societal phenomena, including the legal system.[13] These three assumptions can, even more parsimoniously, be reduced to two core ideas: a theory of individual behaviour based on optimisation and a theory of societal organisation based on the idea of the self-equilibrating market.

The research programme associated with 'behavioural law and economics' has largely focused on the first of these two ideas, to the relative neglect of the second. Prospect theory has identified a number of pervasive behavioural traits that appear to refute aspects of the rational actor model.[14] Yet, on one view, the core of rational actor theory remains intact. This is what Gintis[15] calls the 'beliefs, preferences and constraints' (BPC) model. Actors form preferences that are based on their beliefs about the world. They act 'rationally' with regard to these preferences when they choose from among alternative courses of action in a way that is consistent with respect to anticipated outcomes. Choice-consistency, or stability of preferences, is all that is required here; the more demanding postulates of the expected utility theorem go beyond what is necessary for the basic model to work. The insights of behavioural economics into the circumstances under which individuals behave 'irrationally' — that is, in an apparently less than welfare-maximising way — can all be explained as cases in which individuals maximise with reference to a given preference function. The idea of bounded rationality can be accommodated in this way; actors' preferences are determined by their current state of knowledge of the world, which is a function, in part, of their (limited) cognitive capacity. In addition, other-regarding behaviour — altruism — can be modelled in choice-consistent terms. This is a central finding of the models that have been developed in the past decade in evolutionary and epistemic game theory, and it is supported by a growing body of empirical literature, much of it based on laboratory experiments, but now supplemented by field work studies.[16] Thus, rationality need not imply 'selfishness'. More generally, it is not inconsistent with the BPC model to assume that individuals do not always choose correctly (they may act consistently while still being mistaken about the state of the world), that they change their beliefs over time in response

[12] Luhmann, above n 8; G Teubner, *Law as an Autopoietic System* (Oxford, Blackwell Publishing, 1993).

[13] G Becker, *The Economic Approach to Human Behaviour* (Chicago, University of Chicago Press, 1976).

[14] D Kahneman and A Tversky, *Choices, Values and Frames* (Cambridge, Cambridge University Press, 2000).

[15] Gintis, above n 4, 1.

[16] ibid, at ch 3.

to a changing environment (this is not the same thing as being unable to rank different outcomes at the point of contracting) or that their choices, once made, do not in fact maximise their welfare (this is to confuse the basis for action with its consequences).

With these important qualifications, the rational actor model can be understood as a value-neutral, generalisable account of behaviour under conditions of economic scarcity. However, difficulties begin when the theory is used to generate a theory of societal organisation and, even more so, when it is used to construct a normative theory for use in the design of legal institutions.

The rational actor model alone cannot account for the existence of the structures that make societal coordination possible.[17] Rational actor theory provides the basis for game-theoretical models of decentralised coordination. These models frequently imply a radical disjuncture between individual rationality and optimal societal outcomes. Individual strategies may spontaneously converge on stable states that maximise aggregate welfare, but the conditions under which they do so are extremely restrictive. The game-theoretical concept of 'correlated equilibrium' predicts convergence of this kind only when individual agents possess common knowledge of what other agents will do and hence can predict future societal states.[18] Knowledge of future states cannot be derived from experience of past interactions alone but depends on correlating devices, which include social norms[19] and more formal 'public indicators' such as legal rules.[20] Norms and rules, which are particular types of a more general set of institutional phenomena, serve as summary representations of the recursive patterns or routines around which individual actors expect future strategies to converge. There is a continuum between social norms and publicly-expressed legal rules, with the latter tending to crystallise the former.

How norms evolve and how they operate is a key issue for the behavioural sciences and, by extension, for legal scholars interested in viewing legal phenomena from a social science perspective. To address the question effectively involves an acceptance that public indicators such as norms and legal rules operate at a different level from that of the interactions of individual agents. This does not mean that the indicators of this kind are exogenously supplied, whether by government or by a pre-existing moral order. Norms and rules can be understood as emerging endogenously, that is to say, on the basis of the accumulated experience of individual agents, but, since they also frame the behaviour of those

[17] ibid 44.

[18] R Aumann, 'Correlated Equilibrium as an Expression of Bayesian Rationality' (1987) 55 *Econometrica* 1.

[19] Gintis, above n 4, 240–42.

[20] M Aoki, *Corporations in Evolving Diversity: Cognition, Governance and Institutions* (Oxford, Oxford University Press 2010) 128.

agents, they cannot be described in exclusively behavioural terms. The relationship between norms and behaviour is one of mutual interaction, that is to say, of coevolution.

Normative orders, such as the legal system, make it possible to code, store and transmit the accumulated knowledge on which societal coordination depends. Orders of this kind are 'systemic' in the sense that they are adaptive to their environment. This does not mean that they are precisely aligned to their external context. The accumulation and transmission of knowledge across time and space implies that some kind of inheritance or retention process is in operation, akin to (but not necessarily identical to) the process of genetic transmission.[21] Selection may ensure some kind of 'fit' between the content of norms and rules and the environment in which they are applied, but, unless the context is unchanging or otherwise very stable, the information contained within normative orders can only be completely functional for past environments. As some degree of misalignment between normative orders and their (present) environments is unavoidable, normative solutions to coordination problems are necessarily imperfect and incomplete.

Contract law is an emergent normative order that has evolved over time in a way that loosely matches, in the sense just described, the conditions of the societies in which it operates. It does not literally describe external social 'reality' but instead recreates its external environment in ways that can be understood in terms of its own dynamics. Thus, external economic phenomena have to be redescribed in the conceptual or dogmatic terms of legal analysis.[22] The study of legal concepts (which can be distinguished from the analysis of rules as such) makes it possible to reconstruct, in historical terms, the process by which the legal system has shaped, and has been shaped by, the emergent market order.[23]

From this perspective, the answer to the question of how societal coordination emerges from the micro-foundations of individual agents' behaviour and beliefs is to be found, in part, within contract law itself, that is to say, within the body of doctrine that informs the production and reproduction of legal rules concerning contracts. Contract law has its own accounts of 'individual rationality' and 'societal coordination'.[24]

[21] S Deakin, 'Evolution for Our Time: A Theory of Legal Memetics' (2003) 55 *Current Legal Problems* 1.

[22] Luhmann, above n 8; Teubner, above n 12.

[23] S Deakin and F Wilkinson, *The Law of the Labour Market: Industrialization, Employment and Legal Evolution* (Oxford, Oxford University Press, 2005).

[24] See S Deakin, '*Capacitas*: Contract Law, Capabilities, and the Legal Foundations of the Market' in S Deakin and A Supiot (eds), *Capacitas: Contract Law and the Institutional Foundations of a Market Economy* (Oxford, Hart Publishing, 2009), on which the following section draws.

3. THE CAPACITY CONCEPT AND THE CONCEPTUALISATION OF THE MARKET IN CONTRACT LAW

All contract law systems recognise the principle that a simple exchange, even between otherwise consenting parties, is not enough to found a legally binding contract. It has to be shown, in addition, that each party has the capacity to contract. One aspect of capacity is the ability of a contracting party to assess whether a transaction is in its best interests. The law presumes that this may not be so in the case of the young, on the grounds of their immaturity and inexperience, and with regard to those such as the very old or mentally ill, who for one reason or another may be unable to understand the consequences of their actions.[25] Thus, the concept of capacity is based on the view that one of the preconditions for the enforcement of contracts is that individuals possess the capability for rational economic action, understood as the ability to make decisions about exchange in a choice-consistent way.

The common law concept of undue influence performs a similar function, denying contract enforcement in cases where one party, with the knowledge or assumed knowledge of the other, enters into a transaction in a context where their ability to understand and express their own best interests is limited. This can occur, for example, where family ties, religious or social affiliations, or dependence on another for advice or expertise qualify the ability to exercise independent judgement.[26] Viewed in this way, undue influence and the capacity concept express a similar underlying logic.

However, the capacity concept is not limited to providing an account of individual rationality. It is also predicated upon assumptions about the need for institutional underpinning of market exchange. In this sense, it discloses a theory of the societal organisation needed to make markets function.

Thus, one aim of the doctrine of capacity is, without doubt, the paternalist one of providing protection to the incapable. But the doctrine also protects the market against the incapable,[27] by excluding them from unassisted participation in exchange relations. They may enter into transactions, but only with the aid of intermediaries, thanks to the doctrines of assistance and representation. These ideas, which are formally stated in the civil law and implicit to some degree in the common law rules, are intended to enhance the contractual security of third parties and thereby secure confidence in market transactions in general.[28] Thus, an inference that may be drawn from the structure of contract law is that legal enforcement of contracts matters, along with its corollary, namely selective non-enforcement. The maintenance of the market order depends upon the legal

[25] See E McKendrick, *Contract Law*, 8th edn (Basingstoke, Palgrave, 2009) ch 15.

[26] ibid, at ch 16.

[27] See M Hesselink, 'Capacity and Capability in European Contract Law' in Deakin and Supiot, above n 24.

[28] S Godelain, 'Le concept de capacité dans le droit des contrats français' in Deakin and Supiot, above n 24.

system being able to take a discriminating view on which contracts to enforce and on how, or on what conditions, to enforce them.

To say that this is a basic assumption of contract law systems is not to imply that contract law necessarily works this way in practice. Empirical observation, informed by economic or sociological theory, might be able to confirm the functionality (in this sense) of contract law, but this type of evidence cannot be directly inferred from the study of contract law doctrine. Contract law doctrine provides an insight into how the legal system has come to view the external effects of its own enforcement mechanisms. In the 'internal' discourse of contract law doctrine, the market is seen not as a natural state of affairs but instead as the product of a certain institutional configuration. In this respect, contract law's view of the market is a very different perspective from that of mainstream law and economics, which is itself, of course, no more a description of an external social or economic reality than contract law doctrine is. 'Law and economics' is just a certain economic doctrine's view of the legal system.

A number of other doctrines provide for selectivity in the enforcement of consensual transactions. In the common law systems, the doctrine of 'public policy' sets out a series of such grounds.[29] These consist of a range of apparently ad hoc and unconnected justifications: 'restraint of trade', 'agreements injurious to good government' and 'agreements contrary to family life', and so on. Viewed functionally, these justifications divide into two categories: cases in which non-enforcement is justified by the need to protect the market against itself (or, more precisely, against the market-limiting effects of consensual exchange) and cases in which the aim of selective enforcement is the protection of society against the market.

The doctrine of 'restraint of trade' is concerned with protecting the market against itself or, more precisely, against the freedom of market actors to make agreements that hinder the operation of the market. Market entry and exit rules, price fixing, wage regulation and other forms of contractual self-regulation of the market potentially come within the scope of the restraint of trade doctrine. Contract law recognises that the competitive process on which the market order depends for its successful operation can be undermined by the very value of freedom of contract that the market is meant to uphold. Selective legal enforcement of contracts is a precondition for a functioning market order.

The other heads of public policy cannot be explained as protecting the market against itself. Instead, they involve the assertion of certain social values that take priority over the market. When courts refuse to enforce contracts that are 'contrary to public morals', that undermine governmental authority or that oust their own jurisdiction, they are recognising that certain institutions, such as the family, the apparatus of government and the legal system itself, are not just separate from the market but operate according to a logic that is not that of

[29] McKendrick, above n 25, ch 14.

market relations. For these reasons, they require legal protection from the potentially destabilising effects of the market.

The list of grounds of non-enforcement is, nevertheless, selective and, arguably, outdated. At the turn of the twentieth century, courts in most common law jurisdictions, taking their lead from the House of Lords, held that the heads of public policy, as they then existed, were a closed set.[30] This was, in part, a reflection of the view that the foremost goal of public policy should be to defend freedom of contract itself.[31] But it was also the product of judicial abstention in the face of the growing body of regulatory legislation that was emerging at that time. The English courts recognised that the formulation of social and economic policy was an area in which Parliament was increasingly taking the lead.[32]

In the course of the twentieth century, social and economic legislation displaced both the capacity concept and public policy as a source of contractual regulation. The rise of regulatory legislation gave rise to a process that legal historians refer to as 'derationalisation', signifying the fragmentation of the unitary concept of capacity: new forms of legal protection have arisen, representing new interests.[33] In consumer protection and employment protection law, the law substantially qualified the concept of freedom of contract, but without using the technique of incapacitation to do so. Instead, legislation imposed mandatory and default rules of various kinds as a condition of contractual enforcement.

The relationship between social or regulatory legislation and the notion of contractual capacity has never been less than highly contested. In the early decades of the twentieth century, the language of capacity was invoked to argue that mandatory regulation was an inappropriate and, in some jurisdictions, unconstitutional constraint on freedom of contract.[34] During the 1980s, some of these arguments resurfaced, along with a new emphasis on the alleged inefficiency of social legislation as a mode of contractual regulation. Deregulatory policy initiatives found inspiration in the US-based law and economics movement, which acquired a certain intellectual resonance around this time, as the institutional forms that had been designed for a world of protected national economies and stable economic relationships were unravelling. A principal example of this is the conceptual 'crisis' affecting the legal institution of the employment relationship.[35] However, a simple return to private law, through 'deregulation', has not proved to be feasible. Despite the efforts of political

[30] *Janson v Driefontein Consolidated Mines Ltd* [1902] AC 484.

[31] *Printing and Numerical Registering Co Ltd v Sampson* (1875) 19 LR Eq 462.

[32] The English courts were not able to invoke a higher constitutional authority to review the propriety of regulatory legislation, as the US courts were able to in *Lochner*, above n 3.

[33] A Wijffels, 'Rationalisation and Derationalisation of Legal Capacity in Historical Perspective: Some General Caveats', in Deakin and Supiot, above n 24.

[34] For the use of the term 'capacity' in US constitutional cases on social legislation around this time, see the judgments in *Lochner*, above n 3, and in *Muller v Oregon*, 208 US 412.

[35] See generally A Supiot (ed), *Au delà de l'emploi. Transformations du travail et devenir du droit du travail en Europe* (Paris, Flammarion 1999).

opponents of the welfare state, contractual regulation remains all-pervasive in liberal democracies with a commitment to market-based ordering in the areas of economic and, increasingly, social policy. To consider why this might be the case, we will take a closer look at how contractual regulation works in the context of labour markets.

4. JUSTIFICATIONS FOR THE REGULATION OF LABOUR CONTRACTS

Labour markets in developed economies are intensively regulated. This is just as true of 'liberal market' systems, such as those of the United States and the United Kingdom, as it is of the 'coordinated market' economies of continental Europe and east Asia.[36] The United States lacks employment protection legislation of the kind commonly found in Europe (including the United Kingdom) and its collective labour law system covers a diminishing segment of the workforce, but it has a considerable body of regulatory legislation in relation to such areas as minimum wages, hours of work, occupational safety and health, employment discrimination, social security, employer-based retirement pensions and employer-based health insurance.[37] How much of this regulation can be justified, or at least explained, on paternalistic grounds?

Sunstein and Thaler's influential definition views paternalism as any intervention designed to improve the welfare of individuals whose choices do not reflect their true interests.[38] This is likely to be the case, they suggest, where individuals have less than complete information, limited cognitive capacities and a lack of self-control. 'Drawing', as they put it, 'on some well-established findings in behavioural economic and cognitive psychology', they argue that this is likely to be the case more often than not in the context (among others) of labour contracting.[39] The employment relationship provides an example of a situation in which preferences are likely to be ill-defined and context-dependent: 'contextual influences render the very meaning of the term "preferences" unclear'.[40] Paternalism is not just legitimate, it is unavoidable in the sense that even a default rule of at-will employment (implying no external legal regulation of employment termination decisions) implies a framing effect of a particular kind that will influence behaviour.

'Libertarian paternalism' proposes a set of techniques aimed at enhancing the quality of choice and, hence, of outcomes in situations where individuals act with

[36] On the distinction between 'liberal market' and 'coordinated market' systems, see P Hall and D Soskice, 'An Introduction to Varieties of Capitalism' in P Hall and D Soskice (eds), *Varieties of Capitalism: the Institutional Foundations of Comparative Advantage* (Oxford, Oxford University Press, 2001).

[37] See O Lobel, 'The Four Pillars of Work Law' (2006) 104 *Michigan Law Review* 1539.

[38] C Sunstein and R Thaler, 'Libertarian Paternalism Is Not an Oxymoron' (2003) 73 *University of Chicago Law Review* 1159.

[39] ibid 1162.

[40] ibid 1161.

less than complete transactional capacity. Libertarian paternalism is incompatible with 'any approach that blocks individual choices'[41] — in other words, mandatory legislation. It is, on the other hand, entirely compatible with the wide array of derogations, waivers and opt-outs (or opt-ins) that are increasingly found in employment statutes. These techniques allow the parties some freedom of choice but tend to frame that choice by requiring that derogations from legislative standards are confined in terms of their substantive scope (as in the case of statutory wage premia for over-time work) or by reference to procedural safeguards (such as requirements that individual waivers be in writing, in a certain form or validated by a legal adviser or other representative).[42]

At the core of the libertarian paternalist proposal is the claim that, in many contexts, individual decision-making is irrational but can be made more rational through targeted regulatory interventions. These interventions are paternalistic in the sense of protecting individuals against the consequences of their own decisions but libertarian in the sense of improving the quality of the decisions they take. Private action is moulded, or steered, but not entirely displaced.

The fundamental difficulty with libertarian paternalism is that it employs a notion of 'rationality' that is neither a good descriptive model of human behaviour nor a meaningful benchmark for the design of legal institutions. As we have seen, for behaviour to be rational it simply has to be preference-consistent. Decision-making influenced by the endowment effect, framing, inequality aversion or other heuristic biases identified by prospect theory is not, by virtue of such influence, 'irrational'. None of these effects 'illustrates preference inconsistency once the appropriate parameter (current time, current position, status quo point) is admitted into the preference function'.[43]

The point is not simply a definitional one. The model of rationality that is emerging from empirical studies of strategic interaction (both laboratory experiments and field work) in the last decade is one in which human behaviour is essentially 'pro-social'. Individuals display tendencies towards 'altruistic cooperation' and its converse, the punishment of non-cooperation, in contexts where such behaviour is not in their individual self-interest, even over the long run. Human agents are other-regarding as well as self-regarding, they have 'social preferences' that 'facilitate cooperation and exchange' and 'moral preferences' for the character virtues of honesty and loyalty. Above all, they display a 'meta-preference' for conforming to norms that provide guidance on what constitutes socially appropriate behaviour in a given context. Thus, preferences do not lack 'meaning',[44] but both they and their behavioural consequences are 'situationally specific'.[45]

[41] ibid

[42] ibid 1186–7.

[43] Gintis, above n 4, 25.

[44] Sunstein and Thaler, above n 38, 1161.

[45] Gintis, above n 4, 75.

The origins of the pro-social bias in human behaviour are probably biological: 'human beings did not evolve facing general decision-theoretic problems. Rather, they faced a few specific decision-theoretic problems associated with survival in small social groups'.[46] This is an area in which the key research questions are still being formulated, let alone answered. We do not need to have more complete answers to this set of questions in order to consider the implications of the amended rational actor model for issues of legal policy and design.

A first point to make is that very few if any of the regulatory interventions that take place in modern labour (or other) markets can properly be termed 'paternalistic' in the sense of protecting contracting parties against the consequences of their own decisions. This set of cases should be confined to situations in which individual agents do not display preference consistency (true 'irrational' behaviour). As nineteenth-century contract law recognised, contract enforcement should be denied, or at least conditioned by certain protective devices, in cases where it is not safe to assume that individuals possess the capacity for rational action in this specific sense of the term.[47] This category of instances is of marginal and decreasing relevance for labour law. Early factory legislation may have regulated the working hours and employment conditions of women and children on the grounds, in part, that these groups, in contrast to adult males, did not know their own best interests,[48] but this is not a ground for intervention that has been invoked since at least the early decades of the twentieth century.

A second point to flow from the amendment of the rational actor model is that alternative, non-paternalistic justifications should be sought for labour market interventions. New institutional economics provides part of the answer here, in suggesting a role for regulation in addressing contractual incompleteness, asymmetrical information and externalities of the kind that are commonly found in labour markets.[49] This body of literature suggests that labour law rules can be justified not solely by reference to the protection of the interests of the 'weaker' party to the employment contract but, more generally, in terms of the beneficial effects they confer upon all market actors. In other words, it is the aggregate wealth-enhancing effects of labour law rules that matter, not their redistributional effects for particular contracting agents.

Useful as it is in dispelling some of the more dogmatic and doctrinaire arguments of law and economics scholars against labour market regulation, new institutional economics perhaps claims too much in seeking to portray labour law rules as market-perfecting devices. If they improve market outcomes, they tend to do so in an imprecise way. A more realistic account of labour law rules

[46] ibid 29.

[47] See the discussion in section 2, above.

[48] See S Deakin and F Wilkinson, *The Law of the Labour Market: Industrialisation, Employment and Legal Evolution* (Oxford, Oxford University Press, 2005) 226–31.

[49] B Kaufman, 'Labour Law and Employment Regulation: Neoclassical and Institutional Perspectives' in K Dau-Schmidt, S Harris and O Lobel (eds), *Labor and Employment Law and Economics* (Cheltenham, Edward Elgar Publishing, 2009).

would see them from an evolutionary perspective, that is to say, as emergent solutions to coordination problems of the kind to which labour markets typically give rise.[50] These solutions (factory legislation, collective bargaining, minimum wages, social insurance and so on) are historically contingent, context-dependent and often imperfect in their effects. They may be endogenous in the sense of being generated by conditions in labour markets to which they respond, but they are not spontaneous. While they may enhance aggregate wealth or well-being, they often do so at the expense of certain groups.[51] As such, they almost invariably involve distributional compromises that are the subject of deliberative decision-making processes located, at least partially, in the political domain.

Sunstein and Thaler[52] are right to point to the very widespread use of default rules of various kinds in contemporary labour legislation, but it is not necessary to invoke the theory of libertarian paternalism to explain the origin of these rules or how they work. Their goal can be understood as 'market steering' in the sense of framing overall market outcomes, but this is distinct from the aim of moulding individual transactions.[53] For the most part, labour law rules of this 'reflexive' type involve collectively negotiated derogations rather than the individual waivers favoured by Sunstein and Thaler. As such, they are premised on the assumption that the design and implementation of labour law rules can benefit from collective learning, that is to say, from a process of dialogue and deliberation involving the collective parties (representatives of employers and workers and representatives of the state).[54] Labour law involves an almost endless search for workable solutions in which outcomes are mostly determined, for better or worse, by the interplay of political forces and by the relative strength of the interest groups involved.[55]

Under these circumstances, the libertarian paternalist agenda is highly problematic for labour law. The libertarian aspect of the programme would involve the dismantling of the many mandatory norms still operating in this field and their replacement with default rules of various kinds. Making adherence to labour standards optional may be beneficial if it helps to generate a learning process about which solutions work and which do not, but it can also destabilise social norms that provide a basis for cooperation. The paternalist aspect of libertarian paternalism implies that solutions can be crafted by enlightened regulators deploying the techniques of cost-benefit analysis. This neglects the role

[50] A Hyde, 'What Is Labour Law?'. in G Davidov and B Langille (eds), *Boundaries and Frontiers of Labour Law* (Oxford, Hart Publishing, 2006).

[51] G Davidov, 'Comment on Alan Hyde: The Perils of Economic Justifications for International Labour Standards' (2009) 3 *Law & Ethics of Human Rights* 180.

[52] See above n 38.

[53] J Howe, R Johnstone and R Mitchell, 'Constituting and Regulating the Labour Market for Social and Economic Purposes'. in C Arup *et al* (eds), *Labour Law and Labour Market Regulation* (Sydney, Federation Publishing Group, 2006).

[54] P Gahan and P Brosnan, 'The Repertoires of Labour Market Regulation' in Arup *et al*, above n 53.

[55] A Supiot, 'Introduction', in Supiot, above n 35.

that collective deliberation plays in legitimising the distributional compromises on which labour law rules ultimately rest. Better justifications for labour law regulation are available.

5. MARKET ACCESS AS A CAPABILITY

Whatever their pre-modern roots may be, markets in modern industrialised societies are not natural or spontaneous phenomena. They are complex systems that have evolved alongside other mechanisms of coordination, including the legal system. The market and the legal system complement and, in a deep sense, stabilise each other. While markets may be self-organising, this does not mean that they are always stable. The regulation of exchange is one of the techniques by which the legal system imparts stability to the market and renders its operation compatible, more generally, with societal coordination.

It follows that one of the consequences of the legal regulation of contracts is to facilitate the kind of individual autonomy that exists within a functioning market order. This 'autonomy' is the result of the opportunity, which the market provides to those with access to it, to participate in a system of exchange based on an extensive, societal division of labour. The market, so conceived, makes it possible for the wants of any individual actor to be met to the greatest possible extent that is consistent with the wants of all others. In principle, the preferences of all market actors are factored into the prices against which individuals decide whether or not to trade and, if so, to what extent. Thus, the gains from trade that any one individual can expect to make are contingent not just upon their preferences and the resources available to them but also upon the value others place on them, which in turn is a function of their own preferences and resources. This much is familiar from classical law and economics. But we can go further. The implication of evolutionary law and economics is that without the coordinating devices of (among other things) social norms and legal regulation, there would be no markets in the sense that we are familiar with from the experience of modern societies or only less extensive and less socially valuable ones.

Given the functional role played by norms and laws, in what sense can it be said that contractual regulation infringes the autonomy of the contracting parties? One implication of juxtaposing autonomy and paternalism is that individuals have a right to receive the returns that they would have made if the contract had been struck free of regulation. This is, however, an illusion. Just as there is no such thing as an entirely 'free' (or unregulated) market, so there is no exchange which, at some level, is not being influenced by the normative structures that make market coordination possible.

A more justifiable claim is that the legal system should acknowledge and protect the right of individuals to meaningful participation in the market. This does not mean a right to a particular outcome, such as a wage or income of a certain level, but nor does it mean simply a right to take part in a given, isolated exchange. One of the principles underpinning minimum wage legislation is that wages should reflect as far as possible the social cost of labour, which includes the costs of its reproduction. The claim for a 'living wage' is in essence a claim to a wage that at least meets the costs of subsistence. As nineteenth-century political economy recognised, when wages are paid below subsistence, either the labour supply will shrink (so reducing the scope of the market) or other mechanisms of support, such as the family or the social security system (as the poor law has become), will have to be found.[56] There are strong arguments on incentive-compatibility and resource-allocation grounds for ensuring that the social costs of labour are met as far as possible through the wage system, rather than the social security system.[57] But the point can also be made in ethical terms: minimum wage laws are a more effective means of enhancing labour market opportunities than tax credits, the principal alternative, which have a low take-up in large part because of the punitively high marginal tax rates to which they give rise.

Access to the labour market is a 'capability' that many labour law rules, in particular those in the rapidly developing field of employment discrimination law, protect and promote.[58] A 'capability', in this context, refers to the capacity of an individual agent to realise a range of desired goals through participation in the labour market. These goals (Sen's 'functionings'[59]) are subjectively defined and are not restricted to the material or financial aspects of employment but also include the psycho-sociological benefits from participation in organised economic activity. The capability approach focuses not on the content of functionings (these are individual-specific) or on outcomes according to an objective criterion of individual welfare or well-being such as expected utility but on the environmental preconditions (broadly understood) of effective choice. These preconditions may refer to the physical or institutional environment. Thus, the capability approach opens up a debate, among other things, about the appropriate institutional conditions for substantive choice. While markets are, in principle, capability-enhancing institutions, given the opportunities for social and economic participation that they provide, access to markets depends on a set of prior conditions that are institutional and, to some degree, legal in nature.

The way employment discrimination law works exemplifies this point. The relationship between discrimination law and classical contract law mirrors that between the capability approach and standard law and economics analysis. The capacity-enhancing function of discrimination law is particularly evident in the case of what is arguably the most advanced type of equal treatment legislation, that is, legislation prohibiting disability discrimination. Thus type of legislation is

[56] Deakin and Wilkinson, above n 48, 231–34.
[57] ibid 188–92.
[58] ibid 342–53.
[59] Sen, above n 10, 235–38.

'advanced' in the sense that concepts used elsewhere in discrimination law — 'direct discrimination', referring to unequal treatment on prohibited grounds, and 'indirect discrimination', referring to group disadvantage arising from institutional practices, have been modified in the context of disability to produce a 'duty of reasonable adjustment' on the part of the employer. This means that the employer has a responsibility to organise the workplace in such a way as to enable the individual worker to carry out the duties of the post in question, while taking account of his or her disability. The duty is not absolute; the court in essence applies a proportionality test, taking into account the cost and practicability of adjustments and their impact on the ability of the worker to carry out the task.[60] But even so, the effect is to alter the conceptual framework of discrimination law in ways that point to its potential for enhancing capabilities. Rather than requiring the individual to be 'adaptable' to changing market conditions, the law requires that employment practices be adapted to the circumstances of the individual.[61] If disability discrimination laws go further than most forms of social legislation currently do in imposing affirmative duties on employers in the name of market access, they nevertheless illustrate a general tendency of the law to grant substantive recognition to new forms of contractual capacity or, in economic terms, 'capability'.

The precise way in which legal rules perform this role is a matter for more detailed, applied analysis in particular contexts. An important starting point in this kind of analysis will be to consider how it can be informed by an evolutionary analysis of law. It would be consistent with the capability approach to advocate a methodology that is less concerned with measuring outcomes in welfare terms than with putting forward principles for action of a procedural kind, intended to enrich the process of knowledge accumulation on which societal coordination depends. Thus, 'the capability approach points to an informational focus in judging and comparing overall individual advantages, and does not, on its own, propose any specific formula about how that information may be used'. It does not set out any particular 'blueprint for how to deal with conflicts between, say, aggregative and distributive considerations', and does not prescribe formal equality of capabilities, as opposed to the expansion of capabilities in general, as a meaningful goal.[62] It may be doubted whether the capability approach, so defined, sits entirely happily with a conception of libertarian paternalism based on the assumed ability of an enlightened planner to 'nudge' individuals in the direction of exchanges that, by reference to an external standard, enhance their well-being.[63]

[60] See generally S Deakin and G Morris, *Labour Law*, 5th edn (Oxford, Hart Publishing, 2006) paras 6.116–6.128.

[61] Deakin, above n 24, 26–28.

[62] Sen, above n 10, 232.

[63] C Sunstein and R Thaler, *Nudge: Improving Decisions About Health, Wealth and Happiness* (New Haven, CT, Yale University Press, 2008).

6. CONCLUSIONS

This article has attempted to set out an evolutionary conception of contract law as the basis for assessing claims made in the autonomy-paternalism debate. It has argued that a discriminating approach to contract enforcement is a long-standing feature of contract law systems, which has coevolved with the emergence of market-based economies in liberal democratic societies. The regulation of contracts with a view to establishing norms of societal coordination is at the core of contract law doctrine and is central to the market-supporting role that legal institutions in general perform. Using examples from labour law, the article has also shown how contractual regulation can be justified in normative terms by reference to capability theory. Markets are important capability-enhancing institutions, but this effect depends on regulatory mechanisms that complement the operation of the market.

7

Autonomy and Paternalism from a Common Law Perspective: Setting Aside Disadvantageous Transactions

STEPHEN WADDAMS*

ABSTRACT

English contract law has, by a variety of methods, set aside or refused to enforce transactions that are extremely disadvantageous to one of the parties. The inclusion in the Draft Common Frame of Reference of a general power to this effect suggests that many European systems have often also reached similar results. These cases might, from one perspective, be regarded as instances of paternalism and infringements of autonomy, but other considerations have been relevant, including public policy, avoidance of unjust enrichment and whether the party seeking enforcement has had a legitimate interest in doing so.

1. INTRODUCTION

THE JUXTAPOSITION OF autonomy and paternalism suggests an inquiry into the extent to which it is justifiable for society to restrict individual freedom in the interests of the person whose freedom is restricted. At its widest, this topic has many aspects, crossing over between public and private law. The focus of this article is on contract law. It is often supposed that principles of autonomy, allied with the concepts of freedom (or sanctity) of contract, imply that enforcement of contracts is justified, or even necessary, no matter how one-sided or disadvantageous the contract may be. It will be seen, however, that, by a variety of methods, relief has often been given from disadvantageous transactions of various kinds. The present article is mainly concerned with English law and with systems closely allied with it, but neither the perceived problem nor the shape of the plausible solutions has been peculiar to English law, as will be suggested by references to the recent European *Draft Common Frame of*

* Goodman/Schipper Professor of Law, University of Toronto.

Reference (2009). It might be true to say, as a social observation, that most contracts involve an exchange of approximately equal value, but this assertion is not true in respect of contract *law*. Very many — probably most — contracts that are legally significant involve the exchange of unequal values, and the effect of contract law, where the contract is enforced, is therefore to bring about an unequal exchange. A contract may make a poor person rich, and it may make a rich person poor. To him that has, contract law may give, and, more relevantly to the theme of the present article, from him that has not it may take away even that which he has.

2. CONSIDERATION

English contract law includes a requirement, known as consideration, that came to be generally understood by the eighteenth century as a requirement that value must have been given or promised in exchange for the promise sought to be enforced. Patrick Atiyah remarks that, from the point of view of liberal theory, the doctrine of consideration is 'fundamentally paternalist'.[1] In earlier times, the word 'consideration' had various meanings, but the modern meaning (value given or promised in exchange) was familiar in the early eighteenth century. Jeffrey Gilbert, later Chief Baron of the Exchequer, in an unpublished work written in the early eighteenth century entitled 'Of Contracts', in seeking to explain the doctrine of consideration, gives several explanations, not all consistent with each other. The first reason given in support of the doctrine, namely the need to protect potential defendants from liability for rash promises, has a decidedly paternalistic tone. Having said that some opinions favoured 'the punctuall performance of every verbal promise', Gilbert continues:

> Others held that no obligation arises from a naked promise and that the force of the engagement doth totally depend on the consideration and they take it to be a thing of great rigour that a man should dispose of the fruits and effects of a long and painfull industry and all the certain advantages and conveniences of life by the meer breath of a word and the turn of an unwary expression; they also think that the very laws of self-preservation will not permitt it for what reason of conscience can oblige a man to those words that tend to his own destruction, but if a valuable consideration had been received the bargain is compleat for another man's industry comes in the place of his own. …

Gilbert continues by saying that English law 'hath held the middle between these two extreames', in that formal contracts are enforceable

> so that if a man will oblige himself under the solemnitys of law whereby his contract appears to be seriously intended, it shall ever be obligatory and the consideration shall

[1] PS Atiyah, *Essays on Contract* (1986) 128.

> be intended... but if the contract be verball only it binds in respect of the consideration, otherwise a man might be drawn into an obligation without any real intention by random words, ludicrous expressions, and from hence there would be a manifest inlet to perjury because nothing were more easy than to turn the kindness of expressions into the obligation of a real promise.[2]

Four very different ideas are manifest in this passage, all attributed by Gilbert to the concept of consideration: due deliberation, the reason for making the contract, the reason for enforcing it and reliable evidence that the promise in question had actually been made. From a later perspective, it may be remarked that, by implication, consideration in the sense of exchange also imported into English law the idea of mutual agreement, though this idea was not fully developed until the following century.

The protection of promisors from disadvantageous transactions (Gilbert's first reason) could not, in itself, supply a wholly satisfactory explanation, either historically or functionally, of the doctrine of consideration. Consideration has not usually been thought of as a method of protecting the weak from disadvantageous bargains, because the consideration need not be of equal value with the promise that is to be enforced: a very small value — conventionally, as was said, a peppercorn — is sufficient. It is true also that courts have often shown considerable ingenuity in discovering consideration in circumstances where it might at first appear to be absent.[3] Nevertheless it is also true that one effect of the doctrine of consideration has been to prevent the legal enforcement of purely gratuitous promises, even though they meet all usual tests of voluntariness or autonomy and even though the fact of the promise is convincingly proved, for example by a signed writing.[4] The doctrine of consideration was also employed in the nineteenth century to prevent enforcement of one-sided modifications of obligations, and one effect of this was, in some cases, to give protection to persons who had made disadvantageous modifications of their contractual rights.[5] This branch of the law was heavily criticised by courts and commentators, and more recently other approaches to the question have been advanced.[6]

3. SPECIFIC PERFORMANCE

In English law, specific performance is regarded, conceptually, as an exceptional remedy, available only if damages are inadequate. One effect of this approach has

[2] J Gilbert, *Of Contracts* (manuscript about 1710) (Hargrave, British Library) 265, folios 39–40 (some punctuation added, abbreviations expanded and capitalisation removed).

[3] An example is *North Ocean Shipping Co Ltd v Hyundai Construction Co Ltd (The 'Atlantic Baron')* [1979] QB 705.

[4] *Rann v Hughes* (1778) 7 TR 350n.

[5] *Stilk v Myrick* (1809) 2 Camp 317, 6 Esp 129; *Foakes v Beer* (1884) 9 App Cas 605 (HL)

[6] *Williams v Roffey Bros & Nicholls (Contractors) Ltd* [1991] 1 QB 1 (CA) (duress); *Collier v P & MJ Wright (Holdings) Ltd* [2008] 1 WLR 643 (CA) (estoppel).

been to enable a person who has entered into a very burdensome contract to refrain from performing it, while offering to pay appropriate monetary compensation to the other party. This aspect of the law has been defended by economists as a recognition of 'efficient breach', and this concept, though criticised by some commentators, has been accepted by some courts.[7] The phrase 'efficient breach' appears on its face to be paradoxical, and Daniel Friedmann has usefully suggested that 'tolerated breach' may be a preferable concept.[8]

In the case of contracts for personal services, there is a more fundamental objection to specific enforcement, namely that it would be unduly restrictive of liberty. *De Francesco v Barnum*[9] involved an apprenticeship agreement with a dancing teacher whereby the apprentice agreed to serve for seven years and not to enter into any professional engagements without the teacher's permission during that time. The contract was set aside primarily because the apprentice was a minor, but in discussing the availability of an injunction, Fry LJ commented generally on specific enforcement of contracts for personal services:

> I have a strong impression and a strong feeling that it is not in the interest of mankind that the rule of specific performance should be extended to such cases. I think the courts are bound to be jealous, lest they should turn contracts of service into contracts of slavery; and, therefore, speaking for myself, I should lean against the extension of the doctrine of specific performance and injunction in such a manner.[10]

Specific enforcement was refused, not only because it would have been oppressive to the individual, but because it was 'not in the interest of mankind'. Fry, who was a treatise-writer as well as a judge, commented in the next edition of his treatise after this decision that 'it is not for the interests of society that persons who are not desirous of maintaining continuous personal relations with each other should be compelled to do so.'[11] These comments, in and out of court, show that there is a public interest, as well as a purely private interest, in retention by individuals of some degree of freedom.

It is true that, in *Lumley v Wagner*,[12] an injunction was issued restraining an opera singer from performing for a competitor of the plaintiff, but the court recognised that a decree of specific performance actually compelling the defendant to sing for the plaintiff would have been out of the question. In addition, the restraint on the defendant's freedom of action imposed by the injunction was

[7] *Bank of America Canada v Mutual Trust Co* [2002] 2 SCR 601; *Hillspring Farms Ltd v Walton (Leland) & Sons Ltd* (2007) 312 NBR (2d) 109 (CA); *Delphinium Ltee v 512842 NB Inc* (2008) 296 DLR (4th) 770 at [51].

[8] D Friedmann, 'Economic Aspects of Damages and Specific Performance Compared' in D Saidov and R Cunnington (eds), *Contract Damages: Domestic and International Perspectives* (2008) 65, 82–83.

[9] (1890) 45 Ch D 430.

[10] ibid 438.

[11] Sir Edward Fry, *A Treatise on the Specific Performance of Contracts*, 3rd edn (1892) 49.

[12] (1852) 1 De G M & G 604.

comparatively slight: the injunction was only valid for a period of three months and operated only in England, which was not the defendant's normal sphere of activity. Moreover, there were reasons for the order that are not present in most cases: the singer was a star performer for whom there was no substitute; the plaintiff had invested heavily in her appearance at his opera house; a monetary remedy would have been ineffective; and the defendant was likely (unless restrained by injunction) to confer an unjust benefit on the plaintiff's competitor. It is these considerations that lie behind the rules, adopted in many common law jurisdictions, that an injunction will not be issued unless the defendant's services are unique and that the plaintiff must have an interest in restraining the defendant's conduct that is independent of the interest in inducing performance of the positive side of the contract.[13]

A powerful reason for reluctance in granting a decree of specific performance has been that, if the promisee were entitled to specific performance in a case where the burden to the promisor greatly exceeded the benefit to the promisee of actual performance, the promisee would be in a position to extract from the promisor a sum of money approaching the value to the promisor of release and possibly greatly exceeding the value to the promisee of actual performance.[14] Whatever the terminology, it is a fair summary of the practical effect of the law to say that, where a contract imposes a burden on the promisor that is disproportionate to the legitimate interest of the promisee in actual performance, specific performance will not be granted, and the promisee will be restricted to a monetary remedy. Other legal systems that accept specific performance as a conceptually prior remedy may in practice achieve a similar result in many cases by using other concepts, such as good faith or abuse of rights. As part of recent attempts to harmonise European law, several documents have been published with a view to laying the groundwork for what may eventually become a contract code that incorporates both common law and civil law traditions. The most prominent of these, the *Draft Common Frame of Reference*, in seeking to harmonise English law with continental systems, provides that 'specific performance cannot … be enforced where … performance would be unreasonably burdensome or expensive.'[15] In their comment on this article, the drafters observe that, despite the opposite conceptual approaches of English and civilian law, 'there is

[13] See *Whitwood Chemical Co v Hardman* [1891] 2 Ch 416 (CA); *Macdonald v Casein Ltd* [1917] 35 DLR 443; *Detroit Football Co v Dublinski* (1956) 4 DLR (2d) 688, reversed on other grounds: 7 DLR (2d). 9; AL Corbin, *Corbin on Contracts* (1964) s 1206; ICF Spry, *Equitable Remedies* (Sydney, 1980) 537; RJ Sharpe, *Injunctions and Specific Performance* (Toronto, 1992) para 9.300; EA Farnsworth, *Contracts* (Boston, 1982) 825; M Trebilcock, *The Common Law of Restraint of Trade* (1986) 156–8; SM Waddams, 'Johanna Wagner and the Rival Opera Houses' (2001) 117 *Law Quarterly Review* 431.

[14] Lord Hoffmann in *Co-operative Insurance Society Ltd v Argyle Stores (Holdings) Ltd* [1998] AC 1 (HL).

[15] C von Bar *et al* (eds), *Principles, Definitions and Model Rules of European Private Law.* Draft Common Frame of Reference, full edition prepared by the Study Group on a European Civil Code and the Research Group on EC Private Law (Acquis Group) 6 volumes (2009) III – 3:302 (3)(b).

reason to believe… that results in practice are rather similar under both theories'.[16] In this context, another comment refers to good faith and 'abuse of remedy'.[17] A feature of the law that is especially relevant to the theme of the present article is that even an express contractual provision that the promisor will submit to specific performance is not binding, though it may be relevant to the exercise of the court's discretion. Despite such an express provision, the court will only make a decree of specific performance if satisfied that it is appropriate at the time the order is made.[18]

4. MISTAKE

Relief has been given against various kinds of mistake. Mistakes as to the contents of contractual documents have been dealt with by various means, including a very extensive power of the court to reform or rectify the document, techniques of interpretation and admission of extrinsic evidence to prove the understanding of the parties or to show misrepresentations or collateral contracts. These may be regarded as methods of preventing the enforcement of a transaction that would be disadvantageous to one party, in circumstances where the other party has no reasonable expectation that the document truly represents the mistaken party's intention and therefore has no legitimate interest in enforcing the terms of the document.

Where money is paid or value given in the expectation that certain facts exist, or that certain events will occur, and where those facts or events fail to materialise, an unexpected enrichment may occur. English law has given relief from contracts where unanticipated future events cause a radical change in circumstances.[19] In some cases of mistake as to existing facts relief has been given,[20] though there is considerable doubt about its scope.[21] Relief has been given from a completed gift on proof that the gift was made under the influence of a radical mistake.[22] These cases have often had the effect of granting relief from transactions that, if enforceable, would have turned out to be highly disadvantageous to one of the parties because of the unexpected facts or events.[23]

16 Comment B, Volume 1, at 829.

17 Comment J, Volume 1, at 833–34.

18 *W Bros v Nelson* [1937] 1 KB 209, 220–21; *Sharpe, Injunctions and Specific Performance*, looseleaf edn (2009) paras 7.710–7.810.

19 The doctrine of frustration. See Lord Radcliffe in *Davis Contractors Ltd v Fareham Urban District Council* [1956] AC 696 (HL).

20 *Scott v Coulson* [1903] 2 Ch 249 (CA); *Solle v Butcher* [1950] 1 KB 671; *Magee v Pennine Insurance Co* [1969] 2 QB 507 (CA).

21 *Great Peace Shipping Ltd v Tsavliris Salvage (International) Ltd* [2003] QB 679 (CA).

22 *Lady Hood of Avalon v Mackinnon* [1909] 1 Ch 476.

23 *Eg Krell v Henry* [1903] 2 KB 740 (CA).

5. FAILURE OF COUNTER-PERFORMANCE

An analogous rule, though one not usually considered in this context, is that where reciprocal performance has been promised on each side, the failure of one party's performance excuses the other. Lord Mansfield said in 1760, in what has become the leading case on unjust enrichment in English law, that money paid could be recovered if it had been paid 'upon a consideration which happens to fail'.[24] As mentioned earlier, contract lawyers have commonly used the word 'consideration', as a criterion of enforceability, to mean value given or promised in exchange for the promise sought to be enforced. It is evident that Lord Mansfield was using the word in another sense, and it has often been said, by way of glossing his phrase, that consideration there meant contractual performance. However, it is very probable that Lord Mansfield was using the word in a still wider sense, to mean the reason or basis for the making of the payment. The passage was so understood by Sir William Evans, who equated it with the declaration *causa data causa non secuta* of Roman law,[25] and was also understood in this sense in the mid-nineteenth century and applied outside the contractual context.[26] Birks, writing in 1985, also understood the word in this wide sense, again noting the influence of Roman law:

> The link between 'consideration' and contracts makes it easy to suppose that 'total failure of consideration' must always refer to a failure in contractual reciprocation, whereas in fact that is only the most common species of the genus so described. In the law of restitution the word 'consideration' should be given the meaning with which it first came into the common law. A 'consideration' was once no more than a 'matter considered', and the consideration for doing something was the matter considered in forming the decision to do it. In short, the reason for the act, the state of affairs contemplated as its basis. Failure of consideration for a payment should be understood in that sense. It means that the state of affairs contemplated as the basis or reason for the payment has failed to materialise or, if it did exist, has failed to sustain itself. [The language of the Digest for the same phenomenon is causa data causa non secuta (things given upon a consideration, that consideration having failed)].[27]

In its widest sense, the principle suggested by Lord Mansfield might be extended to the cases of mistake and frustration and to embrace the contractual and restitutionary perspectives of these questions: that money transferred on a

[24] *Moses v Macferlan* (1760) 2 Burr 1005.

[25] W Evans, 'An Essay on the Action for Money Had and Received' (1802) 25, reprinted in (1998) *Restitution Law Review* 1, 9.

[26] *Martin v Andrews* (1856) 7 El & Bl 1 (money paid for anticipated expenses of subpoenaed witness; expenses not incurred).

[27] P Birks, *An Introduction to the Law of Restitution* (1985) 223 and note (same page).

fundamental basis that happens to fail may be recovered and that, if in such circumstances the money has been promised but not yet paid, it ceases to be payable.[28]

Opinions have differed on whether unjust enrichment is subordinate, secondary, supplementary or subsidiary to contract law.[29] Where a forfeiture clause is adjudged valid, it could certainly be said that contract prevails, but unjust enrichment is not irrelevant, because the assessment of the validity of the clause itself involves considerations of unjust enrichment. The validity of the clause is judged by weighing the considerations that favour enforcement of contracts against the desirability of avoiding the unjust enrichment that would be effected by an extravagant forfeiture. Where the claimant is entitled to restitution, whether to avoid a forfeiture or a result that is otherwise unconscionable, or for undue influence or duress, it could be said that unjust enrichment prevails over contract, because entitlement to restitution necessarily implies that the contract is unenforceable. No contract can be valid if performance of it would give rise to an immediate right to restitution.[30]

6. UNFAIRNESS

Since the nineteenth century, writers on English contract law have emphasised the enforceability of contracts and have tended to marginalise the instances in which contracts have been set aside for unfairness. In dealing with consideration it has been common to point out that inadequacy of consideration is not, in itself, a defence against contractual obligation, and from this it has been inferred that, if there is sufficient consideration to meet the test of contract formation, the contract must be enforceable. In the first edition of his treatise on contracts (1876), Sir Frederick Pollock wrote that it was

> a distinguishing mark of English jurisprudence that the amount of the consideration is not material. 'The value of all things contracted for is measured by the appetite of the contractors, and therefore the just value is that which they be contented to give.' It is

[28] Peter Birks suggested failure of basis as the foundation of unjust enrichment in *Unjust Enrichment* (Oxford, 2003).

[29] See R Grantham and C Rickett 'On the Subsidiarity of Unjust Enrichment' (2001) 117 *Law Quarterly Review* 273: 'While the law of unjust enrichment is a core doctrine of the private law, it is a subsidiary doctrine.' L Smith 'Property, Subsidiarity, and Unjust Enrichment'. in D Johnston and R Zimmermann (eds), *Unjustified Enrichment: Key Issues in Comparative Perspective* (2002) 588, 615; 'It begins to appear that unjustified enrichment is not actually subsidiary to contract law. Rather, It Is Excluded by an Operative Distribution of Risks and Benefits.' And H MacQueen, 'Unjustified Enrichment in Mixed Legal Systems' (2005) *Restitution Law Review* 21, 33: 'A general test of subsidiarity seems to pose more questions than answers.'.

[30] See J Beatson 'Duress as a Vitiating Factor in Contract' (1974) *The Cambridge Law Journal* 97, 106–08.

> accordingly treated as an elementary principle that the law will not enter into an inquiry as to the adequacy of the consideration.[31]

Sir William Anson (1879) followed the same line, and made the point more forcefully:

> So long as a man gets what he bargained for Courts of law will not ask what the value may be to him, or whether its value is in any way proportionate to his act or promise given in return. This would be 'the law making the bargain, instead of leaving the parties to make it.'[32]

As both writers were aware, however, this was not the whole story, because courts of equity had often set aside contracts on a variety of grounds relating (in general terms) to unfairness. Pollock mentions this aspect of English law with a somewhat awkward side note in his chapter on consideration (Chapter IV):

> Inadequacy plus other things in Equity: see chap. XI
>
> Inadequacy of consideration coupled with other things may however be of great importance as evidence of fraud, &c., when the validity of a contract is in dispute: and it has been considered (though, it is believed, the better opinion is otherwise) to be of itself sufficient ground for refusing specific performance. This subject, which is by no means free from difficulty, will be examined under the head of Undue Influence, Ch XI., post.[33]

Anson, closely following both the form and the substance of Pollock's work, deals with the matter as follows:

> Equity so far takes adequacy of consideration into account in dealing with contracts, that if a contract is sought to be avoided on the ground of Fraud or Undue Influence, inadequacy of consideration will be regarded as strong corroborative evidence in support of the suit. [Reference follows to what Anson, like Pollock, considers the doubtful power of the court to deny specific performance on this ground.][34]

After 1875, English courts administered law and equity together, and one of the principal stated purposes of Pollock's book was to consider English law and equity as a whole. However, his approach to this question, followed in starker form by Anson, tended to marginalise the power of the court to set aside disadvantageous contracts. The statement of the general principle of law, followed by the mention, two pages later, of a power to set aside contracts 'in equity' suggests that the power is exceptional. The categories of 'fraud, &c.' and 'fraud or undue influence' suggest rare and closely defined instances, scarcely affecting the general principles of contract law. The reference to inadequacy of consideration

[31] F Pollock, *Principles of Contract at Law and in Equity: [...]* (1876) 154, quoting Hobbes, Leviathan (1660) pt 1, c 15.

[32] WR Anson, *Principles of the English Law of Contract* (1879) 63, quoting Alderson B in *Pilkington v Scott* 14 M & W 657, 660.

[33] Pollock, above n 31, 156.

[34] Anson, above n 32, 65.

as a matter only of *evidence* tends to suggest that it has little effect on substantive law, and the emphasis of both writers on the power of the court of equity to refuse specific performance (leaving the promisee with a right to full damages) tends to distract the reader from the far more significant power of the court to *rescind* the contract (leaving the promisee with no remedy at all). The postponement of the subject to a later chapter also tends to suggest that it is not directly relevant to the most basic principles of contract law, and that relief on the grounds of unfairness is conceptually exceptional. The tendency to marginalise the issue reached a peak in Halsbury's Laws of England (1907–15), in which unconscionable contracts are excluded altogether from the article on Contract and are dealt with, anomalously, in a different volume in the article on Fraudulent and Voidable Conveyances.

However, the power of English courts to set aside contracts on grounds broadly relating to unfairness and inequality of exchange was considerably wider than the extracts from Pollock's and Anson's books suggest. The first published treatise on English contract law (by John Joseph Powell, 1790) included a long chapter entitled 'Of the Equitable Jurisdiction in relieving against unreasonable Contracts or Agreements'.[35] Powell states that the mere fact of a bargain being *unreasonable* is not a ground to set it aside in equity,

> for contracts are not to be set aside, because not such as the wisest people would make; but there must be fraud to make void acts of this solemn and deliberate nature, if entered into for a consideration.[36]

However, he goes on to point out that 'fraud' in equity has an unusual and very wide meaning:

> And agreements that are not properly fraudulent, in that sense of the term which imports deceit, will, nevertheless, be relieved against on the ground of inequality, and imposed burden or hardship on one of the parties to a contract; which is considered as a distinct head of equity, being looked upon as an offence against morality, and as unconscientious. Upon this principle, such courts will, in cases where contracts are unequal, as bearing hard upon one party… set them aside[37]

Powell gives as an example the very common provision in a mortgage that unpaid interest should be treated as principal and should itself bear interest until paid. Powell writes that 'this covenant will be relieved against as fraudulent, because unjust and oppressive in an extreme degree'.[38]

The very wide meaning thus given to the concepts of 'fraud' and 'fraudulent' indicates that the power to set aside contracts was much wider than at first appears. Pollock, in his chapter on duress and undue influence, also explains to his readers that 'fraud' could not be taken at face value:

[35] JJ Powell, *Essay upon the Law of Contracts and Agreements*, 2 volumes (1790) Vol 2, 143.
[36] ibid 144.
[37] ibid 145–46.
[38] ibid 146.

> The term fraud is indeed of common occurrence both in the earlier and in the later authorities: but 'fraud does not here mean deceit or circumvention; it means an unconscientious use of the power arising out of these circumstances and conditions' and this does not come within the proper meaning of fraud, which is a misrepresentation... made with the intent of creating a particular wrong belief in the mind of the party defrauded. Perhaps the best word to use would be imposition, as a sort of middle term between fraud, to which it comes near in popular language, and compulsion, which it suggests by its etymology.[39]

It is significant that Pollock, in elucidating the meaning of the word fraud, should consciously look for an equally ambiguous word (imposition), suggesting, on the one hand, the taking of unfair advantage and, on the other hand, actual compulsion.

7. FORFEITURES

The court of equity commonly gave relief against forfeitures of all kinds. The most clearly established case was that of a mortgage. Mortgage documents usually provided that, on default in repayment, the land should be forfeited to the mortgagee. The courts consistently refused to enforce this simple provision, despite the fact that it was well known and perfectly clear. Whatever form of words was used — even if the document evidenced an outright conveyance of the land — the court, if convinced that the substance of the transaction was a mortgage, refused to enforce the document and permitted the borrower to redeem the land:

> So that in every mortgage the agreement of the parties upon the face of the deed, seems to be, that a mortgage shall not be redeemable after forfeiture ... and a mortgage can no more be irredeemable than a distress for rent-charge can be irrepleviable. The law itself will control that express agreement of the party; and by the same reason equity will let a man loose from his agreement, and will against his agreement admit him to redeem a mortgage.[40]

No restriction, even by express agreement, was permitted on the right to redeem. In *Spurgeon v Collier* (1758), Lord Northington said that 'a man will not be suffered in conscience to fetter himself with a limitation or restriction of his time of redemption. It would ruin the distressed and unwary, and give unconscionable advantage to greedy and designing persons'.[41] This last sentence compendiously illustrates the impact of the separate but interlocking concepts that have run

[39] n 31, above, at 527.

[40] *Howard v Harris* (1683) 1 Vern 190, 192. This passage from the argument of successful counsel was cited, with page reference and near quotation, as having assisted in establishing the law on the point, by RH Coote, *A Treatise on the Law of Mortgage* (1821) 22.

[41] (1758) 1 Eden 55 59 (Sir R Henley).

through the unconscionability cases: lack of consent, avoidance of unjust enrichment and deterrence of wrongdoing. A few years later, the same judge again linked the concepts of reason, justice, freedom of consent and deterrence of trickery:

> The court, as a court of conscience, is very jealous of persons taking securities for a loan, and converting such securities into purchases. And therefore I take it to be an established rule, that a mortgagee can never provide at the time of making the loan for any event or condition on which the equity of redemption shall be discharged, and the conveyance absolute. And there is great reason and justice in this rule, for necessitous men are not, truly speaking, free men, but, to answer a present exigency, will submit to any terms that the crafty may impose upon them.[42]

The rule was that the mortgagee could stipulate for no collateral advantage, and so strict was this rule that it came to be applied so as to cause the setting-aside of agreements that were perfectly fair and reasonable. It was easier for the nineteenth-century English legal mind to accept a rigid rule that a mortgagee could in no circumstances stipulate for a collateral advantage (a rule that, for better or worse, happened to be the law) than it was to accept a general power to relieve against unfair transactions (which seemed to admit a dangerous instability). So, ironically, in the name of upholding the sanctity of contracts, transactions were set aside that were not unfair. In a decision of the House of Lords in 1904, Lord Halsbury remarked, with evident irritation, that 'a perfectly fair bargain made between two parties to it, each of whom was quite sensible as to what they were doing, is not to be performed because at the same time a mortgage arrangement was made between them.'[43] Ten years later, the House of Lords restored flexibility by appealing to the underlying original reason for the intervention of the courts:

> It was, in ordinary cases, only where there was conduct which the Court of Chancery regarded as unconscientious that it interfered with freedom of contract. The lending of money, on mortgage or otherwise, was looked on with suspicion and the courts were on the alert to discover want of conscience in the terms imposed by lenders… [I]t is inconsistent with the objects for which [the rules of equity] were established that these rules should crystallise into technical language so rigid the letter can defeat the underlying spirit and purpose.[44]

8. PENALTIES

Forfeiture in its various forms has obvious advantages to the secured party, and it is not surprising that attempts were made by lenders to secure equivalent

[42] *Vernon v Bethell* (1762) 2 Eden 110, 113.
[43] *Samuel v Jarrah Timber and Wood Paving Co*[1904] AC 323 325.
[44] *Kreglinger v New Patagonia Meat and Cold Storage Co Ltd* [1914] AC 25, 36–38 per Lord Haldane.

advantages without the immediate transfer of the property to be forfeited. The growth of the penal bond represented such an attempt. A common form of the bond was a covenant to pay a fixed sum of money unless some other act was performed by a certain date. The effect was to secure the performance of the other act, which might itself be the payment of a sum of money that had been lent by the obligee to the obligor.

The court of equity gave relief from such bonds on much the same principle as in cases of mortgages. The bond was, in substance, a device to secure repayment of a loan, and the legitimate interest of the lender was in repayment of the principal (together with interest and costs) and no more. In 1880, the law on this point, out of keeping though it was with the spirit of the nineteenth century, was explained by Bramwell LJ (who, though not himself sympathetic, accepted that this was the law) as follows:

> [T]he Court of Chancery said that a penalty to secure the payment of a sum of money or the performance of an act should not be enforced; the parties were not held to their agreement; equity in truth refused to allow to be enforced what was considered to be an unconscientious bargain.[45]

In 1900, another judge said:

> The Court of Chancery gave relief against the strictness of the common law in cases of penalty or forfeiture for nonpayment of a fixed sum on a day certain, on the principle that failure to pay principal on a certain day could be compensated sufficiently by payment of principal and interest with costs at a subsequent day.[46]

Also important was the obvious factor that a borrower in urgent need was apt to sign too readily an extravagant penal bond: the need for the funds was always immediate, and the possibility of enforcement of the bond remote.

9. FUTURE INTERESTS IN PROPERTY

The English courts of equity relieved against transactions entered into by persons expecting to own property in the future. The typical case was of the 'expectant heir', and this phrase, together with the otherwise obsolete phrase 'catching bargain', is generally used to denote this branch of English law, although the jurisdiction was not restricted to heirs: it extended to every kind of case in which the borrower expected to become the owner of property in the future. Commonly, the substance of the transaction was a loan, but the transaction took the form of a sale of the expectancy or of the reversion. The court would set aside the transaction unless the purchaser proved that he had given full value. As in the case of mortgages and penalties, the situation is one in which experience shows that a person, pressed by the immediate need for money, is apt to sell a future

45 *Protector Loan Co v Grice* (1880) 5 QBD 592, 596.
46 Re Dixon [1900] 2 Ch 561, 576, per Rigby LJ.

interest at an undervalue — sometimes at a gross undervalue: again, the need for money is immediate, and the interest given up seems remote. So ready was the court to set aside such transactions that the rule came to seem too rigid and legislative intervention was found to be necessary: a statute of 1867 provided that such transactions should not 'be opened or set aside merely upon the ground of undervalue'.[47] The statute, however, did not affect the general jurisdiction of the court to set aside unconscionable transactions,[48] and this line of cases supplies an important illustration of that wider jurisdiction, before and after 1867.[49] In the first edition of his treatise on contracts, Pollock says that 'practically the question is whether in the opinion of the court the transaction was a hard bargain.'[50]

10. UNDUE INFLUENCE

Disadvantageous contractual transactions have frequently been set aside for 'undue influence'. This phrase covers a number of different circumstances. It may apply to an openly hostile relationship where one party threatens the other with adverse consequences if the agreement is not made. This was the case in *Williams v Bayley*,[51] where a son had forged his father's signature to promissory notes and the creditor threatened to prosecute the son unless the father agreed to pay the debt. More commonly, the phrase has been applied to situations related to fiduciary duties where one party reposes trust in the other. Certain categories of cases have been said to give rise to a presumption of undue influence, but it is not necessary for the weaker party to bring his or her case into a recognised category: any case in which there is a relationship of trust or confidence may qualify for relief. A recent instance of a case that does not readily fall into any pre-existing category is one where an employee guaranteed her employer's debts. The guarantee was set aside by the English Court of Appeal. Millett LJ used strong language, very reminiscent of the older equity cases:

> This transaction cannot possibly stand... It is an extreme case. The transaction was not merely to the manifest disadvantage of Miss Burch; it was one which, in the traditional phrase, 'shocks the conscience of the court'. Miss Burch committed herself to a personal liability far beyond her slender means, risking the loss of her home and personal bankruptcy, and obtained nothing in return beyond a relatively small and possibly temporary increase in the overdraft facility available to her employer, a company in which she had no financial interest. The transaction gives rise to grave suspicion. It cries aloud for an explanation.[52]

47 31 & 32 Vic c 4.
48 *Earl of Aylesford v Morris*(1873) 8 Ch 484, 490.
49 See the passage quoted at n 55 below.
50 Pollock, above n 31, 534–35.
51 (1866) LR 1 HL 200.
52 *Credit Lyonnais Bank Nederland NV v Burch* [1997] 1 All ER 144, 152.

Closely related, and perhaps conceptually indistinguishable,[53] are cases where the relationship between the parties is categorised as fiduciary.

11. UNCONSCIONABILITY

The courts of equity exercised a more general jurisdiction to set aside transactions that they regarded as very unfair. In 1818, it was said that

> a court of equity will inquire whether the parties really did meet on equal terms; and if it be found that the vendor was in distressed circumstances, and that advantage was taken of that distress, it will avoid the contract.[54]

In 1888, summarising the cases, Kay J said:

> The result of the decisions is that where a purchase is made from a poor and ignorant man at a considerable undervalue, the vendor having no independent advice, a court of equity will set aside the transaction. This will be done even in the case of property in possession, and a fortiori if the interest be reversionary. The circumstances of poverty and ignorance of the vendor and absence of independent advice throw upon the purchaser, where the transaction is impeached, the onus of proving, in Lord Selborne's words, that the purchase was 'fair, just and reasonable'.[55]

Was undervalue alone a sufficient ground for relief? This question is not easy to answer because of the elusive meaning of 'fraud'. There are, indeed, many statements by courts and commentators to the effect that undervalue alone was insufficient, but these cannot be taken at face value because of frequent indications that a gross undervalue created a 'presumption of fraud': where there was a large inequality of exchange the court could presume, without any separate proof, that the disadvantaged party must have been labouring under some sort of mistake or disability, or else must have been influenced by necessity or by some sort of pressure, or by a relationship with the stronger party.[56] Some cases suggest that the presumption was practically irrebuttable. In *Morse v Royal*, Lord Chancellor Erskine said:

> The authorities, connected with this case, are not many; and the principles are perfectly clear. One class of cases is that of contracts, that may be avoided, as being contrary to the policy of the law; which are interdicted for the wisest reasons. Of that kind are a deed of gift, obtained by an Attorney while engaged in the business of the author of that gift; a deed by an heir, when of age, to his guardian; purchases of reversions from young heirs, when of age... To that class of cases I shall add the case of a trustee selling to

[53] See *Lloyds Bank v Bundy* [1975] QB 326 (CA).

[54] *Wood v Abrey* (1818) 3 Madd 417, 423, per Leach VC.

[55] *Fry v Lane* (1888) 40 Ch D 312, 322. Lord Selborne's words were from *Aylesford v Morris*, above n 48, 491.

[56] *Earl of Chesterfield v Janssen* (1751) 2 Ves Sen 125, *Heathcote v Paignon* (1787) 2 BroCC 167.

himself. Without any consideration of fraud, or looking beyond the relation of the parties, that contract is void... The contract is interdicted by the policy of the law.[57]

In *Lowther v Lowther*, the same judge said that 'though inadequacy of Consideration is not of itself a sufficient ground for setting aside a Contract, it is, when gross, strong evidence of Fraud.'[58] In a note on a case from 1790, it was said that 'under ordinary circumstances even a considerable inadequacy of price will not invalidate a sale... still, the inadequacy may be so gross as, *of itself*, plainly to demonstrate fraud.'[59] In this context, Joseph Story (1836) speaks of 'the most vehement presumption of fraud'.[60]

Inequality of exchange was not, in itself, conclusive, but it does not follow that it was irrelevant: a large inequality of exchange often seems to have called for some sort of explanation (which might be that a part-gift was intended or that the inequality was caused by risks fairly allocated by the transaction).[61] An attempt in the twentieth century by Lord Denning[62] to restate a general principle in terms of unfairness and inequality of bargaining power was rejected by the House of Lords,[63] but the older cases were not overruled.

12. CREDIT TRANSACTIONS

Since the beginning of the twentieth century, legislation has empowered the court to set aside loan and credit transactions that are found to be (broadly speaking) very unfair.[64] A common situation arising in cases of loan guarantees is that the guarantor is induced to enter into the transaction because of some kind of influence exercised by the principal debtor. The problem is whether, and in what circumstances, the lender, not having precise knowledge of the relationship between the guarantor and the principal debtor, should be precluded from enforcing the contract of guarantee. The typical case involves a guarantee given by a wife to secure her husband's debts or those of his business. But many kinds of relationships raise the same problem. In *Credit Lyonnais v Burch*, mentioned earlier, where an employee gave a guarantee to secure the debts of her employer,

[57] (1805) 12 Ves 355 371–72.

[58] (1806) 13 Ves 95.

[59] *Crowe v Ballard* (1790) 1 Ves Jr Supp 91 (note by John Hovenden; emphasis added).

[60] J Story, *Commentaries on Equity Jurisprudence as Administered in England and America* (1836) 250.

[61] *Rotheram v Browne* (1747) 8 Bro PC297 (part gift); *Mortimer v Capper* (1782) 1 Bro CC 156 (inherent risk).

[62] *Lloyds Bank v Bundy*, above n 53.

[63] *National Westminster Bank Plc v Morgan* [1985] AC 686 (HL).

[64] Moneylenders Act 1900 (excessive harsh and unconscionable). *Consumer Credit Act* 1974, ss 137–40 (extortionate, grossly exorbitant, grossly contravenes ordinary principles of fair dealing), Consumer Credit Act 2006s). 140A (unfair).

the English Court of Appeal held that the bank was precluded from enforcing the guarantee, and that it was not sufficient for the bank to recommend independent advice:

> The bank had actual notice of the facts from which the existence of a relationship of trust and confidence between Mr Pelosi and Miss Burch could be inferred. It knew that they were respectively employer and junior employee working in a small business and should have 'appreciated that the possibility of influence exist[ed]'.[65]

In a later case, the House of Lords laid down detailed rules for the guidance of lenders in such circumstances. Dealing with the case of a husband and wife, Lord Nicholls said:

> For the future a bank satisfies these requirements if it insists that the wife attend a private meeting with a representative of the bank at which she is told the extent of her liability as surety, warned of the risks she is running and urged to take independent advice. In exceptional cases the bank, to be safe, has to insist that the wife is separately advised.[66]

The House of Lords was conscious of conflicting policies, desiring, on the one hand, to protect the vulnerable guarantor and, on the other hand, not to make it practically impossible for spouses to raise money on jointly-owned property. Despite the genuine endeavours of the court to satisfy these conflicting objectives, it is difficult to avoid doubts as to the feasibility of the court's enterprise, because a guarantor who is truly under the influence of a stronger spouse will not be effectively protected by the measures proposed. A short private meeting in an office at a bank cannot realistically be expected to displace the continuing influence of a stronger spouse in whose company the weaker spouse will be immediately before and after the meeting. Then there is the consideration that the transaction can easily be restructured in the form of a direct advance of cash to the weaker spouse. If he or she is truly under the influence of the other spouse documents can readily be prepared and executed whereby money is paid into the account of the weaker spouse and paid over, after a shorter or longer interval of time, to the other. The precautions imposed by the House of Lords would not apply in those circumstances. Moreover, there is the awkward consideration that, in the case of a guarantee secured by a mortgage on the matrimonial home, it will, if the spouses are still living together, be the stronger spouse — the very party who allegedly has been responsible for the impugned transaction — who will benefit from having it set aside, thus creating an incentive for self-serving evidence and self-serving admissions. From the public policy point of view, difficult questions arise: is it an essential aspect of freedom that persons should have unrestricted power to borrow money on security of their assets, or are some restraints acceptable or desirable, and, if so, what restraints, and on whom, and in

[65] Above n 52, 155.
[66] *Royal Bank of Scotland Plc v Etridge* (No 2) [2002] 2 AC 773.

respect of what assets? These are questions on which opinions differ widely; they are not questions that the court is well placed to determine.

13. UNFAIR TERMS

There are several other techniques that have been used by English law to control potentially unfair contracts that cannot be discussed here in detail. One of these is the invalidation of disclaimer or exemption clauses, a topic with a long and convoluted judicial and legislative history in the twentieth century. Another is the use of implied terms, which often have the effect of importing obligations of good faith and of converting an apparently one-sided transaction into a more equal exchange. Another method is to find that insufficient consent has been given, in particular circumstances, to a burdensome contractual term. One-twentieth-century judge has said that 'we do not allow printed forms to be made a trap for the unwary'.[67]

The *Draft Common Frame of Reference* incorporates several of these concepts in its provisions on unfair terms. An unfair term, which is 'not binding on the party who did not supply it', is defined differently according to whether the contracting parties are consumers or businesses. The definitions refer to 'transparency', 'significant disadvantage', 'good faith', 'fair dealing' and to whether terms are individually negotiated. A list of terms presumed to be unfair in consumer-business contracts is supplied.[68] The comments and notes on these articles show that this was a difficult and controversial question for the drafters.[69] Although no general duty of good faith has been adopted by English law, many of the concepts mentioned in the articles and comments are also reflected in English cases.

14. THEORETICAL BASIS FOR RELIEF

14.1. Consent

It has frequently been asserted that the underlying reason for the refusal to enforce unfair contracts is the absence of consent on the part of the promisor which is implied by such concepts as cognitive incapacity, undue influence and coercion. Consensual capacity is, no doubt, a relevant, necessary and useful perspective on the problem, but it does not supply a complete explanation, and in certain respects it is misleading.

The principal attraction of the 'consent' approach is that it apparently enables relief for unfairness to be reconciled with a theory that requires enforcement of

[67] *Neuchatel Asphalte Co Ltd v Barnett* [1957] 1 WLR 356, 360 (Denning LJ).
[68] *Draft Common Frame of Reference*, II – 9:401–10.
[69] ibid, Volume 1, 628–67.

all voluntary agreements. Thus, sanctity of contracts can be maintained in theory — those contracts that are not enforced being not, truly speaking, contracts at all. The objections to this, as a complete explanation, are that this approach is fictitious, artificial and circular and that it distorts the concept of consent in cases where that concept is really needed, such as mistake.

In many cases where relief is given, consent, in every ordinary sense of the word, is present. The vendor of land who sells for a tenth of its value or the accident victim who settles a claim for a small sum in cash usually knows what the terms of the agreement are and intends to agree to those terms. Relief has regularly been given against forfeitures and penalties, even to sophisticated and knowledgeable parties. In such cases, it is not plausible to argue that the party seeking to set aside the contract has not assented to its terms. The ordinary tests of assent, subjective and objective, are fully met in most such cases. If it were argued that, in cases where the contract is unfair, there is no 'true' assent,[70] the answer would be that a test would then be needed of what amounts to 'true' assent, and this necessarily reintroduces some test of fairness.

14.2. Wrongdoing

A second general approach to unconscionability has been to focus on the wrongful conduct of the party seeking enforcement. This is suggested by concepts such as equitable fraud and duress. There is confusion regarding the usage of the word 'unconscionable'. The older usage was to refer to the *transaction* as unconscionable. The attitude of the party seeking enforcement might be described as 'unconscientious' or 'unconscionable' or 'fraudulent', but these usages referred to the impropriety of seeking enforcement (after the transaction had been adjudged unfair) not to any wrongful conduct at the time of the transaction itself.[71] On the other hand, a number of modern courts have suggested that it is the *conduct* of the party seeking enforcement that must be shown to be unconscionable, thereby implying the need to establish some kind of wrongdoing.[72]

Many older cases cannot be explained as depending on the defendant's wrongful conduct. In 1864, in setting aside a sale of land at a large undervalue, Turner LJ said:

> I say nothing about improper conduct on the part of the appellant; I do not wish to enter into the question of conduct… I am content to believe that in this case there has

[70] J Murray, 'Unconscionability, Unconscionability' (1969) 31 *University of Pittsburgh Law Review* 1.

[71] See LA Sheridan, *Fraud in Equity: a Study in English and Irish Law* (1957).

[72] eg *Hart v O'Connor* [1985] AC 1000 (PC); *National Westminster Bank v Morgan*, above n 63.

> been no actual moral fraud on the part of the appellant in the transaction; but, for all that, in my judgment an improvident contract has been entered into.[73]

In 1873, in granting relief to a plaintiff from an improvident bargain, Lord Selborne said that the defendant

> is not alleged or proved to have been guilty of deceit or circumvention, and the plaintiff has no merits of his own to plead. He comes into court to be relieved from the consequences of a course of very wilful and culpable folly and extravagance. I think him entitled to the relief which he asks; but I think it is not unjust that he should obtain it at his own expense[74]

Costs were refused, and in some analogous cases a successful plaintiff has actually been ordered to pay the defendant's costs.[75] These cases plainly show that proof of wrongdoing on the part of the stronger party was not required. Even though the party seeking enforcement has acted perfectly properly and entirely in good faith, there are cases where the transaction has been set aside. If, as in the 1873 case mentioned, the plaintiff has 'no merits of his own' and has caused the difficulties entirely by his own 'wilful and culpable folly and extravagance', he may still be entitled to relief. He should pay the expenses attributable to his folly, but this does not mean that he should suffer the consequences of full enforcement of what might be a disastrous contract; justice is sufficiently done if he pays the costs (to both parties) of the legal proceedings that his folly has made necessary.

There are many other cases in which relief has been given despite the absence of wrongful conduct on the part of the party seeking enforcement. Maritime salvage cases supply two kinds of examples. Salvage agreements were not infrequently set aside both on the ground that too small a sum had been agreed (undue advantage being taken of the salvors) and on the opposite ground that too large a sum had been agreed (undue advantage being taken of the ship in distress). Wrongdoing, in any ordinary sense, was not required in either kind of case. In one of the cases setting aside a receipt 'in full payment' of salvage services on the ground that the payment was too small, the judge (Dr Lushington) said: 'I do not mean to say that this receipt was not honestly obtained, but the inclination of the court is to look at the circumstances of the case, and not to allow a paper to operate as a bar.'[76] In the opposite case, where a salvor took advantage of a ship's difficulties in order to obtain what the court considered to

[73] *Baker v Monk* (1864) 4 De G J & S 388, 393–94. See J Devenney, 'Book Review' (2008) 28 *Legal Studies* 477, 480.

[74] *Earl of Aylesford v Morris*, above n 48, 499.

[75] L Field *et al*, *Daniell's Chancery Practice*, 6th edn (1884) 1180: 'Where securities are ordered to be delivered up because the bargain has been unconscientious judgment is generally given for the plaintiff upon the terms that he shall repay the defendant the amount actually advanced or paid by him, with interest; and the defendant being looked upon as a mortgagee for that amount, he was treated as such, and the plaintiff ordered to pay him his costs.'

[76] *The Silver Bullion* (1854) 2 Sp 70, 75. Also *Akerblom v Price Potter Walker & Co* (1881) 7 QBD 129 (CA).

be an extravagant payment, the agreement was again set aside.[77] The agreement was described by the court as 'inequitable', 'unjust', 'unreasonable' and 'extortionate',[78] but it does not appear that the salvor had committed or threatened any legal wrong. Again, undue influence may be established without proof of wrongdoing.[79]

14.3. Unjust Enrichment

The concept of unjust enrichment has been very influential, though not under that name until the twentieth century. In a treatise published anonymously in 1737, the author, generally taken to be Henry Ballow, asserted the power of the court of equity to set aside very burdensome contracts, giving as the reason that 'no man should be a Gainer by another's Loss'.[80] This phrase, like phrases in many old and modern cases, such as 'advantage taken of weakness'[81] and 'deriving immoderate gain',[82] strongly suggests that the principal underlying value to be weighed against the value of enforcing the contract is the avoidance of unjust enrichment. Since the middle of the twentieth century, unjust enrichment has been recognised as a source of obligations independent of contract. In this context, however, the two concepts are closely inter-related: if the contract is enforceable the enrichment is not unjust, but if the enrichment is unjust the contract is unenforceable. It is not satisfactory to say that, before unjust enrichment can be considered, the contract must *first* be set aside, because the concept of unjust enrichment has itself been highly relevant in determining the enforceability of the contract. Nevertheless, unjust enrichment, standing alone, does not explain every case. A person who agrees to sell or to purchase property or services, even at fair market value, may be entitled to set aside the contract if it was induced by undue influence[83] or by wrongful threats.[84] Thus, the concepts of consent and wrongdoing cannot be entirely dispensed with.

[77] *The Port Caledonia and The Anna* [1903] P 184.
[78] ibid 189–90 (Bucknill J).
[79] *Allcard v Skinner* (1887) 36 Ch D 135; *Williams v Bayley* (1866) LR 1 HL 200. See P Birks, 'The Burden on the Bank'. in F Rose (ed), *Restitution and Banking Law* (1988) 199–200.
[80] [Henry Ballow] A Treatise of Equity (1737) 11.
[81] *Earl of Chesterfield v Janssen*, above n 56, 157.
[82] See B Crawford, 'Comment' (1966) 44 *The Canadian Bar Review* 142.
[83] See *Griesshammer v Ungerer* (1958) 14 DLR (2d) 599(agreement to purchase dancing lessons).
[84] See M Trebilcock, *The Limits of Freedom of Contract* (1993) 81.

14.4. Public Policy

Public policy has sometimes been directly invoked to set aside disadvantageous contracts. Contracts in restraint of trade,[85] in restraint of marriage[86] or otherwise unduly restrictive of personal liberty[87] have been held to be unenforceable. These cases involve a mixture of public and private considerations. As Lord Diplock said, in relation to contracts struck down for restraint of trade:

> If one looks at the reasoning of 19th-century judges... one finds lip service paid to current economic theories, but if one looks at what they said in the light of what they did, one finds that they struck down a bargain if they thought it was unconscionable as between the parties to it, and upheld it if they thought it was not.[88]

There is much debate, and little consensus, about the theoretical basis of contract law.[89] To every theory that seeks to explain why contracts are enforced, unconscionability appears as an exception, anomaly or limitation: the criteria of enforceability are apparently satisfied, yet the contract is not enforced. This is true whether the fundamental purpose of contract law is taken to be giving effect to the will of the promisor or protecting the reliance or expectation of the promisee, whether it deals with promises or bargains, whether it rests on principles of morality or social utility and whether it is primarily concerned with justice between individuals or with social welfare.

Naturally enough, theories seeking to explain the positive reasons for enforcement of contracts do not usually emphasise the excuses for non-performance, but some attempts have been made to discern in the doctrine of unconscionability the positive implementation of valuable social policy. It has been suggested that the willingness of courts to set aside contracts reflects the egalitarian values of the welfare state.[90] There is undoubtedly some substance to this suggestion: a society that acknowledges a duty to give positive assistance to its poorest members can hardly fail to sympathise with a poor and weak person who seeks relief from a very disadvantageous contract.

Nevertheless, there are several reasons why contract law cannot be satisfactorily viewed as a primary tool for the redistribution of wealth. With some exceptions (mainly in monopoly situations), the law does not compel the making of contracts. Even where power is given to reopen or to rewrite a contract, there is

[85] *Mason v Provident Clothing and Supply Co* [1913] AC 724. See M Trebilcock, *The Common Law of Restraint of Trade* (1986).

[86] *Lowe v Peers* (1768) 4 Burr 2225.

[87] *Horwood v Millar's Timber & Trading Co. Ltd* 1917) 1 KB 305 (CA).

[88] *A Schroeder Music Publishing Co v Macaulay* [1974] 1 WLR 1308 1315 (HL).

[89] The principal theories are discussed by S Smith, *Contract Theory* (2004).

[90] See R Brownsword, G Howells and T Wilhelmsson (eds) *Welfarism in Contract Law* (Aldershot, Dartmouth Publishing 1994); E Posner 'Contract Law in the Welfare State: A Defense of the Unconscionability Doctrine, Usury Laws and Related Limitations on the Freedom to Contract' (1994) 24 *Journal of Legal Studies* 283; S Waddams 'Unconscionable Contracts: Competing Perspectives' (1999) 62 *Saskatchewan Law Review* 1.

usually no power to compel parties that have not dealt with each other at all to enter into a contract. Because of this, the ability of contract law to redistribute wealth in society will always be very strictly limited. Its scope of operation is restricted, on the whole, to granting relief to those who happen to have entered into disadvantageous contracts.

The extent of relief for mistake or unconscionability is usually the restoration of the status quo before the contract was made. If there was an inequality of wealth between the parties before the contract was made, the most that the court will do, if it grants relief, is to restore that situation. It may prevent the weaker party from throwing away some of the little wealth that he or she has, but it will not make that party wealthier.

Contract law focuses on individual transactions and not, generally, on the overall wealth of the parties. Thus, wealthy parties benefit at the expense of the poor under doctrines of mistake, as when a bank erroneously credits a customer's account or when a wealthy party signs a contract that contains a clerical error. Even in the case of relief for unconscionability, a wealthy party may benefit at the expense of a poorer party, as in the case of a wealthy farmer who sells his farm to an impecunious speculator for one-tenth of its value. The court, if inclined to give relief, will not be deterred by the consideration that the farmer is wealthier than the buyer, and that he would remain wealthier even if the transaction were enforced. It should be noted too that the court, in a contract case, lacks the mechanism to assess the wealth of the parties. If redistribution of wealth were to become a central feature of contract law, the court would have to contemplate a full examination of both parties' wealth, including an assessment of income and a valuation of capital assets, with opportunity for the other party to dispute the evidence. Such a process would, to say the least, be inconvenient in the course of a civil action.

Relief from contractual obligation is specific to the parties. Even if the court had the means to judge the wealth of the parties, it could not compare the plaintiff with other potential recipients of welfare, who might be more deserving, nor could it compare the defendant with other potential contributors, who might have a greater ability to pay. Apart from the fact that the court lacks the machinery to operate a means test and a system of taxation, there are grave political and institutional objections to ad hoc taxation and distribution of the proceeds by individual judges.

The beneficiaries of the relief that contract law can give are rarely the very poor. They are people with something to lose and with the means and energy to seek to regain it. As we have seen, the courts gave relief to expectant heirs who squandered their inheritance and to landowners who sold their land at an undervalue. These were deserving cases, but they were by no means representative of the poorest members of society. The greater the wealth lost, the more useful is the law to the party seeking relief. Thus, the benefit of a judicial power to set aside contracts increases with the wealth of the weaker party. Litigation is often inaccessible to the poor.

The law of insolvency must also be considered. If a debtor has many creditors, but only one is before the court, as is usual in a contract case, it cannot be right for the court to give relief against one creditor only. The effect will probably be to the benefit not of the debtor but of the other creditors. There may well be a case for consumer bankruptcy or a stay of proceedings against a needy debtor, but such a stay should bind all the creditors, and the court, in contract litigation, lacks the mechanism to achieve that result.

The considerations mentioned in the preceding paragraphs tend to suggest reasons why policy, standing alone, has not been adopted by courts as the primary criterion for setting aside unfair contracts. But it does not follow that policy has been irrelevant. The word 'policy' has often been used in the sense of general residual considerations of justice between the parties, and in this sense it weighs in favour of giving relief from very harsh transactions. 'Policy' has also been used in the sense of giving due attention to the effect that a proposed rule or principle is likely to have on future cases. In this latter sense, policy considerations have frequently been adduced not as a primary reason for granting relief but as a reason for restraint, lest, in the words of an eighteenth-century judge, the court should 'throw every thing into confusion and set afloat all the contracts of mankind'.[91] Relief given from a particular transaction will benefit the disadvantaged party in the particular case, but it may disadvantage persons in similar circumstances in the future by taking away from them the means of obtaining credit.

15. A COMMON EUROPEAN SOLUTION?

The *Draft Common Frame of Reference* (2009) includes the following provisions:

II –7:207 Unfair exploitation

(1) A party may avoid a contract if, at the time of the conclusion of the contract:

(a) the party was dependent on or had a relationship of trust with the other party, was in economic distress or had urgent needs, was improvident, ignorant, inexperienced or lacking in bargaining skill; and

(b) the other party knew or could reasonably have been expected to have known this and, given the circumstances and purpose of the contract, exploited the first party's situation by taking an excessive benefit or grossly unfair advantage.

(2) Upon the request of the party entitled to avoidance, a court may if it is appropriate, adapt the contract in order to bring it into accordance

[91] *Griffith v Spratley* (1787) 1 Cox Ch 383, 388 (Eyre LCB).

with what might have been agreed had the requirements of good faith and fair dealing been observed....

II –7:208 Third persons

(1) Where a person for whose acts a party is responsible or who with a party's assent is involved in the making of a contract:
   (a) causes a mistake, or knows of or could reasonably be expected to know of a mistake; or
   (b) is guilty of fraud, coercion, threats or unfair exploitation,

   remedies under this Section are available as if the behaviour or knowledge had been that of the party.

(2) Where a third person for whose acts a party is not responsible and who does not have the party's assent to be involved in the making of a contract is guilty of fraud, coercion, threats or unfair exploitation, remedies under this Section are available if the party knew or could reasonably be expected to have known of the relevant facts, or at the time of avoidance has not acted on the contract.[92]

The comment states that 'the Article adopts the principle that a contract which gives one party excessive advantage and which involved unfair exploitation may be avoided at the request of the disadvantaged party.'[93] Here are several concepts very familiar to English lawyers. The 'principle' mentioned in the comment is reminiscent of proposed tests of unconscionability along the lines of taking undue advantage of inequality of bargaining power.[94] The factors mentioned in 7:207 (1)(a) (dependence, trust, economic distress, urgent needs, improvidence, ignorance, inexperience or lack of bargaining skill) largely echo expressions used in English courts and tend to suggest lack of consent. The concept in paragraph (1)(b) of 'knew or could reasonably be expected to have known' echoes the equitable concept of constructive notice. The requirement of the means of knowledge on the part of the stronger party tends to suggest an element of wrongdoing, but the open-ended indication of what it is that might reasonably have been known — 'this' referring to the list in 7:207 (1)(a) and 'the relevant facts' in 2:708 (2) — leaves much flexibility. The phrases 'excessive benefit' and 'grossly unfair advantage' echo phrases like 'immoderate gain' and 'undue advantage' and suggest unjust enrichment. But there is no express requirement to prove lack of consent, wrongdoing or unjust enrichment. The provision in 7:208 concerning third persons echoes the above-mentioned concerns of the English courts in attempting to deal with the responsibility of lenders to guarantors influenced by family members and others.[95] The inclusion of these various

[92] Draft Common Frame of Reference, above n 15.

[93] Comment A, Volume 1, at 507.

[94] The English law on undue influence and unconscionability is referred to in n 4, as is the Consumer Credit Act, in Vol 1, 511–12.

[95] The two principal English cases on the subject are mentioned in n 3, Vol 1, 518.

elements in a carefully considered international document suggests that it may not be possible to reduce the issue to a single governing concept: several concepts, not wholly commensurable, appear to be simultaneously in play.

One interesting phrase in 7:207 (1)(b) is 'given the circumstances and purpose of the contract'. This invites the court to look at the real substance of the transaction and ask whether the enrichment can be justified by the allocation of risks properly inherent in the particular kind of transaction. The sale of a reversionary interest in land was, on the face of it, a sale of an interest in land. If that were the real substance of the transaction, that is, if the seller were dealing in a fair market for the purchase and sale of future property interests, a very large enrichment to *either* party would be wholly defensible if it arose from risks inherent in the purchase and sale of property, for example an unexpected rise in land values after the date of the contract. The allocation of that risk is the very nature of the contract, and the buyer takes a corresponding risk of a fall in values: general contractual principles give strong support for enforcement *even if there is a substantial enrichment to the buyer*. The buyer, in that case, would simply have made a profitable, legitimate bargain. But, if the real substance of the transaction is a loan, the court will compare the net effect of the transaction with the terms on which money could be borrowed in a fair market for the lending of money, and will not allow the lender to extract what is, in effect, an extravagant rate of interest. The point was made in an eighteenth-century case:

> An annuity may be purchased at as low a rate as you can, provided it was the original negotiation to purchase and sell an annuity: but if the treaty began about borrowing and lending, and ends in the purchase of an annuity, it is evident, that it was only a method or contrivance to split the payment of the principal and usurious interest into several instalments, and consequently that it was a shift... So, in the case of goods or merchandise it is lawful to sell as dear as you can, on a clear bargain by the way of sale: but if it is first proposed to borrow, and afterwards to sell goods beyond the market price, this is usurious.[96]

The fact that these provisions have been included in a draft to which European civil and common lawyers have both contributed strongly suggests that it is no less important now than it was 250 years ago to avoid transactions that would 'ruin the distressed and unwary, and give unconscionable advantage to greedy and designing persons'.[97]

Another interesting phrase appears in the closing words of 7:208, allowing avoidance of a contract induced by a third party 'if the [other contracting] party ... at the time of avoidance has not acted on the contract', even if that party had no means of knowing the relevant facts. This phrase recognises a distinction between what Anglo-American lawyers might call the 'expectation interest' and the 'reliance interest'. The party seeking enforcement may be deprived of the right

[96] *Earl of Chesterfield v Janssen*, above n 56 (Lord Hardwicke).
[97] See above n 41.

of full enforcement unless there has been reliance. It must follow that, if there has been limited reliance, the disadvantaged party may escape the consequences of full enforcement on compensation of the other party's reliance, for it can scarcely be a working legal rule that a million-euro transaction becomes fully enforceable because the party seeking enforcement has incurred the cost of a postage stamp. Where the weaker party has, by its own foolishness, caused *actual out-of-pocket loss*, there is a strong argument for requiring the weaker party to reimburse the other party's actual loss, *as a condition of relief*. But this concept does not support full enforcement of the stronger party's expectation interest. The distinction corresponds to that made in some of the above-mentioned English equity cases,[98] where the weaker party was successful in setting aside the impugned transaction but was required to pay the other party's costs. This suggests that a choice between 'all or nothing' is not always necessary or desirable.

16. CONCLUSIONS

As has been seen, English law has, by a variety of methods, granted relief against very disadvantageous transactions of various kinds. It would be true to say that, taken as a whole, these methods manifest an element of what may be called paternalism, in the sense of concern for the welfare of the disadvantaged party. It may also be said that these are instances in which autonomy, in the sense of the voluntary desire of the disadvantaged party to enter into the transaction under review, has proved insufficient to justify enforcement. Autonomy and paternalism represent important and relevant considerations, but they cannot be visualised as opposite ends of a simple linear scale. Refusal to enforce an unequal transaction does not restrict the autonomy of the disadvantaged party at the time when enforcement comes into question. On the other hand, considerations other than paternalism have been influential in inducing courts to withhold enforcement.

First, there is a public interest in the freedom of persons not to be unduly restrained by law. This interest has been reflected in the setting-aside of transactions that are in unreasonable restraint of trade or other freedoms. These cases have reflected considerations that are specific to the contracting parties, as well as a public interest that individuals should be free of undue restraints — not only for their own good but for the good of the community. These two kinds of considerations are not entirely separable, because it has been perceived to be in the public interest that individuals should retain a certain degree of freedom. Related to public policy, but conceptually distinct, is the idea that some transactions have been held to be unenforceable because the court sees enforcement as an inappropriate use of the court. Thus, certain kinds of contracts have been held to be non-justiciable, and other kinds of contracts, such as gaming and wagering contracts — which are often highly disadvantageous to one of the parties, even

[98] See above nn 74–75.

though they are not illegal or directly affected by statute — have evoked a marked reluctance on the part of courts called upon to enforce them.

Second, there is the question whether the party seeking to enforce the transaction has a legitimate interest in doing so. The cases discussed here suggest that the autonomy, will or consent of the promisor has not been sufficient to justify the imposition of an obligation unless the other party also appears to have a legitimate interest in the enforcement of the transaction in question. The transaction must be looked at from both sides.[99] The cases on forfeitures and penalties reflect the courts' view that the legitimate interest of the party seeking to enforce such clauses is in securing performance of the primary obligation, not in obtaining an unexpected windfall from a clause that was secondary to the main purpose of the contact. Many of the cases involving written documents suggest that the party seeking enforcement must show that he or she honestly and reasonably thought that the document reflected the actual intention of the other party. In one of the leading Canadian cases on rectification, the US government sought and obtained rectification of a formal contractual document by reason of a mistaken omission in the document.[100] This result is not easily explained as paternalism. The United States did not ask for, or require, the fatherly assistance of the Canadian courts. The US government intended to execute the document as a final expression of its agreement, and its advisers were no doubt very careless in overlooking the omission. But it is not sufficient that the defendant deserves to be made liable: it must also appear that the party seeking to enforce the terms of the document has a legitimate interest in doing so. In this case, there was no such legitimate interest, because that party was found to have agreed to the terms as understood by the United States.

Third, attention needs to be devoted to the law relating to unjust enrichment. Unjust enrichment may offer a firmer conceptual ground for judicial intervention than the concept of paternalism, which, standing alone, may seem an insufficient reason for intervention, or at least one requiring special justification. Forestalling and reversing unjustified transfers of wealth is evidently within the normal range of judicial activity. On the other hand, an unjust enrichment perspective might restrict the scope of intervention by suggesting the need to show not only that the weaker party had incurred a loss but also that the stronger party had made a corresponding gain. Two further related points may be added. One is that the questions addressed here require at least a minimal coherence between the principles of contract law and those relating to restitution for unjust enrichment, because a transaction cannot be legally enforceable if it would have caused an immediate unjust enrichment when it was executed. The other, more general point is that a legal rule might be justifiable because it tends, *in general*, to prevent undesirable consequences (for example, a rule against disclaimer clauses

[99] This concept was developed in respect of tort law in Ernest Weinrib's influential *The Idea of Private Law* (1995).

[100] *USA v Motor Trucks Ltd* [1924] AC 196 (JC).

in consumer contracts, which tends to prevent unfair exclusion of liability), even though there might be no actual unfairness in individual applications of the rule. Many legal rules, once established, have operated independently of what may be thought to have been their original underlying reasons, such as the doctrine of consideration with which this article commenced. Reverting to the theme of the juxtaposition of autonomy and paternalism, we may conclude that relief from disadvantageous contracts, while restricting autonomy in one sense, has enlarged it in others. While such relief may properly be called an instance of paternalism, it has often been supported for additional and independent reasons.

8

Informing Consumers about Themselves

OREN BAR-GILL* AND FRANCO FERRARI**

ABSTRACT

Consumers make mistakes. Imperfect information and imperfect rationality lead to misperception of benefits and costs associated with a product. As a result, consumers might fail to maximise their preferences in product choice or product use. A proposed taxonomy of consumer mistakes draws attention to a less-studied category of mistakes: use-pattern mistakes — mistakes about how the consumer will use the product. Use-pattern mistakes are prevalent. Sellers respond strategically to use-pattern mistakes by redesigning their products, contracts and pricing schemes. These strategic design responses often exacerbate the welfare costs associated with consumer mistakes. From a policy perspective, focusing on disclosure regulation, the importance of use-pattern mistakes requires more, and better, use-pattern disclosure. In particular, sellers should be required to provide individualised use-pattern information.

* Professor of Law and Co-Director, Center for Law, Economics and Organization, New York University School of Law.

** Inge Rennert Distinguished Professor of Law, New York University School of Law. We wish to thank Jenifer Arlen, Ian Ayres, Lucian Bebchuk, Omri Ben-Shahar, Richard Craswell, Clay Gillette, Ofer Grosskopf, Christine Jolls, Marcel Kahan, Ehud Kamar, Daryl Levinson, Ronald Mann, Florencia Marotta Wurgler, Avishalom Tor, Elizabeth Warren and workshop participants at Harvard, NYU, the University of Haifa and the University of Illinois for helpful comments. Special thanks to Anthony Ogus, Willem van Boom and the participants in the Rotterdam Workshop on Juxtaposing Autonomy and Paternalism in Private Law for valuable comments and discussions. We are also grateful to an anonymous referee for helpful comments and suggestions. Robin Moore, Tal Niv and Rebecca Stone provided excellent research assistance. Financial support from the Filomen D'Agostino and Max E. Greenberg Research Fund and from the Cegla Center for Interdisciplinary Research of the Law in Tel-Aviv University is gratefully acknowledged.

Oren Bar-Gill and Franco Ferrari

1. INTRODUCTION

CONSUMERS MAKE MISTAKES. Imperfect information and imperfect rationality lead to misperception of benefits and costs associated with a product. As a result, consumers might fail to maximise their preferences in product choice or product use. In this chapter, we offer a taxonomy of consumer mistakes, drawing attention to a less-studied category of mistakes: use-pattern mistakes. We argue that use-pattern mistakes are prevalent. Sellers respond strategically to use-pattern mistakes by redesigning their products, contracts and pricing schemes. These strategic design responses often exacerbate the welfare costs associated with consumer mistakes. From a policy perspective, focusing on disclosure regulation, we argue that the importance of use-pattern mistakes requires more, and better, use-pattern disclosure.

We begin, in Part 2, by distinguishing between two categories of information — information about product attributes and information about product use.[1] For example, the interest rate on a credit card and the penalty for late payment are attributes of the credit card product. Borrowing patterns and the incidence of late payment describe how the product is used. The total benefits and costs associated with a product are a function of both product attributes and use patterns. Total interest paid depends both on the interest rate and on the consumer's evolving balance. Total penalty charges depend both on the late fee and on the frequency of late payment. The important role of information has been recognised both in the economic analysis of consumer markets and in consumer protection law. To a large degree, however, both the law and the economics of consumer markets have focused on information about product attributes. This chapter emphasises the importance of product use information or lack thereof in explaining market behaviour and in effectively regulating consumer markets.

The relevance of consumer mistakes — descriptively, normatively and prescriptively — depends on the robustness and persistence of these mistakes in a market setting. A naive view would dismiss mistakes based on imperfect use information as short-lived or even non-existent. Product use depends on consumer wants and needs, and consumers are supposed to know their own wants and needs. The ideal *homo oeconomicus* consumer has perfect information about his preferences. But his real-world counterpart does not. Moreover, product use depends on external influences as well as on internal preferences. Accordingly, even the ideal, perfectly rational consumer might suffer from imperfect use information.

After describing the two main subjects of consumer mistakes — product attributes and product use — we proceed, in Part 3, to consider regulatory responses to such market failure. In particular, we consider disclosure regulation.

[1] Product attributes affect product use. How a consumer uses a product depends on the product's functionality and on the product's price — both product attributes.

We focus on disclosure regulation for several reasons. First, disclosure is the most benign form of intervention, facilitating, rather than inhibiting, the operation of markets.[2] Second, and related, disclosure mandates have proven to be the most politically feasible, often the *only* politically feasible form of regulation in many contexts.[3] Finally, this chapter studies the problem of consumer mistakes. Since mistakes can often be traced back to lack of information, disclosure of information is the natural starting point for solving the mistake problem. This does not mean that disclosure is a perfect fix in all mistake cases. Nor does it mean that disclosure is always superior to other forms of regulation or to no regulation at all. The costs and limits of information disclosure are well known. Our goal is not to idealise disclosure. Rather, recognising the prevalence of disclosure regulation, our goal is to help regulators design more effective disclosure mandates. We argue that disclosure requirements should match the type of information deficit that caused the market failure. When market failure is caused by mistakes about product attributes, the solution is disclosure of product attributes. And when market failure is caused by mistakes about product use, the solution is disclosure of use patterns.

A brief survey of existing disclosure requirements demonstrates the prevalence of disclosure mandates focused on product attributes. Use-pattern disclosure requirements are more limited and less effective. Consumers receive information on the proper use of products. For example, the Federal Trade Commission (FTC) in the United States, as well as parallel agencies in several European states, require clothes manufacturers to provide information on how to properly clean the clothes.[4] Consumers also receive indirect use information when product attribute information is based — explicitly or implicitly — on some assumption about average or typical use. For example, a cigarette's tar and nicotine ratings, which are certified by the FTC, assume a certain intensity of smoking — a 2-second, 35-millilitre puff every minute.[5] We argue for enhanced use-pattern disclosure. In particular, we argue for direct disclosure of average use-pattern information. For example, credit card issuers can be required to disclose the average likelihood of paying late (and triggering a penalty fee) or, even better, the amount that an average consumer pays in late fees each year. More importantly, we argue that in certain markets sellers should be required to provide individual-use information. Elaborating on the previous example, credit card issuers can be

[2] See C Camerer *et al*, 'Regulation for Conservatives: Behavioral Economics and the Case for "Asymmetric Paternalism"' (2003) 151 *University of Pennsylvania Law Review* 1211); CR Sunstein and RH Thaler, 'Libertarian Paternalism Is Not an Oxymoron' (2003) 70 *University of Chicago Law Review* 1159.

[3] See, eg O Bar-Gill, 'Seduction by Plastic' (2004) 98 *Northwestern University Law Review* 1373) 1374, fn 3 (describing the failed attempts to enact usury ceilings for credit cards and the resort to disclosure regulation); RJ Mann, *Charging Ahead: The Growth and Regulation of Payment Card Markets*, (2006) 159 (describing disclosure mandates as 'a common compromise solution in the American regulatory regime').

[4] See below Section 3.1. However, there is no such regulation at the European level. Ibid.

[5] See below Section 3.2.

required to tell each consumer how much he or she paid in late fees over the past year. This prescription is feasible and desirable in markets, such as the credit card market, where sellers maintain long-term relationships with their customers and thus voluntarily collect individual-use information.

The call for enhanced use-pattern disclosure, and specifically the emphasis on individual-use disclosure, challenges the conventional wisdom about information and disclosure in consumer markets. This conventional wisdom recognises that sellers often have superior product attribute information and that it may be desirable to require them to disclose this information to consumers. On the other hand, the conventional wisdom largely overlooks the welfare-enhancing potential of use-pattern disclosure, because it assumes that consumers, not sellers, have superior use-pattern information. We argue that this assumption, while clearly true in some markets, is false in others. In important consumer markets, sellers know more about the consumers' use patterns than the consumers themselves. In these markets, use-pattern disclosure may well be desirable.[6]

Finally, disclosure mandates can be more important when the subject of the mandate is use-pattern information. Sellers have strong incentives to voluntarily disclose product attribute information. By disclosing this seller-specific information, high-quality sellers can convince consumers to buy from them, rather than from a low-quality competitor. (And since only low-quality sellers remain silent, consumers will be able to easily identify the low-quality sellers.) Voluntary disclosure of use-pattern information is less likely. Since the information is consumer-specific, not seller-specific, if one seller discloses the use-pattern information, the now-informed consumer may well purchase the product from a different seller. When voluntary disclosure is less reliable, the case for disclosure mandates becomes stronger.

We focus on mandatory disclosure as the prototypical autonomy-enhancing, minimally paternalistic regulatory technique. But our analysis also questions whether disclosure mandates are as benign as they are believed to be. First, the notion of informing consumers about themselves smacks of paternalism. Second, and more important, our analysis highlights the complex set of regulatory design choices that result in a mandatory disclosure rule. Since imperfectly rational consumers cannot process endless amounts of information, optimal disclosure rules must carefully pick what information is disclosed and what information remains undisclosed (or what information is emphasised and what information is de-emphasised). In effect, the regulator must decide what information is more important for consumers and what information is less important for consumers. Even with disclosure, some measure of paternalism cannot be avoided.

[6] While the conventional wisdom, and the regulatory landscape that is based on it, focus on product attribute disclosure, there are important examples of use-pattern disclosures, including direct average-use disclosures and individual-use disclosures, both in existing law and in law reform proposals. See below Part 3. These examples, however, serve as the exception that proves the rule.

2. THE OBJECT OF CONSUMER MISTAKES: TWO CATEGORIES

This chapter is about mistakes, specifically, consumer mistakes affecting product choice and product use. A mistake can be the result of imperfect information or imperfect rationality. Why do consumers have only imperfect information? Why and in what way do consumers deviate from the perfect rationality ideal? These are all important questions — important questions that are largely sidestepped in this chapter. Rather, our goal is to conceptualise and categorise mistakes, in Part 2, and to study regulatory responses to mistakes, in Part 3.

2.1. Two Categories of Consumer Mistakes

Informed choice assumes two distinct categories of information: information about product attributes and information about how the product will be used. One way to view the distinction between product-attributes information and product use information is by tracing the source of the information. Product attribute information, like the product itself, is created by the manufacturer. The manufacturer is the source of the information. Product use is a function of both the product's attributes and the consumer's wants and needs. Product-use information has two sources — the manufacturer and the consumer. A different categorisation would focus on these two sources and distinguish between manufacturer (or seller) information and consumer information. Consumer information, ie information on consumer wants and needs, can be further divided into two categories or sources of information: an internal source, consisting of consumer preferences, and an external source, consisting of the sum of external forces that affect the benefit to the consumer from using the product.

Consumer protection law is concerned with imperfect information on the part of consumers. Traditional consumer protection analysis and policy focus on lack of information about product attributes.[7] This emphasis on product attribute information can be traced back to the rational choice foundations of traditional consumer protection analysis. Rational choice theory assumes that individuals have perfect information about their own preferences. To the extent that use is determined by consumer preferences, the rational choice model assumes perfect information about use patterns. Unfortunately, few consumers are perfectly rational. And imperfectly rational consumers might have imperfect information concerning their own preferences.[8] Moreover, as explained above, how a consumer

[7] See below Part 3.

[8] We are assuming that consumers have fixed preferences, but might be imperfectly aware of these preferences at the time when they decide whether to buy a certain product or which type of product to buy. Our departure from the neoclassical model is thus limited. A more substantial departure would recognise that some preferences are not fixed, but rather constructed, and that information, including information provided by sellers, affects the construction of preferences. Relaxing the fixed-preferences assumption raises important descriptive and normative questions; questions which we do not address in this chapter.

will use a product depends on external influences as well as on internal preferences. Even a perfectly rational consumer may have only imperfect information about these external influences.

Consider a lawnmower. The value of a lawnmower to a consumer depends on attributes of the lawnmower and on how frequently the consumer will want or need to mow his or her lawn. How often the lawnmower will be used depends, in turn, on attributes of the lawnmower, on consumer preferences and on external factors influencing the consumer's need to mow the lawn. The attributes of the lawnmower matter, for example, because, a better lawnmower is less burdensome to operate and thus will be used more often. Consumer preferences matter, because a consumer who cares more about his or her lawn will use the lawnmower more often. And external forces, like rainfall and soil condition, matter, because they affect the speed with which grass grows. To make a fully-informed decision whether to purchase a lawnmower and which lawnmower to purchase the consumer must have information on all of these factors. Yet consumer protection law, with its focus on product attribute information, pays insufficient attention to other factors affecting product use.

Or consider a credit card. Focusing on the financing component of the credit card product, the value of a credit card depends on product attributes, specifically the interest rate. The value of the product also depends on how it will be used — on how much the consumer will borrow. The extent of borrowing, in turn, depends on: (1) product attributes such as the interest rate; (2) the consumer's intertemporal consumption preferences; and (3) external forces affecting the consumer's desire to borrow or need to borrow, such as present and expected available income and conditions affecting the demand for funds, eg illness or divorce. Policy-makers have been concerned about mistakes in the credit card market. Their response, however, has largely been targeted at product attribute information. The Truth in Lending Act, for example, mandates conspicuous disclosure of credit card interest rates. Use-pattern mistakes that are not caused by imperfect information about interest rates have received less attention.[9]

2.2. The Persistence of Use-Pattern Mistakes

Many consumer mistakes are short-lived. Consumers quickly learn to avoid these mistakes and market forces work to eliminate them. Accordingly, consumer mistakes are important, descriptively and normatively, only if they can withstand these mistake-correction forces. The persistence of any mistake, including use-pattern mistakes, is an empirical question.[10] A market-specific inquiry is necessary to

[9] See below Part 3.

[10] See A Tversky and D Kahneman, 'Rational Choice and the Framing of Decisions' in RM Hogarth and MW Reder (eds), *Rational Choice: the Contrast Between Economics and Psychology,*

determine whether the specific market is afflicted by a mistake-driven market failure. But before we turn to empirics, we offer several observations on the theoretical possibility of persistent use-pattern mistakes. We argue that learning, an important mistake-correction force, might be weaker in the use-pattern context. We then argue that another mistake-correction force, education efforts by sellers, might also be less effective in curing use-pattern mistakes.

2.2.1. Learning by Consumers

Use-pattern mistakes are based on misperception about product attributes as well as about the consumer's own wants and needs. Learning about internal factors influencing a consumer's wants and needs — about preferences — should be easy and quick. Learning about external factors, namely product attributes and external forces influencing the consumer's wants and needs, can be more or less effective depending on context.[11] But there are general forces working against learning of use-pattern information. Learning can be both intrapersonal and interpersonal. In many markets, interpersonal learning is an important safeguard against persistent consumer mistakes. And interpersonal learning is less effective in curing use-pattern mistakes.[12]

Interpersonal learning is quick and effective when the object of learning is a standardised product.[13] But not all products are standardised. And when the product is not standardised interpersonal learning becomes slower. With a standardised good, when a consumer discovers, through use, a certain hidden feature of the product, he or she can share this information with family and friends. Since the information pertains to a standardised good it is relevant to others. But if the good is not a standardised good such interpersonal learning will be less effective. With a non-standardised good the information obtained by one

(1987) 91 ('The claim that the market can be trusted to correct the effect of individual irrationalities cannot be made without supporting evidence.').

[11] Learning from one's mistakes relies on timely, clear and painful feedback that the decision was in fact a mistake. See C Camerer, 'Comments on "Some Implications of Cognitive Psychology for Risk Regulation", by R. Noll and J. Krier' (1990) 19 *Journal of Legal Studies* 791,794 (learning occurs when the outcome is prompt and unambiguous); R Korobkin, 'Bounded Rationality, Standard Form Contracts, and Unconscionability' (2003) 70 *University of Chicago Law Review* (citing references). An impediment to learning is that people attribute good outcomes to skill and bad outcomes to (bad) luck. See J Arlen, 'Comment: The Future of Behavioral Economic Analysis of Law' (1998) 52 *Vanderbilt Law Review* 1765 at 1783 (citing M Bazerman, *Judgment in Managerial Decision Making* (1998)). On the limits of learning, see generally Tversky and Kahneman, above n 10, at 90–91; H Latin, '"Good" Warnings, Bad Products, and Cognitive Limitations' (1994) 41 1193 *University of California at Los Angeles Law Review* 1252–55. Generally, infrequent mistakes or mistakes that generate infrequent feedback are less susceptible to correction by learning.

[12] Learning — both intrapersonal learning and interpersonal learning — can occur within markets and across markets. Some use-pattern mistakes transcend market boundaries and are more amenable to cross-market learning than product attribute mistakes.

[13] See eg RA Epstein'Behavioral Economics: Human Error and Market Corrections' (2006) 73 *University of Chicago Law Review* 111, 120 (arguing that mistakes with respect to the value of a standardised product are unlikely to persist in the marketplace).

consumer might not be relevant to another consumer who purchased a different version of the non-standard good.[14]

When the nature of the product is more broadly defined to include the potential uses of the product, then the group of standardised products shrinks. In particular, even an otherwise standardised product is non-standardised with respect to use patterns, when different consumers use the product in different ways. And this can inhibit learning of use-pattern information. After using a product for some time, a consumer will obtain valuable use-pattern information. But this information, while valuable to this specific consumer, may be of little value to another consumer who will use the same product differently.[15]

An important factor that facilitates learning is seller reputation. Seller reputation is commonly based on the quality of the seller's product, not on how consumers use the product. Accordingly, reputation, as facilitator of consumer learning, plays a smaller role in the learning of use-pattern information. Another form of learning is based on expert advice. Consumers, recognising their imperfect rationality and the imperfect information at their disposal, take steps to limit the mistakes that they make. In particular, consumers seek advice and consult experts before entering the market.[16] This indirect form of learning is also less effective when product use information is concerned. Experts and other advice-providers can assist the consumer by providing information about typical uses of the product, but they generally do not have information about an individual consumer's expected use patterns.

2.2.2. Correction by Sellers

In addition to learning by consumers, sellers may invest in correcting consumer misperceptions.[17] Consider the following, arguably common, scenario. Seller A offers a product that is better and costs more to produce than the product offered by seller B Consumers, however, underestimate the added value from seller A's product and thus refuse to pay the higher price that seller A charges. In this scenario, seller A has a powerful incentive to educate consumers about its

[14] See O Bar-Gill, 'The Behavioral Economics of Consumer Contracts' (2008) 92 *Minnesota Law Review* 749.

[15] This is not to say that meaningful information cannot be conveyed, eg one consumer can indicate to another: 'This is a good printer if you don't print more than 100 pages a month, otherwise it is expensive.' This information is useful to consumers with different use patterns. Interpersonal learning about use-pattern information is plausible if the 'teacher' conveys generic information that the 'learner' can adapt to his or her own circumstances.

[16] See eg RA Epstein'Second-Order Rationality' in EJ McCaffery and J Slemrod (eds), *Behavioral Public Finance*, (2006) 355 at 361–62.

[17] See, eg Epstein, above n 13, at 120. The line between consumer learning and seller advertising is not always clear. Sellers can and do influence information transmission between consumers (word-of-mouth). See DB Godes and D Mayzlin, 'Firm-Created Word-of-Mouth Communication: A Field-Based Quasi-Experiment' (2004) Harvard Business School Marketing Research Paper No 04–03.

product — to correct their underestimation of the product's value. Underestimation of value is often the product of a use-pattern mistake. For example, consumers who underestimate the intensity with which they will use a product will underestimate the value of a higher-quality, more resilient product. Accordingly, seller A will want to correct consumers' use-pattern mistake.

But what if both seller A and seller B and many other sellers offer identical low-quality products? If seller A increases the quality of its product and invests in correcting the use-pattern mistake that led consumers to undervalue high-quality products, then seller A will attract a lot of business and make a supra-competitive profit. But this is not an equilibrium. After seller A invests in consumer education, all the other sellers will free ride on seller A's efforts. They will similarly increase quality and compete away any profit that seller A would have made. Anticipating such a response, seller A will realise that, if it invests in consumer education, it will not be able to recoup its investment. It will thus choose not to increase the quality of its product, and instead will continue to offer a low-quality product. This collective action problem can lead to the persistence of consumer misperception.[18]

Even apart from this collective action problem, sellers might prefer not to correct consumer mistakes and might even invest in creating misperception. Arguably, manipulation of consumer perceptions, and even preferences, is a main purpose of advertising.[19] For example, to increase demand for their product, sellers will often try to persuade consumers that they will use a product more than they actually will. Therefore, while competing sellers may often choose to educate consumers, this mistake-correction force is limited.

[18] See H Beales, R Craswell and S Salop, 'The Efficient Regulation of Consumer Information' (1981) 24 *Journal of Law and Economics* 491, 527 (explaining why sellers might not disclose both positive and negative information). See also RT Cruz and JJ Hinck, 'Not My Brother's Keeper: The Inability of the Informed Minority to Correct for Imperfect Information' (1996) 47 *Hastings Law Journal* 635, 659. In some markets, the first-mover advantage will be large enough to overcome the collective action problem. Branding and product differentiation can also reduce the collective action problem. See Epstein, above n 13, at 120. But see Bar-Gill, above n 14, at § I.B. (identifying the limits of Epstein's branding and differentiation argument). In this sense, monopoly power, including limited monopoly power conferred by patent or trademark, by geographic proximity and so forth, can facilitate mistake correction by reducing the collective action problem. See Beales, Craswell and Salop, see above, at 503–509, for a general discussion of information failures in consumer markets. On the limits of advertising as a mistake-correction mechanism, see also X Gabaix and D Laibson, 'Shrouded Attributes, Consumer Myopia, and Information Suppression in Competitive Markets' (2006) 121 *Quarterly Journal of Economics* 505; Korobkin, above n 11, at 1242–43).

[19] See EL Glaeser, 'Psychology and the Market' (2004) 94 *American Economic Review Papers and Proceedings* 408 at 409–411 ('Markets do not eliminate (and often exacerbate) irrationality.... The advertising industry is the most important economic example of these systematic attempts to mislead, where suppliers attempt to convince buyers that their products will yield remarkable benefits.... It is certainly not true that competition ensures that false beliefs will be dissipated. Indeed in many cases competition will work to increase the supply of these falsehoods.'). Glaeser argues, however, that government decision-makers have weaker incentives than consumers to overcome errors, and thus intervention in markets might make things worse. ibid See also EL Glaeser, 'Paternalism and Psychology' (2006) 73 *University of Chicago Law Review* 133.

Moreover, use-pattern mistakes are less susceptible to correction as compared with product attribute mistakes. Sellers have a powerful incentive to correct product attribute mistakes, and specifically to undo any underestimation of product quality, because these product attribute mistakes hurt the seller's reputation and thus adversely affect not only the demand for this one product but also the demand for the seller's other products. Since use-pattern mistakes do not have a similar effect on the seller's reputation, the incentive to correct such mistakes is weaker.

Finally, and most importantly, while sellers have powerful incentives to voluntarily disclose product attribute information, they do not have similar incentives to disclose product use information. First, consider the case of product attribute information. Rational but uninformed consumers, facing different sellers offering products of varying quality, would be willing to pay for only average quality. A seller with an above-average product would thus have a strong incentive to disclose the quality of its product (product attribute information). But this is not the end of the story. Since all above-average sellers disclose the quality of their products, consumers would know that any seller who remains silent is in the bottom half of the quality distribution. Consumers who face a silent seller would thus be willing to pay for only average quality *in the bottom half of the quality distribution.* A bottom-half seller whose product exceeds the average quality in the bottom half of the quality distribution would thus have a strong incentive to disclose the quality of its product. Now consumers would know that any seller who remains silent is in the bottom quarter of the quality distribution. This dynamic of disclosure and inference continues until all sellers, except for the lowest quality seller, disclose the quality of their products.[20]

Such voluntary disclosure is less likely with respect to product use information. Product-attribute information is seller-specific. Sellers disclose this information to attract buyers, by demonstrating that their product is superior to what their competitors are offering. Product-use information, on the other hand, is consumer-specific, at least in part. If a seller discloses product use information, there is no guarantee that the consumer will purchase the product from the disclosing seller. As long as the disclosed use patterns are common to the entire product category, ie they are not seller-specific, the now-informed consumer may just as well purchase the product from a non-disclosing seller. Accordingly, sellers have little reason to voluntarily disclose use-pattern information. The standard argument for voluntary disclosure of product attribute information does not extend to product use information.[21]

[20] See SJ Grossman and OD Hart, 'Disclosure Laws and Takeover Bids' (1980) 35 *Journal of Finance* 323.

[21] See O Bar-Gill and O Board, 'Product Use Information and the Limits of Voluntary Disclosure' *American Law and Economics Review* (forthcoming).

3. DISCLOSURE REGULATION

Consumer mistakes are costly. Sellers' response to these mistakes often increases their cost. An identification of a market failure, here a behavioural market failure, opens the door to the possibility of welfare-enhancing legal intervention. In many markets the primary form of regulation is disclosure mandates. Disclosure is preferred because it does not constrain market forces. Instead it facilitates the efficient operation of markets.[22] Disclosure mandates are perhaps the most widely used tool for regulating consumer products and contracts. Disclosure regulations are promulgated at both the federal and state levels. And disclosure requirements are based on both statutory law and common law.

Product attribute information features prominently in the vast landscape of disclosure regulation. A comprehensive survey of product attribute disclosure mandates is beyond the scope of this chapter. Yet even a few examples demonstrate the range of product attribute information that is subject to disclosure mandates. Starting with price information, the Truth in Lending Act (TILA) requires disclosure of interest rates and fees by lenders,[23] and the same is true under EU law.[24] TILA also mandates transparent disclosure of different price components as well as total price in consumer lease contracts.[25] Parallel legislation, the Truth in Savings Act, requires depository institutions to disclose fees and other terms concerning deposit accounts.[26] And regulations promulgated by the Securities and Exchange Commission require disclosure of mutual fund fees,[27] as does a very recent Proposal for a Directive of the European Parliament and of the Council on Alternative Investment Fund Managers.[28] Mandated disclosure of price information is not limited to financial services. For example, the Real Estate Settlement Procedures Act requires disclosure of closing costs in real estate transactions.[29] And the FTC requires various price disclosures in its Funeral Industry Practices Rule.[30]

Moving on to product quality information, FTC trade regulations require gasoline stations to post octane ratings of gasoline,[31] sellers of insulation to disclose the

[22] Yet disclosure is not without cost. See below Section 3.6.

[23] 15 United States Code [hereinafter USC] § 1601 *et seq*; 12 Code of Federal Regulations [hereinafter CFR] § 226.

[24] See Art 5(1)(l) of EP and Council Directive 2008/48/EC, OJ L 133/66.

[25] 12 CFR § 213. See also Press Release, Federal Reserve, available at: //www.federalreserve.gov/boarddocs/press/boardacts/1996/19960927/default.htm (last visited 27 September 1996).

[26] 12 USC § 4301 *et seq*; 12 CFR § 230 (2000).

[27] Shareholder Reports and Quarterly Portfolio Disclosure of Registered Management Investment Companies, Exchange Act Release, 33–8393, 34–49 333, IC-26372, File No. S7–51–02, 17 CFR §§ 210, 239, 249, 270 and 274; RIN 3235-AG64, 2004 SEC LEXIS 474.

[28] See Art 20(1)(h) of the EP and Council Proposal for a Directive of 30 April 2009, COM (2009) 207 final.

[29] 12 USC §§ 2601–2617; HUD, RESPA, available at: www.hud.gov/offices/hsg/sfh/res/respa_hm.cfm (last visited 8 August 2007).

[30] 16 CFR § 453 (especially § 453.2). See also Federal Trade Commission, *Facts for Business: Complying with the Funeral Rule*, (2004) available at: www.ftc.gov/bcp/edu/pubs/business/adv/bus05.shtm.

[31] 16 CFR § 306.10.

effectiveness of the insulation,[32] sellers of home amplifiers to disclose the power output of the amplifier,[33] and the list goes on.[34] The Nutrition Labeling and Education Act, enforced by the Food and Drug Administration (FDA), directs that food labels list information concerning 12 of the most important nutrients.[35] The FDA also regulates drug labelling.[36] For example, labels of non-prescription, over-the-counter (OTC) drugs must provide information on active ingredients and on the purposes and uses of the drug.[37] The Motor Vehicle Information and Cost Savings Act, enforced by the National Highway Traffic Safety Administration, requires car dealers to disclose information about a vehicle's damage susceptibility, crashworthiness and ease of diagnosis and repair.[38] And the courts, enforcing contract law doctrine, require disclosure of material facts about any contractual transaction.[39] Contract law also provides incentives for disclosure of contract terms,[40] which, given the collapse of the product-contract distinction,[41] are also considered quality information.[42]

[32] ibid, at §§ 460.13–460.14.

[33] ibid, § 432.

[34] For an exhaustive list of the disclosure rules that the FTC enforces, see PC Ward, *Federal Trade Commission: Law, Practice and Procedure* (2006). The FTC is also engaged in negative disclosure regulation, working to prevent disclosure of false or misleading information. The FTC has general authority to police unfair or deceptive acts or practices. See Federal Trade Commission Act, 15 USC §§ 41–58. It also has authority under specific statutes such as the Nutrition Labeling and Education Act, which regulates health claims on food labels and in food product advertising. 21 USC § 301; 21 CFR § 101. See also: <http://www.cfsan.fda.gov/label.html> (last visited 12 March 2010). The FTC regulates food advertising, while the FDA is responsible for food labelling. See Working Agreement Between the FTC and FDA, 3 *Trade Reg Rep (CCH)* 9851 (1971).

[35] 21 USC § 301; 21 CFR § 101. See also: www.cfsan.fda.gov/label.html.

[36] 21 USC § 352 (n); 21 CFR § 201 (prescription drugs); 21 CFR § 201.66 (non-prescription drugs). The FDA supervises labelling of both prescription and non-prescription drugs. With respect to advertising, the FDA has the authority to supervise advertising for prescription drugs, while the FTC supervises non-prescription drug marketing. See Memorandum of Understanding Between Federal Trade Commission and the Food and Drug Administration, 36 *Fed Reg* 18539 (16 September 1971).

[37] 21 CFR § 201.66. See also FDA, OTC Drug Facts Label available at: http://www.fda.gov/Drugs/ResourcesForYou/Consumers/ucm143551.htm last visited: 11 March 2011.

[38] 15 USC §§ 1901–12.

[39] See Restatement (Second) of Contracts § 161b (1981) (unilateral mistake doctrine). See also R Craswell, 'Taking Information Seriously: Misrepresentation and Nondisclosure in Contract Law and Elsewhere' (2006) 92 *Virginia Law Review* 565, 575 (discussing the duty to disclose product attributes and contract terms); MA Eisenberg, 'Disclosure in Contract Law' (2003) 91 *California Law Review* 1645.

[40] In particular, unconscionability doctrine provides an indirect incentive for sellers to inform consumers about contract terms. See Beales, Craswell and Salop, above n 18, at 493–94. See also Craswell, above n 39, at 575 (discussing the duty to disclosure product attributes and contract terms.); Eisenberg, above n 39. In insurance law, the 'reasonable expectations' doctrine provides insurers with an incentive to disclose policy terms to consumers. See, eg RE Keeton, 'Insurance Law Rights at Variance with Policy Provisions' (1970) 83 *Harvard Law Review* 961 at 968; D Schwarcz, 'A Products Liability Theory for the Judicial Regulation of Insurance Policies' (2007) 48 *William and Mary Law Review* 1389, 1395.

[41] See AA Leff, 'Contract as Thing' (1970) 19 *American University Law Review* 131 144–51 and 155; LA Kornhauser, 'Unconscionability in Standard Forms' (1976) 64 *Commonwealth Law Reports* 1151; DG Baird, 'The Boilerplate Puzzle' (2006) 104 *Michigan Law Review* 933.

[42] See also Magnuson-Moss Consumer Warranty Act, 15 USC §§ 2301–12 (requiring a seller or manufacturer who provides a written express warranty to properly disclose warranty or service

In Europe, too, disclosure of product quality information is required in many contexts. For example, pursuant to EU law, food labels must provide product quality information to consumers,[43] including mandatory front-of-pack nutrition information.[44] EU law also regulates drug labelling, requiring, for instance, that the packaging contain a statement of the active substances expressed qualitatively and quantitatively per dosage unit or according to the form of administration for a given volume or weight.[45] Also, as in the United States, disclosure of material facts relating to certain transactions is required in Europe, too.[46] In effect, this duty to disclose constitutes a core principle[47] of European contract law, as recently acknowledged by the drafters of the 2009 Draft Common Frame of Reference, which states that

> [b]efore the conclusion of a contract for the supply of goods, other assets or services by a business to another person, the business has a duty to disclose to the other person such information concerning the goods, other assets or services to be supplied as the

contract terms). In addition, both federal and state law facilitates the meaningful disclosure of certain contract terms, especially warranty and liability-related terms, by requiring that they be conspicuously disclosed. See, eg 15 USC § 2303 (consumer product warranties must be labelled conspicuously); Uniform Commercial Code § 2–316(2) (any disclaimer of the implied warranty of merchantability must be conspicuously disclosed); New York Personal Property Law § 335.1 (liability of an automobile lessee for the total loss of a vehicle must be conspicuously disclosed). See also J Sovern, 'Toward a New Model of Consumer Protection' (2006) 47 *William and Mary Law Review* 1635, 1688.

[43] See most recently the EP and Council Proposal for a Regulation of 30 January 2008, COM (2008) 40 final; see also EP and Council Directive 2000/13/EC, OJ 2000 L 109/29 (Corrigendum to Directive 2000/13/EC, OJ 2000 L 124/66) as amended by EP and Council Directive 2003/89/EC, OJ 2003 L 308/15, and Commission Directive 2001/101/EC, OJ 2001 L 310/19, and Council Directive 2006/107/EC, OJ 2006 L 363/411, and Commission Directive 2006/142/EC, OJ 206 L 368/110, and Commission Directive 2007/68/EC, OJ 2007 L 310/11, and EP and Council Regulation (EC) No 1332/2008, OJ 2008 L 354/7; Commission Directive 87/250/EEC, OJ 1987 L 113/57; Council Directive of 14 June 1989, OJ 1989 L 186/21, as amended by Council Directive 91/238/EEC, OJ 1991 L 107/50, and Council Directive 92/11/EEC, OJ 1992 L 65/32; Commission Directive 94/54/EC, OJ 1994 L 300/14, as amended by Council Directive 96/21/EC, OJ 1996 L 88/5; EP and Council Regulation (EC) No 1829/2003, OJ, 2003 L 268/1, as amended by Commission Regulation (EC) No 1981/2006, OJ 2006 L 368/99, and EP and Council Regulation (EC) No 298/2008, OJ 2008 L 97/64; EP and Council Regulation (EC) No 1830/2003, OJ, 2003 L 311/1.

[44] Apart from some of the provisions contained in the statutory material referred to in the previous note, see Council Directive 90/496/EEC, OJ 1990 L 276/40, as amended by EP and Council Regulation (EC) No 1882/2003, OJ 2003L 284/1, and by the Commission Directive 2003/120/EC, OJ 2003 L 333/51, and Commission Directive 2008/100/EC, OJ 2008 L 285/9 (making nutrition labelling mandatory where a nutrition claim appears on labelling, in presentation or in advertising, with the exclusion of generic advertising).

[45] See eg EP and Council Directive 2001/83/EC, OJ 2001L 311/67.

[46] See eg Council Directive 85/577/EEC, OJ 1985 L 372/31; Council Directive 90/314/EEC, OJ 1990 L 158/59; EP and Council Directive 94/47/EC, OJ 1994 L 280/83 (recently amended by EP and Council Directive 2008/122/EC, OJ 2009 L 33/10, which set forth information duties as well); EP and Council Directive 97/7/EC, OJ 1997 L 144/19, as amended by EP and Council Directive 2002/65/EC, OJ 2002 L 271/16, and EP and Council Directive 2005/29/EC, OJ 2005 L 149/22, and EP and Council Directive 2007/64/EC, OJ 2007 L 319/1; EP and Council Directive 98/6/EC, OJ 1998 L 80/27; EP and Council Directive 2008/48/EC, OJ 2008 L 133/66.

[47] See eg P Giliker'Regulating Contracting Behaviour: The Duty to Disclose in English and French Law' (2005) *European Review of Private Law* 621, 622623.

other person can reasonably expect, taking into account the standards of quality and performance which would be normal under the circumstances.[48]

Finally, as with US law, European law also provides incentives for disclosure of contract terms.[49]

The quality dimension that is most often subject to disclosure regulation is product risk. The Federal Hazardous Substances Act requires that certain hazardous household products bear cautionary labelling to alert consumers to the potential hazards that those products present.[50] FDA regulations require that OTC drug labels include warnings about possible side-effects and other risks associated with the use of the drug.[51] Under regulations promulgated by the Environmental Protection Agency (EPA) and the Department of Housing and Urban Development (HUD), sellers, landlords and agents must disclose the use of lead-based paint on the property and provide purchasers and tenants with an EPA-approved lead hazard information pamphlet.[52] And tort law, through its 'duty to warn', provides strong incentives for the disclosure of product risk information. In particular, the failure to provide a reasonable warning about a product risk is considered a product defect that might trigger tort liability.[53]

[48] Draft Common Frame of Reference, Chapter II. -3:101(1) (2009). See also EP and Council Proposal for a Directive of 8 October 2008, COM (2008) 614 final (Chapters II and III).

[49] See, eg Council Directive 85/577/EEC, OJ L 372/31; EP and Council Directive 1999/44/EC, OJ L 171/12; Directive 2008/48/EC, OJ 2008 L 133/66; EP and Council Proposal for a Directive of 8 October 2008, COM (2008) 614 final.

[50] 15 USC §§ 1261–1278; 16 CFR §§ 1500–1512. See also US Consumer Products Safety Commission, 'Federal Hazardous Substances Act' available at: www.cpsc.gov/businfo/fhsa.html last visited: 12 March 2010. Among the disclosures that such labels must include are: the name and business address of the manufacturer, packer, distributor or seller; the common or usual or chemical name of each hazardous ingredient; the signal word 'Danger' for products that are corrosive, extremely flammable or highly toxic; the signal word 'Caution' or 'Warning' for all other hazardous products; an affirmative statement of the principal hazard or hazards that the product presents, for example, 'Flammable', 'Harmful if Swallowed', 'Causes Burns', 'Vapor Harmful', etc.; the word 'Poison' for a product that is highly toxic, in addition to the signal word 'Danger'. See Office of Compliance, Consumer Product Safety Commission, *Requirements Under the Federal Hazardous Substances Act: Labeling and Banning Requirements for Chemicals and Other Hazardous Substances*, (2002) 3 available at: www.cpsc.gov/businfo/regsumfhsa.pdf.

[51] 21 CFR § 201.66 (c) (warnings for non-prescription drugs, including side-effects).

[52] See Residential Lead-Based Paint Hazard Reduction Act of 1992, 42 USC §§ 2681–92, 4851–56; Requirements for Disclosure of Known Lead-Based Paint and/or Lead-Based Paint Hazards in Housing, 24 CFR § 35, 40 CFR § 745. See also Toxic Substances Control Act, 15 USC § 2686.

[53] See Restatement (Third) of Torts: Product Liability § 2 (1998); W Page Keeton *et al*, *Prosser and Keeton on the Law of Torts* (1988) at 96; Craswell, above n 39, at 566; JA Henderson, Jr and AD Twerski, 'Doctrinal Collapse in Products Liability: The Empty Shell of Failure to Warn' (1990) 65 *New York University Law Review* 265; [Latin], above n 11; JD Hanson and DA Kysar, 'Taking Behaviorism Seriously: The Problem of Market Manipulation' (1999) 74 *New York University Law Review* 630. Accordingly, the Restatement (Third) of Torts: Products Liability instructs sellers to 'provide reasonable instructions and warnings about risks of injury posed by products'. See Restatement (Third) of Torts: Products Liability § 2, cmt. i (1998). See also *Liriano v Hobart Corp*, 170 *F3d* 264 (1999).

In Europe, one of the most famous examples of required product risk disclosure relates to tobacco products. Pursuant to EU law, the use of warnings (both a general one — 'smoke kills/can kill' — and an additional one that must cover no less than 40 per cent of the external surface of the packet) is compulsory.[54] Of course, many more examples can be given. The packaging of paints or varnishes containing lead in quantities above a certain amount must disclose that the paints and varnishes contain lead.[55] Similarly, the packaging of medicinal products must provide product risk information, such as information regarding the product's effects on the ability to drive and to use machines.[56]

The preceding examples demonstrate the prevalence of product attribute disclosures. Information about product attributes is clearly valuable. It is important to know what APR is charged on a credit card balance. It is important to know that orange juice contains vitamin C. And it is important to know that the paint in an apartment contains lead. With most products, however, the benefit or cost to a consumer from any product attribute depends on how the consumer will use the product. The APR on a credit card is more important for consumers who borrow more. Drinking orange juice is a good source of vitamin C, but only if the juice is consumed soon after the container is first opened. And lead paint is especially dangerous when chewed on by toddlers. Accordingly, if consumers make mistakes not only with regard to product attributes but also with regard to product use, it is important to provide use-pattern information in addition to product attribute information.

While many disclosure mandates focus on product attribute information, product use disclosure is not absent from the current regulatory scheme. Still, current use-pattern disclosures are insufficient — both in quantity and in quality. We begin by surveying existing use-pattern disclosure mandates in Sections 3.1 and 3.2. Existing product use disclosures fall into two categories: (1) proper-use disclosures; and (2) average-use information that is indirectly disclosed as a benchmark for product attribute disclosures. This survey of existing product use disclosures highlights the limits of the current regulatory scheme. We respond to these limits by advocating improved use-pattern disclosure. In Section 3.3, we argue for direct average-use disclosures. And, more importantly, in Section 3.4, we argue for the disclosure of individualised use-pattern information. After arguing that use-pattern information should be disclosed, we turn in Section 3.5 to the regulatory design question: how should use-pattern information be disclosed? Finally, Section 3.6 recalls the main costs and limits of disclosure regulation. The limited efficacy of disclosure and the costs of disclosure regulation caution against a broad expansion of the disclosure landscape. We do not argue for more disclosure. Rather, we argue for a more balanced division of

[54] See EP and Council Directive 2001/37/EC, OJ 2001 L 194/26.
[55] See Commission Directive 2006/8/EC, OJ 2006 L 19/12.
[56] See EP and Council Directive 2001/83/EC, OJ 2001 L 311/67.

disclosure mandates between product attribute information and use-pattern information and for better-designed use-pattern disclosures.[57]

3.1. Proper-Use Information

Use information is provided through disclosures that specify the proper use of a product. The Consumer Products Safety Commission (CPSC) has general authority to promulgate 'requirements that a consumer product be marked with or accompanied by clear and adequate warnings or *instructions*'.[58] The purpose of this provision is to provide information on how to use the product properly. Under this authority, the CPSC has issued regulations requiring the disclosure of proper-use information for numerous products.[59] For example, sellers of bicycle helmets must provide instructions telling riders how to make sure the helmet fits properly and how to wear it properly.[60] Sellers of television antennas must provide instructions on how to avoid the hazard of electrocution during the installation of the antenna.[61] And sellers of bunk beds must provide instructions for safe use, including: 'Do not allow children under 6 years of age to use the upper bunk'; 'Use guardrails on both sides of the upper bunk'; 'Prohibit horseplay on or under beds'; 'Prohibit more than one person on upper bunk'; and 'Use ladder for entering or leaving upper bunk'.[62]

The CPSC-enforced, Federal Hazardous Substances Act provides another example. The Act requires that certain hazardous household products bear cautionary labelling to alert consumers to the potential hazards that those products present and to inform them of the measures they need to take to protect themselves from those hazards.[63] Specifically, such labels must include the following disclosures: precautionary statements telling users what they must do

[57] An important question that we do not address in this chapter is the question of who should be entrusted with designing and enforcing disclosure regulations. One of us begins to address this question in the context of consumer credit products in O Bar-Gill and E Warren, 'Making Credit Safer' (2008) 157 *University of Pennsylvania Law Review* 1 (arguing that regulation of consumer credit markets, including disclosure regulation, should be entrusted to a federal administrative agency). See also A Schwartz and L Wilde, 'Intervening in Markets on the Basis of Imperfect Information: A Legal and Economic Analysis' (1979) 127 *University of Pennsylvania Law Review* 630 678–82 (arguing that administrative agencies are better suited than courts to address the market failure); Craswell, above n 39, at 700 (same); *Ford Motor Credit Co v Mihollin*, 444 US 555, 568–569 (1980).

[58] 15 USC § 2056 (emphasis added).

[59] Beyond the examples provided below, CPSC regulations are listed on the CPSC's website, available at: www.cpsc.gov/cgi-bin/regs.aspx last visited 12 March 2010.

[60] See Office of Compliance, Consumer Product Safety Commission, *Requirements for Bicycle Helmets*, (2002) 4 available at: www.cpsc.gov/businfo/regsumbicyclehelmets.pdf.

[61] 16 CFR § 1402 (§ 1402.1 describes the scope of the regulation; §1402.4 requires the disclosure of a specific warning: 'Warning: Installation of this Product Near Powerlines is Dangerous. For Your Safety, Follow the Installation Directions.').

[62] See CPSR Safety Standard for Bunk Beds, 16 CFR §§ 1213, 1500, 1513See also Office of Compliance, Consumer Product Safety Commission, *Safety Standard for Bunk Beds* (2001) 2 available at: www.cpsc.gov/businfo/regsumbunkbed.pdf.

[63] 15 USC §§ 1261–78; 16 CFR §§ 1500–12. See also CPSC, 'Federal Hazardous Substances Act' available at: www.cpsc.gov/businfo/fhsa.html last visited: 8 August 2007.

or what actions they must avoid to protect themselves; instructions for first aid treatment to perform in the event that the product injures someone; if a product requires special care in handling or storage, instructions for consumers to follow in order to protect themselves; and the statement 'Keep out of the reach of children'.[64]

The FTC, in its trade regulations, also requires disclosure of proper-use information. For example, the FTC requires clothing manufacturers to provide information on proper care.[65] The FDA requires disclosure of proper-use information on drug labels. In particular, drug manufacturers must provide dosage and other proper-use information for non-prescription drugs.[66] Moving on to real estate, the EPA and HUD require sellers, landlords and agents to provide purchasers and tenants with an EPA-approved lead hazard information pamphlet, which contains proper-use information on ways to minimise lead-based paint hazards.[67]

And tort law, through its 'duty to warn', provides strong incentives for the disclosure of proper-use information. As mentioned above, the failure to provide reasonable instructions and warnings is considered a product defect.[68] And on the flip side, adequate warnings often provide an effective shield against liability.[69] The subject of these instructions and warnings is commonly proper-use

[64] See Office of Compliance, Consumer Product Safety Commission, *Requirements Under the Federal Hazardous Substances Act: Labeling and Banning Requirements for Chemicals and Other Hazardous Substances*, (2002) 3 available at: www.cpsc.gov/businfo/regsumfhsa.pdf.

[65] FTC, 'Trade Regulation Rule: Care Labeling of Textile Wearing Apparel', 16 C.F.R. § 423 (1980). See also EP and Council Working document on the proposal for a regulation of 8 April 2009, COM (2009) 31 final (stating that '[t]here is currently no EU-wide legislation on care labeling, i.e. information on washing and ironing conditions'. But noting that '[s]ome Member States have introduced national provisions for compulsory care labelling', and that 'most manufacturers include this kind of information on the label of the textile product on a voluntary basis').

[66] 21 USC § 352 (n); 21 CFR § 201.66 (c). See also Food and Drug Administration, *Drug Interactions: What You Should Know*, (2004) available at: www.fda.gov/Drugs/ResourcesForYou/ucm163354.htm ('The "Directions" section of the [over-the-counter drug] label tells you: the length of time and the amount of the product that you may safely use' and 'any special instructions on how to use the product'). For general information on the regulation of over-the-counter drugs see: www.fda.gov/cder/offices/otc/default.htm last visited: 12 March 2010). Disclosure of dosage and other proper-use information is also required on prescription drug labels. See 21 CFR § 201.5. See also FDA Requirements on Content and Format of Labeling for Human Prescription Drug and Biological Products, 21 CFR §§ 201, 314, 601. But this information is mainly for healthcare professionals, not consumers.

[67] HUD Requirements for Disclosure of Known Lead-Based Paint and/or Lead-Based Paint Hazards upon Sale or Lease of Residential Property, 24 CFR § 35.8; EPA Requirements on Lead-Based Poisoning Prevention in Certain Residential Structures, 40 CFR § 745; EPA, 'Protect Your Family from Lead in Your Home', available at: www.epa.gov/lead/pubs/leadpdfe.pdf last visited 12 March 2010.

[68] See above n 53.

[69] Tort law often exempts manufacturers from liability whenever the harm could be avoided had the consumer followed the warning. See Restatement (Second) of Torts, § 402A, cmt. j (1965) ('Where [adequate] warning is given, the seller may reasonably assume that it will be read and heeded; and a product bearing such a warning, which is safe for use if it is followed, is not in defective condition, nor is it unreasonably dangerous.'); *Ellsworth v Sherne Lingerie, Inc*, 495 A2d 348, 356 (Md 1985), fn 12 ('If a product otherwise unreasonably dangerous can be made safe for reasonably foreseeable uses by adequate warnings or instructions, liability will be avoided, and the focus in such

information.[70] As emphasised by Judge Calabresi in *Liriano v Hobart Corp*,[71] a warning does more than provide information about a product's dangerousness — product attribute information; it also provides information about how the product should be used — product use information.

Proper-use information is also publicised by government agencies. The CPSC's public information disclosures include safety suggestions, ie suggestions on how to use products safely.[72] For example, the CPSC's website includes an Extension Cords Fact Sheet with suggestions on how to avoid risks associated with extension cords.[73] Similarly, the FTC publicises information on the proper use of different products and services, including credit cards and automobiles.[74] The Security and Exchange Commission (SEC) provides information on the proper use of investment products. For example, it emphasises the importance of diversification.[75] And the FDA publicises information on the proper use of food and drug products.[76]

In Europe, as well, many products must be marked with, or accompanied by, clear and adequate instructions. For instance, where skates, roller skates, online

cases is generally on the adequacy of the notice. If the warnings or instructions are adequate the product is not defective, and the plaintiff cannot recover under a theory of strict liability in tort. The cause of the injury in such cases is the failure to read or follow the adequate warnings or instructions, and not a defective product.'). See also Latin, above n 11, at 1258 (describing and criticising Section 402A, Comment J, and other tort doctrines, like proximate cause and the unforeseeable misuse defence, that have been used to exempt manufacturers from liability based on warnings). The Restatement (Third) of Torts: Products Liability takes a less extreme approach but still counts the existence of a warning as a relevant consideration in establishing liability. See Restatement (Third) of Torts: Product Liability § 2, cmt. f (1998) (listing instructions and warranties accompanying the product as a relevant factor 'in determining whether an alternative design is reasonable and whether its omission renders a product not reasonably safe').

[70] See Restatement (Third) of Torts: Product Liability § 2, cmt. i (1998) ('Commercial product sellers must provide reasonable instructions and warnings about risks of injury posed by products. Instructions inform persons how to use and consume products safely.'). In fact, tort law often allows manufacturers to get away with an unsafe product design as long as they provide proper-use warnings, eg the manufacturer of a toy BB-gun with lethal power was able to avoid liability by including a warning that the gun should not be pointed at any person. And the manufacturer of a lawnmower with inadequate protective skirts was able to avoid liability by including a warning that the lawnmower should not be operated when any person (other than the operator) is in its vicinity. See Latin, above n 11, at 1195–1196 (citing *Sherk v Daisy-Heddon*, 450 A2d 615 (Pa 1982) (BB-gun case) and *Dugan v Sears, Roebuck and Co*, 454 *NE2d* 64 (1983) (lawnmower case)).

[71] *Liriano v Hobart Corp.*, 170 *F.3d* 264 270–1 (1999). See also JA Henderson, Jr and AD Twerski, 'Doctrinal Collapse in Products Liability: The Empty Shell of Failure to Warn' (1990) 65 *New York University Law Review* 265 285.

[72] 15 USC §§ 2054–55 (the CPSC can collect and disclose information on product risks).

[73] See CPSC, 'Extension Cords Fact Sheet', CPSC Document No. 16 available at: www.cpsc.gov/cpscpub/pubs/16.html last visited: 13 March 2010 (on extension cords).

[74] See: www.ftc.gov/bcp/consumer.shtm last visited: 13 March 2010.

[75] SEC, 'Beginners' Guide to Asset Allocation, Diversification, and Rebalancing' available at: www.sec.gov/investor/pubs/assetallocation.htm last visited: 13 March 2010.

[76] See eg FDA, 'Produce Safety' available at: http://www.fda.gov/Food/ResourcesForYou/Consumers/ucm114299.htm last visited 11 March 2011. For information on the proper use of drugs/medicine, see FDA, Ensuring Safe Use of Medicine, available at: http://www.fda.gov/Drugs/ResourcesForYou/Consumers/BuyingUsingMedicineSafely/EnsuringSafeUseofMedicine/default.htm last visited: 11 March 2011

skates, skateboards, scooters and toy bicycles for children are offered for sale as toys, they must bear the warning 'Protective equipment should be worn. Not to be used in traffic.'[77] More generally, EU law expressly requires that toys be accompanied by 'instructions ... which ... shall draw the attention of users or their supervisors to the inherent hazards and risks of harm involved in using the toys, and to the ways of avoiding such hazards and risks.'[78] Medicinal products, too, must be accompanied by the necessary and usual instructions for proper use, in particular: the dosage, the method and, if necessary, route of administration, the frequency of administration, specifying if necessary, the appropriate time at which the medicinal product may or must be administered, and, as appropriate, depending on the nature of the product: the duration of treatment, where it should be limited, the action to be taken in the case of an overdose (eg symptoms, emergency procedures), the course of action to take when one or more doses have not been taken, indication, if necessary, of the risk of withdrawal effects.[79]

Disclosure of proper-use information is clearly important. But proper-use information also suffers from an important limitation. Although it is appropriate for use dimensions that have a single, well-defined proper use, not all use dimensions have a single, well-defined proper use. There is one proper way to wash a pair of jeans. There is no single, well-defined way to use a credit card.[80] When proper use is not well defined, and even when it is well defined, sellers can disclose another type of product use information — actual-use information. We next consider statistical actual-use information, ie average-use or typical-use information.

3.2. Product-Attribute Information with Average-Use Benchmarking

Use-pattern information is sometimes provided indirectly through product attribute disclosures. We have argued that product use depends on product attributes.[81] But product attributes can also depend on product use. For example, the fuel efficiency of an automobile depends on technical features of the vehicle and on how the vehicle is driven, eg city driving versus highway driving. A pure product attribute disclosure would include only technical information on the car's engine, weight and so forth. Most consumers will find it difficult to effectively use such a disclosure when choosing among different cars. Alternatively, the law may prefer a more comprehensible 'impure' product attribute disclosure that presumes a certain use pattern. For example, car manufacturers

[77] See EP and Council Directive 2009/48/EC, OJ 2009 L 170/1.

[78] See Art 10(2) of EP and Council Directive 2009/48/EC, OJ 2009 L 170/1.

[79] Art 59(1)(d) of EP and Council Directive 2001/83/EC, OJ 2001 L 311/67.

[80] General statements like 'Do not borrow too much' or 'Use your card prudently' will not be very helpful.

[81] See above Part 2.

can be required to disclose miles-per-gallon information that necessarily presumes specific driving behaviour. Indeed, mandated disclosures sometimes assume, explicitly or implicitly, a certain use pattern and provide information on price, quality or risk based on this use pattern.[82]

Elaborating on the fuel efficiency example, expenditures on gasoline are a major cost of car ownership. As noted above, these expenditures are a function of a vehicle's inherent fuel efficiency and its owner's use patterns. The Environmental Protection Agency (EPA) decided that the best way to communicate gasoline cost information is through miles-per-gallon disclosures. Of course, the same vehicle will drive 10 miles-per-gallon under certain conditions and 20 miles-per-gallon under different conditions. The EPA chose two use patterns, 'city driving' and 'highway driving', and provided miles-per-gallon ratings for these two uses. Obviously, most consumers drive both in the city and on the highway and they divide their driving between these two uses in different proportions. Moreover, there is more than one way to drive in a city and more than one way to drive on the highway. But some benchmark had to be chosen.[83]

Similarly, in the European Union, fuel consumption is generally expressed in either litres per 100 kilometres (l/100 km) or kilometres per litre (km/l).[84] Moreover, EU law expressly recognises the importance of different use patterns. Directive 1999/94/EC of the European Parliament and of the Council of 13 December 1999 relating to the availability of consumer information on fuel economy and CO_2 emissions in respect of the marketing of new passenger cars requires that fuel economy labels for new passenger cars state: 'driving behaviour as well as other non-technical factors play a role in determining a car's fuel consumption'.[85]

The energy efficiency feature of home appliances is similarly disclosed using a typical-use benchmark. A major cost of home appliances is energy cost. The energy cost depends on product attributes, ie on the technical features of the appliance, and on the consumer's use patterns. The Federal Trade Commission (FTC) has constructed an energy efficiency index for appliances based on typical use and requires manufacturers to disclose their product's 'Energy Efficiency Rating'.[86]

[82] To take a banal example, disclosure requirements under the Federal Hazardous Substances Act include the warning: 'Harmful if Swallowed'. See 15 USC § 1261; 16 CFR § 1500; Consumer Product Safety Commission, *Office of Compliance, Labeling and Banning Requirements for Chemicals and Other Hazardous Substances*, (2002) 3 available at: www.cpsc.gov/businfo/regsumfhsa.pdf (US law); EP and Council Regulation (EC) No 1272/2008, OJ 2008 L 353/1 (EU law).

[83] Energy Policy and Conservation Act, 42 USC § 6201. See also Craswell, above n 39, at 581–82 ('the EPA publishes only two indices of automobile gasoline consumption ("city" and "highway" miles-per-gallon ratings), each of which is a rough attempt to reflect the driving habits of millions of different drivers.').

[84] See EP and Council Directive 1999/94/EC, OJ 2000 L 12 16.

[85] ibid, at Annex I(6).

[86] 16 CFR § 305 (Rule Concerning Disclosures Regarding Energy Consumption and Water Use of Certain Home Appliances and Other Products Required under the Energy Policy and Conservation

Nutrition information listed on food labels provides another example. The Nutrition Labeling and Education Act of 1990 requires disclosure, on food product labels, of the quantities of 12 important nutrients.[87] The quantity of a nutrient is pure product attribute information. But the health benefits or risks of a product do not depend only on this quantity measure. Use-pattern information, specifically how much one consumes of this and other food products, is as important as the quantity of nutrients per 100 grams. And food labels do include some indirect information on product use. Specifically, labels provide information on the quantity of nutrients *per serving*. The assumption is that the average consumer consumes one serving (or, alternatively, that the per-serving information will be used by the consumer to calculate total value). Food labels also provide 'percent daily value' information for the included nutrients. Per cent daily value information depends not only on how much one consumes of the particular product but also on the consumer's overall diet. Food product manufacturers must include the statement 'Percent Daily Values are based on a 2,000 calorie diet'. And, in some cases, a more detailed disclosure of daily values based on both a 2000-calorie and a 2500-calorie diet is required.[88]

Required disclosure of the risks associated with cigarette smoking also makes certain assumptions about use patterns. We focus on the US Surgeon General's warnings that appear on cigarette labels and advertisements,[89] although similar warnings are required in Europe.[90] One warning reads: 'Smoking Causes Lung Cancer, Heart Disease, and May Complicate Pregnancy.' Another reads: 'Quitting Smoking Now Greatly Reduces Serious Risks to Your Health.' And a third reads: 'Smoking by Pregnant Women May Result in Fetal Injury, Premature Birth, and Low BirthWeight.' The risks of smoking depend on the number of cigarettes smoked. The risk from smoking one cigarette a month is not equal to the risk of smoking two packs a day. The Surgeon General's warnings implicitly assume that most smokers smoke more than one cigarette a month.

These Surgeon General's warnings are required by law. But tobacco companies voluntarily provide additional information about the risks of smoking. Specifically they provide information about the levels of tar and nicotine produced by

Act — 'Appliance Labeling Rule'). See also Craswell, above n 39, at 581–582 ('the energy used by a home appliance will vary depending on consumers' usage patterns, and the actual cost of that energy will also vary depending on local electricity rates. It might have been possible to present these data in a complicated table, so that consumers could use their own electric bills (and their knowledge of their own usage patterns) to estimate their energy costs with some precision. However, the FTC believed that few consumers had the time or the patience to calculate their actual costs in this way, so it constructed its own index of likely energy costs which allowed the costs of different appliances (relative to other appliances of the same type) to be disclosed in the form of a single 'Energy Efficiency Rating".).

[87] 21 USC § 301.

[88] 21 CFR § 101.9(d)(9).

[89] The Comprehensive Smoking Education Act, 15 USC §§ 1331–41.

[90] See Directive 2001/37/EC of the European Parliament and of the Council of 5 June 2001 on the approximation of the laws, regulations and administrative provisions of the Member States concerning the manufacture, presentation and sale of tobacco products.

the cigarette. This information, while voluntarily disclosed, is certified by the FTC. Tar and nicotine levels depend on product attributes as well as on use patterns. The FTC developed a machine-based test to objectively measure tar and nicotine levels, and the tar and nicotine measures provided by the FTC test assume a certain intensity of smoking — a 2-second, 35-millilitre puff every minute.[91] It is now understood that the FTC's machine-based test does not reflect any reasonable assumption about typical smoking behaviour.[92] First, the machine-based FTC test has been shown to only poorly represent actual smoking by humans.[93] Second, if a cigarette provides less nicotine and less tar per puff, smokers will compensate by taking deeper, longer or more frequent puffs from their cigarettes,[94] or simply by smoking more cigarettes, ie by changing their use patterns.[95] The FTC rating ignores the critical impact of such compensation.

Cigarette manufacturers use the FTC's nicotine and tar ratings to promote 'low tar' and 'light' cigarettes.[96] Moreover, a 1981 Surgeon General's report encouraged smokers who are unable to quit to switch to cigarettes that scored better on the FTC rating.[97] These inducements worked. Some 85 per cent of all smokers today use the supposedly safer cigarettes.[98] But it is now clear that these cigarettes are not safer, because of the compensation effect.[99] The FTC recognised the importance of use patterns and how the compensation effect limits the informative value of its nicotine and tar ratings. A consumer alert published by the FTC emphasises the importance of use patterns:

[91] FTC News Release, 'FTC Proposes New Method for Testing Amounts of Tar, Nicotine, and Carbon Monoxide in Cigarettes: New System Will Provide Consumers With Improved Info. About Cigarette Tar and Nicotine Yields', 9 September 1997 [hereinafter FTC News Release]. The FTC proposed to make disclosed tar and nicotine levels more informative by adding a second, high-intensity rating, based on a 2-second, 55-millilitre puff every 30 seconds. ibid. The FTC ratings are voluntarily disclosed by the major cigarette companies in all cigarette advertisements. ibid. In particular, these ratings are used to promote 'low tar' and 'light' cigarettes. See, eg Advertisement for Merit, Merit Low Tar Kings Soft, Merit Ultima Kings Soft and Merit Ultra Lights Kings Soft, 'Now you're on the road. You've got Merit', Philip Morris, USA Advertising Archive, Document ID 2 061 038 984, available at: www.pmadarchive.com last visited 13 March 2010 [hereinafter Merit Advertisement].

[92] See also J Foulds *et al*, 'Health Effects of Tobacco, Nicotine, and Exposure to Tobacco Smoke Pollution' in J Brick (ed), *Handbook of the Medical Consequences of Alcohol and Drug Abuse*, (2008) 423, 435 *et seq.*

[93] See FTC Consumer Alert, 'Up in Smoke: The Truth About Tar and Nicotine Ratings' (May 2000) [hereinafter FTC Consumer Alert] ('people don't smoke cigarettes the same way the machine does'); Editorial, 'The Safer Cigarette Delusion' 28 August 2006) *New York Times* A14 [hereinafter The Safer Cigarette Delusion].

[94] See Foulds *et al*, above n 92, at 437.

[95] See FTC Consumer Alert, above n 93; FTC News Release, above n 91; *US v Philip Morris, USA, Inc*, 449 FSupp 2d 1, 337–38 (DDC, 2006); The Safer Cigarette Delusion, at A14 ('More than 95 percent of all smokers compensate, with many replacing every bit of tar and nicotine they thought they were avoiding.').

[96] See, eg Merit Advertisement, above n 91.

[97] The Safer Cigarette Delusion, at A14.

[98] ibid.

[99] See also Foulds *et al*, above n 92, at 438.

> The Federal Trade Commission wants you to know that cigarette tar and nicotine ratings can't predict the amount of tar and nicotine you get from any particular cigarette. That's because how you smoke a cigarette can significantly affect the amount of tar, nicotine, and carbon monoxide you get from your cigarette.[100]

The FTC even proposed required disclosures that emphasise use patterns. The two alternative disclosures proposed by the FTC were:

1. There's no such thing as a safe smoke. Even cigarettes with low ratings can give you high amounts of tar and nicotine. It depends on how you smoke; or
2. How much tar and nicotine you get from a cigarette depends on how intensely you smoke it.[101]

These proposals were not implemented.[102] The tar and nicotine disclosures described above demonstrate the importance of choosing accurate typical-use assumptions. Inadequate provision of use-pattern information renders the product attribute information meaningless, even misleading. Of course, product attribute disclosure based on accurate typical-use benchmarking can be helpful.

3.3. Direct Disclosure of Average-Use Information

The previous section provides examples of average-use information indirectly disclosed as a benchmark for product attribute disclosures. While average-use information is helpful even when it is disclosed indirectly, in some markets law-makers should consider mandating direct disclosure of average-use information. For example, there is evidence suggesting that consumers are too quick to purchase extended warranties and other insurance riders that are commonly offered as add-ons with basic consumer products. The small likelihood of an event that would trigger the warranty or insurance coverage, coupled with the relatively small cost that the consumer would bear if such an event occurs, cannot justify the price of the add-on. One possible remedy for this category of mistakes — overestimation of the value of the insurance product — is to provide use-pattern information. As suggested by Professors Ian Ayres and Barry Nalebuff, sellers could be required to provide information on the probability that an extended warranty would be invoked.[103] Or, even better, sellers could be required to provide an estimate of the total repair or replacement costs that a typical consumer would save by purchasing the extended warranty. With this use-pattern

[100] See FTC Consumer Alert, above n 93.
[101] FTC News Release, above n 91.
[102] See 15 USCA § 1333 (specifying the required disclosures); 15 USCA § 1334 (preemption — 'No statement relating to smoking and health, other than the statement required by section 1333 of this title, shall be required on any cigarette package.').
[103] See B Nalebuff and I Ayres, *Why Not?* (2003) 181 ('Circuit City or Ford could tell you the odds of actually making a claim against an extended warranty.'). See also I Ayres, *Super Crunchers*, (2007).

information, extended warranties and similar insurance add-ons would likely suffer a sharp decline in sales.[104]

In the rebates context, Jeff Sovern has recently proposed that sellers offering rebates be required to disclose the low redemption rates.[105] Similarly, if Blockbuster's customers underestimate the likelihood, and hence the cost, of tardiness in returning their video rentals, then Blockbuster could be required to disclose the number of late returns and the total fee payments that an average consumer pays over a one-year period. If Hewlett–Packard (HP) customers, when purchasing a home printer, underestimate the number of ink cartridges that they will purchase over the life of the printer, then HP can be required to provide the missing use-pattern information, perhaps based on an FTC-designed average-use index. Even better, HP could be required to disclose average Total Cost of Ownership (TCO) information that combines the use-pattern information with ink prices. Similar average-use or total price information could be provided by sellers of base goods and add-ons bundles. With such information, for example, a consumer choosing between two hotels could compare not only room rates but also total price figures, based on an average add-on use index (eg two phone-calls, one in-room meal, one movie, etc). And health clubs could be required to disclose the effective per-visit fee paid by an average subscription holder. If this effective per-visit fee is eight times higher than the club's actual per-visit fee, some consumers may reconsider their decision to purchase a subscription.[106]

Direct average-use disclosures could also be effective in the credit card market. Some consumers are sometimes late in paying their credit card bill. And when they are late, they are assessed for a 'late fee'. This late fee is prominently disclosed in credit card solicitations, in accordance with the disclosure regulations issued under the Truth in Lending Act (TILA).[107] But this product attribute disclosure will not be very effective if consumers underestimate the likelihood of paying late. TILA disclosures, especially disclosures in card solicitations, are supposed to help consumers make an informed choice among the many competing credit card products. Such informed choice is crucial for the efficient operation of the credit card market. A consumer who underestimates the likelihood of paying late

[104] Interestingly, use-pattern information for the insurance add-on is a function of both product attribute information and product use information for the base good, eg the likelihood that an extended warranty will be invoked depends on the reliability of the base good and on how the base good is used.

[105] See Sovern, above n 42, at 1703. See also JG Lynch and G Zauberman, 'When Do You Want It? Time, Decisions and Public Policy' (2006) 25 *Journal of Public Policy and Marketing* 67, 71 (making a similar proposal).

[106] See S DellaVigna and U Malmendier, 'Paying Not to Go to the Gym' (2006) 96 *American Economic Review* 694. Many consumers might think that they will attend the health club more often than the average consumer. Thus health clubs could also be required to provide information on the effective per-visit price paid by an above-average consumer, eg a consumer at the eightieth percentile of the distribution. The disclosure could read: 'For 80% of subscription holders the effective per-visit fee is more than X.'

[107] 12 CFR §§ 226.18, 226.5a.

and triggering a late fee will not make a truly informed choice, even if he or she has perfect information about the magnitude of the late fee. The TILA disclosure apparatus can and should be amended to include use-pattern disclosures. Specifically, issuers can be required to disclose the number of late payments that an average consumer makes in a year or the amount that an average consumer pays in late fees in one year.

Moving from late payments to debt repayment rates, a recent amendment to the Truth in Lending Act requires issuers to provide average-use information. Congress was concerned that consumers lack information on the cost of slow repayment. Specifically, many consumers who make only the minimum monthly payment underestimate the amount of time that it will take them to repay their credit card debt and, consequently, underestimate the total amount of interest that they will end up paying. In response, Congress required issuers to disclose on the monthly statement the length of time it will take an average consumer to repay a typical balance in full if he or she makes only the minimum required payment each month.[108]

Credit card issuers engage in intertemporal bundling in response to underestimation of future use by offering low teaser interest rates for an introductory period. Issuers could be required to disclose information on average switching rates or information on the average interest rate that the consumer will pay, accounting for borrowing patterns in both the introductory and post-introductory periods. The evidence suggests that such disclosures would reduce the attractiveness of teaser rate offers. Overestimation of switching affects not only the perceived value of teaser rate offers but also the perceived cost of other mid-stream changes that issuers make. Disclosure of switching rates can help reduce these cost misperceptions as well.

Direct average-use disclosure can also be helpful in other consumer credit markets. Mortgage lenders that offer loans with increasing interest rates could be required to disclose the average balance-weighted interest rate, or the average monthly payment, over the life of the loan. Lenders could also be required to disclose the average likelihood of incurring each of the many penalty fees included in the loan contract and, perhaps, the total fees paid by an average consumer. And in response to consumer optimism about refinancing options, lenders could disclose the average likelihood of refinancing. Payday lenders could

[108] The Bankruptcy Abuse Prevention and Consumer Protection Act of 2005, Public Law 109–8, 119 Stat 23 [hereinafter BAPCPA] § 1301 (the required disclosure is 'Minimum Payment Warning: Making only the minimum payment will increase the interest you pay and the time it takes to repay your balance. For example, making only the typical 2% minimum monthly payment on a balance of $1,000 at an interest rate of 17% would take 88 months to repay the balance in full.'). See also TA Durkin, *Requirements and Prospects for a New Time to Payoff Disclosure for Open End Credit Under Truth in Lending,* (2006) FEDS Working Paper No 2006–34, available at: www.federalreserve.gov/Pubs/feds/2006/200634/200634pap.pdf (describing the new disclosure requirement). The typical balance stated in Section 1301 is $1000. To what extent this balance is in fact typical is questionable. Moreover, there is a risk that a consumer with a balance of $5000 will simply multiply the disclosed repayment period for a $1,000 balance by five, leading to underestimation of the repayment period.

also be required to provide average-use information. Specifically, they could be required to disclose the average number of roll-overs and, based on the average number of roll-overs, the total fee paid by an average consumer. For example, the disclosure could read: 'The fee is $30 for a two-week, $200 advance. The average borrower renews his or her loan three times (ie takes three consecutive advances) before repaying. Therefore, the total fee on a $200 loan is $90 for an average borrower.'

Average-use disclosures can also prove helpful in the cell-phone market. A common feature of the wireless service contract is the lock-in clause, which ties the consumer to a specific provider for as long as two years. Consumers might underestimate the cost of lock-in.[109] In fact, in the absence of significant fixed costs, this lock-in feature of wireless service contracts may well be a strategic response to consumers' underestimation of the cost of lock-in. Average-use disclosure can reduce this underestimation bias. Sellers can be required to provide information about the percentage of consumers who stop using their phones, but continue paying for them, before the end of the lock-in period. Sellers can also be required to disclose the percentage of consumers who break the contract and pay the exit penalty.

We have argued that proper-use information is appropriate for use dimensions that have a single, well-defined proper use. When there are many proper uses for a product, proper-use disclosure loses its bite. In such cases, the alternative is average-use disclosure. But average-use disclosure suffers from a similar limitation. When heterogeneous consumers use the same product in many different ways, average-use information might be of little value. The value of average-use information depends on the degree of heterogeneity. The degree of heterogeneity is a function of both product characteristics and characteristics of the consumer group. But the degree of heterogeneity is also a function of the disclosure regime. The question is whether the seller discloses average-use information where the averaging is done across the entire group of consumers or whether the averaging on which the disclosure is based is done across a smaller, more homogenous subgroup of consumers.

At one extreme, the seller considers the average consumer who enters its store or even the average consumer in the market. Average use, under these assumptions, contains little information. But often the seller has more information — based on demographics, product choice and so forth. Based on this information, the seller can place the consumer in a subgroup of consumers who share a set of observed characteristics. Now average use becomes average use within this

[109] Consumers will underestimate the cost of lock-in if they underestimate the likelihood of contingencies that would induce them to end the contract earlier, eg the appearance of a more attractive offer from another provider, a change in their need for wireless services or an unanticipated financial hardship that reduces the available income left for non-necessities like wireless phone services. Simple myopia might also lead to underestimation of the cost of lock-in.

subgroup. As the subgroup becomes smaller, the consumer heterogeneity problem decreases and the value of the average-use information increases. Disclosure of average-use information, when averaging is done over smaller subgroups, is advantageous and should be expanded.

3.4. Individual-Use Information

The consumer heterogeneity problem limits the efficacy of average-use disclosure. It also supports individual-use disclosure.[110] In certain markets, where sellers enter into long-term relationships with consumers, sellers can be required to provide the consumer with individualised information on his or her use patterns. An immediate objection to this prescription is that sellers have better information than consumers about the attributes of their product, and that they generally have better information about proper use and average use, but that they do not have better information than the consumer about the individual consumer's use patterns. This is surely true about some products. It is not true about all products. The following examples demonstrate the feasibility of individual-use disclosures in several consumer markets.[111]

3.4.1. Credit Cards

The credit card market is an example of an economically significant market where sellers can disclose individual-use information to consumers. Credit card issuers often have more information about how a consumer will use the credit card than the consumer him or herself. First, issuers have detailed statistics about card use, including statistics about card use in the consumer's demographic and socio-economic group. Second, issuers have information on the individual consumer from the credit card application and from credit bureaus. Third, and most importantly, since issuers often maintain long-term relationships with consumers, they quickly obtain information about how the individual consumer uses his or her specific card. Most of this information is available to the consumer, but many consumers do not know or do not remember all the relevant information. Also, many consumers do not consolidate information from these different

[110] See also Ayres, above n 103 (arguing for individualised disclosure).

[111] Scepticism about the feasibility of regulations requiring disclose of actual individualised information was recently expressed by Christine Jolls and Cass Sunstein. See C Jolls and CR Sunstein, 'Debiasing Through Law' (2006) 35 *Journal of Legal Studies* 199 209 (rejecting the possibility of requiring the disclosure of individualised information about product risk). Jolls and Sunstein write that 'it is difficult to imagine incorporating such individualised information into a general legal standard'. The disclosure regulation proposed below is not in the form of a general legal standard. Rather, we advocate market-specific disclosure mandates. In addition to the feasibility concern, individualised disclosure raises a privacy concern. At this point, however, we propose disclosure only of information that sellers collect anyway. However, if disclosure requirements affect sellers' information collection and retention practices, then the privacy concern will have to be addressed.

sources and do not use sophisticated algorithms to analyse the information and predict future use based on this information. Issuers, on the other hand, consolidate all relevant information, store it in databases, update it regularly and analyse it using sophisticated algorithms that can also predict future use.[112]

Recall the late payment and late fee example. We argued that the disclosure of the late fee — a product attribute disclosure — might be less effective if many consumers underestimate the likelihood of paying late. In discussing average-use disclosures, we suggested mandating disclosure of the number of late payments that an average consumer makes over a one-year period. We also noted the limits of such a disclosure, as most consumers will optimistically believe that they will pay late less often than the average consumer. A better solution is to require disclosure of individualised late payment information.[113] Issuers keep records on consumers' late payments. They can be required to disclose the number of late payments made by the specific consumer or the total amount of late fees paid by the consumer over the past year.[114]

We now move from late fees to over-limit fees. Disclosure of individualised use-pattern information can also be effective when provided at the point of sale. Professor Ronald Mann proposed that issuers be required to disclose, through merchants, when a certain purchase would take the consumer over his or her credit limit, triggering an over-limit fee. Such a disclosure could help the consumer to avoid inadvertently exceeding his or her credit limit, perhaps by switching to another card or to another payment system.[115] With respect to the debt-repayment dimension, we noted the recent addition of an average-use disclosure mandate requiring issuers to provide, on the monthly statement, information on the average length of time it will take to pay off a typical balance

[112] See M Furletti, 'Credit Card Pricing Developments and Their Disclosure 6–9' (2003) Federal Reserve Bank of Philadelphia, Payment Cards Center, Discussion Paper' available at: www.philadelphiafed.org/pcc/papers/2003/CreditCardPricing_012003.pdf Duncan McDonald, former general counsel of Citigroup's Europe and North America card businesses, notes: 'No other industry in the world knows consumers and their transaction behavior better than the bank card industry. It has turned the analysis of consumers into a science rivaling the studies of DNA.... The mathematics of virtually everything consumers do is stored, updated, categorized, churned, scored, tested, valued, and compared from every possible angle in hundreds of the most powerful computers and by among the most creative minds anywhere. In the past 10 years alone, the transactions of 200 million Americans have been reviewed in trillions of different ways to minimize bank card risks.' See DA MacDonald, 'Viewpoint: Card Industry Questions Congress Needs to Ask' (2007) *American Banker* 10.

[113] There may still be optimism at play, limiting the effectiveness of even individualised disclosure. A consumer might be forced to acknowledge that he or she, not some average consumer, has paid a lot of money in late fees over the past year, but may still believe that he or she will not repeat this behaviour in the future. Of course, such optimism will become less likely as the disclosed history reveals year after year of high penalty payments.

[114] Issuers provide year-end summaries with individualised information. These summaries, however, focus more on spending behaviour and less on borrowing behaviour (see, eg the 'Year-End Summary' feature offered by several credit card companies, which provides an annual itemised list of all charges). Accordingly, the total amount paid in interest charges or late fees is not disclosed.

[115] See Mann, above n 3, at 162. A proposed bill, HR 1052, 107th Cong (2001). in Section 10, goes beyond disclosure and prohibits the imposition of over-limit fees for creditor-approved transactions.

if the consumer makes only the minimum payment each month. The new disclosure has an individual-use component as well. Issuers must provide a phone number that the consumer can call to receive information on the length of time it will take that consumer to pay off his or her specific balance if the consumer makes only the minimum payment each month.[116] While this option to receive individualised repayment rate information is a step in the right direction, it would probably be more effective if the individualised disclosure was provided automatically on each monthly statement.[117]

3.4.2. *Cell Phones*

The cellular phone market is an example of another economically significant market where the long-term relationship between providers and consumers allows for the provision of individualised use-pattern information. Evidence of consumer mistakes in the cell phone market suggests that such individualised disclosure may be helpful. A notable design feature of mobile service contracts is the steep jump in per minute charges when the consumer exceeds the plan limit. Many contracts specify an increase of over 100 per cent in the per-minute price, with some contracts specifying increases of 200 per cent and beyond.[118] Arguably, the high prices set for minutes beyond the plan limit target consumers' underestimation of their future use of the cellular phone.[119]

Individualised disclosure can reduce consumer mistakes about cell phone use. In particular, sellers can provide individualised use information, focusing the consumer's attention on use exceeding the plan limit.[120] This disclosure could be supplemented by information on alternative service plans that would reduce the total price paid by the consumer, given his or her current use patterns.[121]

[116] BAPCPA, § 1301. See also Durkin, above n 108 (describing the new disclosure requirement).

[117] Compare § 2 of the proposed bill, HR 1052, 107th Cong (2001). See also Mann, above n 3, at 160–61 (proposing an individualised disclosure on the monthly bill and arguing that such a disclosure is not too costly to implement).

[118] See S DellaVigna and U Malmendier, 'Contract Design and Self-Control: Theory and Evidence' (2004) 119 *Quarterly Journal of Economics* 353, 380; Verizon Wireless, America's Choice® Basic Plans, available at: www.verizonwireless.com last visited: 5 June 2007 (quoting mark-ups in excess of 300% for minutes beyond the plan limit). See also Nalebuff and Ayres, above n 103, at 178–79 (describing the high post-plan minute prices as 'hidden pricing').

[119] Clearly, these huge increases do not reflect a corresponding change in the provider's per-minute cost. See MD Grubb, *Selling to Overconfident Consumers*, (2007) (unpublished manuscript), available at: ssrn.com/abstract=721701; O Bar-Gill and R Stone, 'Mobile Misperceptions' (2009) 23 *Harvard Journal of Law and Technology*.

[120] Or to use that is substantially below the plan limit and would merit a switch to a lower limit/lower fee plan. Carriers, both in the United States and in Europe, already provide certain use information on the monthly bill.

[121] Utility companies in Germany have voluntarily adopted an even more pro-consumer policy. At the end of the year, they retroactively match each consumer to the service plan under which the consumer pays the lowest total price given his or her use over the past year. See Nalebuff and Ayres, above n 103, at 27.

Individual-use information can be especially helpful for consumers who inadvertently exceed the plan limit. The challenge of keeping track of cumulative use has increased with the invention of multiple-limit plans, eg plans with different limits for peak and off-peak minutes. To reduce the incidence of inadvertently exceeding the plan limit, issuers could be required to notify consumers, via a recorded message or a text message, when they are about to exceed the plan limit. A consumer receiving such notification may well decide to cut the conversation short, switch to a land line or postpone the conversation until off-peak hours.[122]

3.4.3. Other Markets

Sellers have individual-use information in many other markets. Some of this information is currently being disclosed to consumers, but enhanced disclosure requirements may be desirable. For example, phone (not cell phone) companies disclose certain use information to consumers on their monthly bills. More effective disclosure would include use patterns averaged across several months, perhaps accompanied by total cost information under the consumer's current plan as well as under alternative plans offered by the phone company.[123] Health clubs could also be required to disclose individualised use-pattern information. Specifically, health clubs could disclose attendance records for the past year and even for the preceding year (or years). They could also calculate and disclose the per-visit fee paid by the individual subscription-holder. Faced with such information when asked to renew the subscription, the consumer may well decide to forgo the subscription and pay on a per-visit basis. Similarly, a retailer asking a consumer to renew a membership card or a discount card could be required to disclose the total savings enjoyed by the individual consumer over the past year. This information would assist the consumer in making a more informed decision as to whether to pay the annual fee and renew the membership.

Netflix effectively competes with traditional video rental stores through a unique business model. For a constant monthly fee, the consumer can have a specified number of movies, say three movies. The consumer can keep these three movies for as long as he or she likes. Whenever a movie is sent back to Netflix, the company promptly replaces it with the next movie on the consumer's priority list. Under this model, a consumer who sees two movies a month pays the same price as a consumer who sees 20 movies a month. The question is whether

[122] cp 'usage alert' mandates in Art 6(a)(2) of Regulation (EC) No. 544/2009 of the European Parliament and of the Council of 18 June 2009, amending Regulation (EC) No. 717/2007 on roaming on public mobile telephone networks within the Community and Directive 2002/21/EC on a common regulatory framework for electronic communications networks and services. In the United States, the FCC is considering similar regulations. See Federal Communication Commission, Public Notice: Comment Sought on Measures Designed to Assist U.S. Wireless Consumers to Avoid 'Bill Shock', CG Docket No. 09–158, 11 May 2010.

[123] Utility companies also provide some individualised use-pattern information on the monthly statement. For instance ConEdison provides information on the individual consumer's average daily use of electricity for previous months.

consumers correctly anticipate their in-home movie-viewing patterns. Netflix could easily prevent consumers from making use-pattern mistakes. It could disclose the average number of videos that an individual consumer receives in a month, as well as the average price that the consumer pays per movie. With this information, the consumer would be able to compare prices across the different business models and make a more educated choice between Netflix and, say, Blockbuster.[124]

Finally, simple disclosure could assist consumers who forget to cancel a service at the end of the introductory period. Service providers know precisely when the introductory period ends for each individual consumer. The service provider could be required to send a notice to each consumer two weeks before the introductory period ends for the individual consumer. This notice would remind the consumer that the low introductory price will soon be replaced by a higher post-introductory price and describe a low-cost way to discontinue the service. This disclosure would prevent many inadvertent continuances of service beyond the introductory period.[125]

3.5. Designing Optimal Use-Pattern Disclosure

One of the main goals of this chapter is to establish use-pattern disclosure as a complement to product attribute disclosure in addressing behavioural market failures. Product-use information is clearly important for consumer decision-making and for the efficient operation of consumer markets. But this is not enough. Successful disclosure regulation must effectively convey use-pattern information to consumers. The question is how to optimally design disclosure regulation. We do not purport to provide a comprehensive answer in this

[124] To further facilitate a comparison between Netflix and video rental stores that follow a traditional business model with late fees, Netflix's competitors could be required to disclose the number of late payments made by the specific consumer or the total amount of late fees paid by the consumer over the past year. Of course, such individual-use disclosure is only feasible for consumers who maintain a long-term relationship with the video rental store (eg consumers who hold a membership card).

[125] There is evidence that such inadvertent continuances are common. A recent Bill introduced in the Israeli parliament (the Knesset) proposes a regulatory response similar to the one described in the text. Opposition to this Bill by service providers suggests that inadvertent continuances are common and constitute a substantial revenue source for these service providers. See R Linder-Ganz and Z Zarhiya, 'Bill Prohibiting Automatic Contract Renewal Stuck in Committee', *Haaretz* (2007). In the United States, state legislators have also been concerned about the problem of automatic contract renewal following a low-price introductory period. See, eg Illinois Automatic Contract Renewal Act, 815 ILCS 601/1 *et seq* (sellers must provide consumers with written notice of the automatic renewal no less than 30 days or more than 60 days prior to the date of the cancellation deadline for the renewal). Other state laws require only that sellers provide a general notice about cancellation rights, not an individualised notice prior to the end of the introductory period for the specific consumer. See, eg Act Concerning Enforceability of Automatic Contract Renewal Provisions, HR 7204, Gen Assem, Jan Sess (Conn. 2007). See also HB 1702, 80th Leg (Tex 2007); S. 527, 2007 Gen Assem, Reg Sess (NC 2007).

chapter.[126] Still, the preceding discussion offers some general guidelines. First, when possible, use-pattern disclosure should be based on individual-use information. And when use-pattern disclosure is based on average-use information, the averages should be taken over a cost-effectively small subgroup of consumers.

Second, in many cases, disclosure mandates should combine product attribute and product use information. For example, a consumer will benefit from a disclosure stating the number of late payments he made on a credit card over the past year. He or she will likely benefit even more from a disclosure that by combining price information and use information states the total amount that the consumer paid in late fees during the previous year. And the most informative disclosure would combine price and use information in multiple dimensions. Such disclosure would state the total amount that the consumer paid in penalty fees and interest, including late fees, over-limit fees, penalty interest payments and so forth. The goal is to come as close as possible to TCO information. Due to the existence of multiple price dimensions and the fact that the relative importance of different price dimensions depends on use patterns, calculating total price can be difficult. Sellers should be required to make these calculations for consumers. Disclosure regulation should strive to provide consumers with meaningful price information in a simple, accessible way.[127]

3.6. The Costs and Limits of Disclosure

This chapter focuses on disclosure regulation because, compared with other forms of regulation, it is more compatible with free markets and, in most cases, more politically feasible. This does not mean that disclosure is always effective. Nor does it mean that disclosure, when effective, is without cost. We now consider the main costs of disclosure mandates and the main limits on the efficacy of disclosure regulation. We begin with the general costs and limits of disclosure regulation. We then describe additional costs and limits specific to average-use disclosure. The shortcomings of average-use disclosure indirectly support an expansion of individual-use disclosure.[128]

[126] On the optimal design of disclosure regulation, see, eg Jolls and Sunstein, above n 111; Beales, Craswell and Salop, above n 18, at 529–31; Craswell, above n 39; L Froeb *et al*, 'Economic Research at the FTC: Information, Retrospectives, and Retailing', (in press) Review of Industrial Organisation, available at: papers.ssrn.com/sol3/papers.cfm? abstract_id=592101 last visited 13 March 2010; JM Lacko and JK Pappalardo, 'The Effect of Mortgage Broker Compensation Disclosures on Consumers and Competition: A Controlled Experiment' (2004) available at: www.ftc.gov/os/2004/01/030123mortgagesummary.pdf (the FTC is studying the efficacy of different disclosure techniques in the home mortgage market).

[127] See Craswell, above n 39, at 692–94 (discussing single-price disclosures and detailing the costs of such disclosures).

[128] The costs and limits described below reduce the appeal of disclosure regulation even when designed and administered by regulators seeking to advance the public good. Unfortunately, not all regulators share this goal, and regulatory decision-making is too often guided by politics, not by the

3.6.1. *The Costs of Disclosure*

We begin with the direct costs of disclosure. These include the cost to sellers of collecting, compiling and distributing the information. They also include the cost to consumers who need to read the disclosure and process the disclosed information. In many of the examples provided in this chapter, the direct cost to sellers only amounts to the relatively minor cost of distributing the information. The reason for this is that sellers collect and compile the relevant information anyway. Credit card issuers, for example, have a powerful business motivation to obtain information on consumers' use patterns.

This relates to another, indirect cost of disclosure regulation. If sellers are required to disclose the information they collect, then they will have a weaker incentive to collect information.[129] While this adverse incentive effect is undeniably true, its magnitude can be expected to be small in many markets, as the business reasons for collecting information will often outweigh the disclosure disincentive.[130] Moreover, disclosure mandates commonly imply an obligation to collect the information to be disclosed. Of course, when the information would not have been collected absent the mandate, the cost of collection constitutes a cost of the disclosure regulation — a cost that will be passed on, at least in part, to consumers. And, in some markets, this cost might be so large that it would drive sellers out of the market.

3.6.2. *The Limited Efficacy of Disclosure*

One of the main limits on the efficacy of disclosure regulation concerns information overload. There is a limit on the amount of information that the average consumer can effectively process. Accordingly, disclosed information might be ignored or might replace other information, perhaps more important information, in the consumer's decision-making process. The information overload problem cautions against increasing the amount of information disclosed.[131]

public good. Of course, these concerns apply to all forms of regulation and not specifically to disclosure regulation or to use-pattern disclosure.

[129] cp AT Kronman, 'Mistake, Disclosure, Information, and the Law of Contracts' (1978) 7 *Journal of Legal Studies* 1 (arguing that contract law disclosure obligations might deter the acquisition of information).

[130] Kronman distinguishes between deliberately acquired information and casually acquired information and argues that casually acquired information can be subject to disclosure mandates. ibid. In Kronman's terms, much of the information that sellers should disclose is casually acquired, ie it would have been acquired by sellers anyway for business reasons.

[131] See, eg Craswell, above n 39 (arguing that provision of additional information dilutes the effectiveness of existing disclosures); Korobkin, above n 11 (consumers can process only limited amounts of information); Government Accountability Office, 'Credit Cards: Increased Complexity in Rates and Fees Heightens Need for More Effective Disclosures to Consumers' (2006) 46, available at: www.gao.gov/new.items/d06929.pdf (finding that credit card disclosures contain too much information); Furletti, above n 112, at 19 (concluding that it is not clear that requiring more details in regulatory disclosures would be useful for consumers.); Latin, above n 11.

Even if consumers can process the disclosed information, it is not clear that they will do so. Provision of information, specifically use-pattern information, can be helpful if consumers follow a deliberative decision-making process (even if this decision-making process is not fully rational). However, there is evidence that, in some cases, consumer decision-making is driven by an emotional response rather than by a deliberative process or that emotions influence the deliberative process.[132] In these cases, disclosure regulation will be less effective.

Finally, even if consumers can process use-pattern information and would like to do so, the required information might not exist. This problem is especially acute with respect to new products. It takes time to collect information about average use. And the absence of historic information precludes individual-use disclosure. Moreover, these practical impediments to effective disclosure regulation can be manipulated by sellers. For example, in order to evade disclosure mandates, sellers might try to present a slightly modified version of a product as a new product.

3.6.3. The Limited Efficacy of Average-Use Disclosure

Average-use disclosure is subject to additional limitations. These limitations reinforce the case for individual-use disclosure. The first, inherent limitation is an immediate implication of consumer heterogeneity. Averaging, by its very nature, implies loss of information. As the degree of heterogeneity among the relevant group of consumers increases, the value of average information decreases. For this reason, if sellers segment the market into small subgroups of consumers and can be required to disclose average-use information within these more homogeneous subgroups, the value of the disclosure increases.[133]

Optimism imposes another limit on the efficacy of average-use disclosure. Most consumers will optimistically think that they are above average — that they will be late less often than the average consumer in paying their credit card bill, that they will repay their bill more quickly than the average consumer, that they are less likely than the average consumer to break their lock-in cell-phone contract and so forth. Still, average-use information can be helpful. Consumers suffer from two types of misperception: (1) misperception about the mean; and (2) misperception about their position relative to the mean.[134] Average-use information can be helpful in curing the former misperception.

Moreover, optimally designed average-use information can minimise the optimism problem. First, measuring and disclosing average-use across smaller, more homogeneous groups of consumers should reduce the 'we are all above average' problem. Second, more sophisticated use of statistical information can reduce the

132 See eg J O'Shaughnessy and NJ O'Shaughnessy, *The Marketing Power of Emotion*, (2002).

133 See Craswell, above n 39, at 691–692 (discussing heterogeneity as a limit of disclosures based on averages; Craswell does not focus on average use).

134 See Latin, above n 11, at 1243–44.

optimism problem. Statistical use information need not be limited to straight averages. To take a specific example, the fact that an average consumer pays $200 in penalty fees over the course of the year might be dismissed by most consumers as irrelevant to them. These consumers will find it more difficult to dismiss the fact that 80 per cent of consumers pay more than $100 a year in penalty fees. Disclosure of statistical use information describing the behaviour of a super-majority of consumers should reduce the optimism problem.[135]

Finally, average-use disclosure might suffer from an endogeneity problem. Consider the rebates example. Assume that, absent disclosure, only 5 per cent of consumers redeem the rebate. If the seller discloses this 5 per cent figure, then most consumers will respond by ignoring the rebate and focusing on the pre-rebate price. These consumers will purchase a product with no rebate and a lower spot price. Still, a minority of highly motivated rebate users will prefer rebate pricing. And, in time, the rate of redemption, among this minority of rebate users, will rise to, say, 90 per cent. If the seller updates the disclosure from a 5 per cent redemption rate to a 90 per cent redemption rate, there is a risk that the majority of consumers will again opt for rebate pricing. The redemption rate will then drop back to 5 per cent, the disclosure will be updated again and so forth. This dynamic is undesirable. But the endogeneity problem will often be mitigated by market forces. In the rebates example, if a seller expects that after disclosing the 5 per cent redemption rate only highly motivated rebate users will prefer rebate pricing, it will have to reduce the magnitude of the rebate significantly to avoid a loss. Accordingly, the seller will be able to advertise a 90 per cent redemption rate only for minor rebates.[136]

3.6.4. Voluntarily-Supplied Use-Pattern Information

A cost-benefit analysis of any use-pattern disclosure mandate should consider the use-pattern information that is being voluntarily provided in the marketplace.

[135] Of course, individual-use disclosure, when feasible, is the best way to minimise the optimism effect. But even individualised disclosure is not a perfect cure for optimism. Individualised disclosure is based on historic information. An optimistic consumer might convince him or herself that he or she will not repeat the mistakes of the past, eg a consumer who is confronted with information about the amount of late fees that he or she paid over the past year might refrain from switching to a credit card with lower late fees because he or she optimistically believes that he or she will not be late next year.

[136] Health club subscriptions provide another example. Assume that the average consumer who purchases a health club subscription attends the club 10 times a year. If this information is disclosed, and if this disclosure is effective, many consumers who previously purchased a subscription will now choose the per-visit pricing option, and only heavy users will purchase a subscription. Accordingly, the average attendance of a subscription holder would rise to, say, 50 visits a year. The health club would have to update its disclosure. And there is a risk that with the new disclosure consumers will again opt for a subscription. Of course, if they do, then the disclosure will need to be updated again: back to an average attendance of 10 times a year. Again market forces mitigate the problem. If, following the initial disclosure, only heavy users purchase subscriptions, then the subscription price will increase significantly. And this increased price will minimise the number of light users who opt for a subscription, even when the disclosure is updated to the new 50 visits per year average.

The benefit of a disclosure mandate will generally be smaller when use-pattern information is already available.[137] And this smaller benefit may no longer justify the cost of the disclosure regulation. Use-pattern information is voluntarily provided by sellers and by third parties in some cases. For example, sellers routinely provide proper-use information, even absent a legal mandate. Tobacco companies voluntarily disclose tar and nicotine levels. Utility companies, cell phone service providers, credit card issuers and other sellers provide some use information on the monthly bill. Amazon and Netflix compile use-pattern information and use it to inform consumers about books and movies enjoyed by other consumers with similar use patterns. And more.

Use-pattern information is also provided by third parties, like Consumer Reports and CNet.com. For example, Consumer Reports provides proper-use information about child car seats, lawnmowers and many other products.[138] And CNet.com provides use information and Total Cost of Ownership information on home printing, for example.[139] When information is provided by the market — by sellers or by third parties — the need for disclosure regulation is diminished. The problem, of course, is that the market will not always provide sufficient information. When buyers understand the extent and cost of their ignorance, they will become informed or generate demand for information that would motivate both sellers and third parties to provide this information. But buyers are not always aware of their ignorance (or of the cost of their ignorance). And, absent such rational demand for information, the imperfect alignment between seller interests, and even third-party interests, and consumer interests might lead to failure in the market for information.[140] When such a market failure exists, disclosure regulation may be socially desirable.

3.6.5. *The Costs and Limits of Disclosure — Summary*

Disclosure regulation is only partially effective, and its limited benefits are often offset by countervailing costs. This chapter is not a call for expanded disclosure. Rather, it argues that, within the vast landscape of disclosure regulation, too little

[137] We assume that anti-fraud law effectively polices the accuracy of the voluntarily disclosed use-pattern information.

[138] See ConsumerReports.org, '*Buying Advice*: Child Car and Booster Seats', available at: www.consumerreports.org/cro/babies-kids/child-car-booster-seats/reports/how-to-choose/index.htm last visited 8 August 2007 (child car seats); ConsumerReports.org, 'Equipment Care', available at: www.consumerreports.org/cro/home-garden/news/october-2006/end-of-season-lawn-and-equipment-guide-10–06/equipment-care/0610_end-of-season-lawn-and-equipment-guide_equipment-care.htm last visited 8 August 2007 (lawnmowers).

[139] See CNet.com, 'Printer Buying Guide', available at: reviews.cnet.com/4520–7604_7–1 016 838–5.html?tag=tnav last visited 8 August 2007.

[140] See also above Section 2.2.2.

attention has been paid to use-pattern disclosure.[141] Accordingly, the implications of our analysis are not necessarily more disclosure. In many markets, applying the analysis developed in this chapter will require substituting some product attribute disclosure with use-pattern disclosure or modifying existing use-pattern disclosures. To the extent that disclosure regulation is socially desirable, the goal is to design the best possible disclosure regime. This regime will feature an optimal mix of product attribute disclosures and use-pattern disclosures.

Most importantly, the cost-benefit analysis that should guide regulators in designing an optimal disclosure regime must be a market-specific analysis. Only an in-depth inquiry into the specific market can identify a behavioural market failure — a persistent consumer mistake that causes substantial welfare loss. And only an in-depth market-specific analysis can determine the optimal regulatory response to the identified market failure. This chapter establishes the framework for identifying use-pattern mistakes and for designing a disclosure-based regulatory response to use-pattern mistakes. Applying this framework to specific consumer markets must be left for future research.[142]

4. CONCLUSIONS

Before purchasing a product, the consumer forms a mental image of how he or she will use the product. This image is not always accurate. Mistakes in estimating product use affect the perceived benefits and costs associated with a product and can lead to welfare-reducing transactions. The law plays an important role in facilitating the efficient operation of markets by requiring disclosure of information that minimises consumer mistakes. And when the problem is use-pattern mistakes, the cure must be use-pattern disclosure. Existing use-pattern disclosures are largely confined to proper-use information and to average-use information, indirectly disclosed as a benchmark for product attribute disclosures. Policy-makers should consider increasing the number and quality of use-pattern disclosure requirements. In particular, disclosure of individual-use information should be considered in markets characterised by long-term relationships between sellers and consumers.

While this chapter focuses on disclosure regulation as a policy response to use-pattern mistakes, other, structural responses should be considered when

[141] As the preceding discussion makes clear, the costs and limits of disclosure affect both product attribute disclosures and use-pattern disclosures.

[142] In theory, the call for a market-specific analysis invokes the problem of defining the relevant market. While the market-definition problem is a major problem in antitrust law, it should not pose a significant hurdle in the present consumer protection context. At the very least, there is a sufficiently large number of consumer markets where the proposed framework can be fruitfully applied without bumping against boundary questions of market definition. And, in many contexts, regulators should be able to base their policy analysis on a largely uncontroversial market definition that is functionally based on the identified objectionable design feature.

applying the proposed framework to specific consumer markets. In particular, legal intervention establishing a time-limited consumer right to return a product or discontinue a service provides another regulatory response tailored to the unique characteristics of use-pattern mistakes. Ideally, after using the product or service for a period of time, the consumer will learn the necessary use-pattern information and will be better equipped to choose among competing products.[143]

[143] Of course, the details of such a policy will have to be worked out on a market-by-market basis. Moreover, the policy will be inapplicable in many markets. Still, the structural connection of this policy to use-pattern mistakes and the potentially small burden it imposes on the operation of markets justify its consideration by policy-makers. cp Camerer *et al*, above n 2 (noting cool-off periods as an example of asymmetrically paternalistic regulation).

9

Forms of Imposed Protection in Legal History, Especially in Roman Law

LAURENS WINKEL*

1. INTRODUCTION

LEGAL MEASURES TO protect economically and socially weaker parties are supposedly a rather recent phenomenon in legal history. Indeed, at first glance they are not clearly present in Roman law and cannot be found earlier than the nineteenth century. During the latter period, they were a necessary consequence of the blatant forms of inequality that resulted from the Industrial Revolution. On a legislative level, measures to protect weaker parties may also be understood as a reaction to the ultra-liberal ideas behind the codifications of the early nineteenth century.[1] However, imposed legal protection sometimes takes another form that already existed in classical Roman law or that developed during the reception of Roman law in civil law countries.

2. PROTECTION THROUGH THE EXPANDING APPLICATION OF THE CONCEPT OF *BONA FIDES* (GOOD FAITH)

In Roman law, economic or social inequality as such was not regarded as a reason to institute special legal remedies for the protection of weaker parties. However, within the framework of the ever-expanding number of contractual *iudicia bonae fidei*, the judge could take forms of undue influence or duress into account and so protect a weaker party. In classical Roman law, those *iudicia bonae fidei* already

* Professor of Legal History, Erasmus School of Law, Erasmus University Rotterdam. This chapter is an expanded version of a paper 'Feminae comme personae privilegiatae', which was presented in French at the 54th session of the Société Fernand de Visscher in Antalya in September 2000.

[1] For an interesting account of the behaviour of a liberal jurist in the nineteenth century, see G Baert 'François Laurent. Zijn Leven, zijn tijd en zijn Strijd (1810–1887)'. in J Erauw & M Storme (eds), *Liber Memorialis François Laurent* (1989) especially 40ff.

covered the most important commercial transactions, like the four types of consensual contract: sale (*emptio/venditio*), letting and hiring (*locatio/conductio*), partnership (*societas*) and mandate (*mandatum*). Other *iudicia bonae fidei*, for example those following most forms of *contractus re*, like pledge (*pignus*),[2] contract of loan for use (*commodatum*) and contract of deposit (*depositum*), were instituted by the praetor during the period of classical Roman law, during the first 250 years of the Christian era. In this way, standards of good faith gradually came to be more widely applied.

A special remedy against abuse was created by the so-called rules of *laesio enormis* (prejudice of more than half the market price), introduced by the Emperor Diocletian in two constitutions concerning the sale of a plot of land, in which he seemed to protect the vendor.[3] In the Middle Ages, these constitutions were given a wider application, beyond the scope of contracts of sale, under the influence of the Aristotelian concept of justice, which became popular during the mid-thirteenth century. In some later national codifications, the rules concerning *laesio enormis* in the law of sale survive until this day.[4]

All of this does not imply that the *iudicia stricti iuris*, in which the judge does not automatically apply standards of good faith, afforded absolutely no protection to weaker parties. As early as 69 BC, we find such protection in the form of an *exceptio doli*, a legal remedy awarded by the praetor to the defendant in cases in which the defendant was treated dishonestly, such as when a debtor was absolved informally but was nevertheless summoned to court by the plaintiff on the grounds that the obligation still existed in the strict sense of the law. In such cases, the *exceptio doli* was granted to the defendant and the claim was dismissed. Somewhat later, an active legal remedy for the plaintiff was granted in the form of a praetorian *actio de dolo*.[5]

Other examples include cases of duress and intimidation (*metus*).[6] Here the praetor provided legal remedies in the form of a *restitutio in integrum propter metum*. Other passive and active legal remedies in these cases were the *exceptio metus* and a delictual remedy called *actio quod metus causa gessum sit*. This action could lead to a fine.[7] The difference with the application of *bona fides* was that

[2] This contract of pledge provides the debtor, who gave the pledge, with the *actio pigneraticia in personam*, to be distinguished from the *actio pigneraticia in rem (= actio Serviana)*, an *actio in rem* for the benefit of the creditor to reclaim the pledge from third parties as well.

[3] C. 4.44.2 and C. 4.44.8.

[4] R Zimmermann, *The Law of Obligations — Roman Foundations of the Civilian Tradition* (1990) 259 at fn 156, with many further references. See recently, Th Finkenauer, 'Zur Renaissance der laesio enormis beim Kaufvertrag' in L Aderhold *et al* (eds), *Festschrift für HP Westermann* (Cologne, 2008) 183–207; R Hardy, 'De iustum pretium-leer. (Nieuwe) inzichten uit de rechtseconomie, het mededingingsrecht en empirie' (2010) *Nederlands Juristenblad* 1160–64.

[5] A Wacke 'Zum dolus-Begriff der actio de dolo'. in *Revue Internationale des Droits de l'Antiquité*, 3ème Série, XXVII (1980) 349–86.

[6] AS Hartkamp *Der Zwang Im Römischen Privatrecht* (1971) passim.

[7] On *actiones populares*, see L Winkel 'Quelques remarques sur l'accusation publique en droit grec et romain'. in *Revue Internationale des Droits de l'Antiquité, 3ème Série, XXIX* (1982) 281–94.

none of these legal remedies were ever granted automatically: the party concerned had to specifically request such a remedy during the first stage (*in iure*) of the proceedings.

3. PROTECTION THROUGH EARLY INSTITUTIONS OF FAMILY LAW

The following examples of imposed protection may be found in early Roman law, but the notion of protection may be a later historical retro-projection. The original purpose of the measures may well have been to secure the authoritarian family order under the *patria potestas*, but they were subsequently understood in a different way, namely as protection for socially weaker persons.

One example of this is the *tutela impuberum* (tutelage for children).[8] In the absence of paternal authority, children under the age of 12 (girls) or 14 (boys) were placed under the tutelage of a tutor. This form of protection was focused mainly on the patrimonies of children, but it was also a consequence of the structure of the Roman family in the early Roman republic, where the *pater familias* had quasi-patrimonial rights as far as his wife and children were concerned. At this time, there was even an *ius vitae necisque*— the father decided on the life or death of family members under his authority. Excesses were not punished directly at the legal level, but only at the religious level by a magistrate called the *censor*, when he gave a *nota censoria*. This *nota censoria* had consequences for the religious and social position of the person concerned, as well as indirect consequences for his legal position.[9] For example, it led to *infamia*, which meant that the person in question could no longer play a role in political life and could never in the future become a *tutor* or *curator*.

When the father (*pater familias*) died, he could appoint a *tutor* in his will, or one could be nominated by a magistrate. The first appearance of this *tutela impuberum* was in the Law of the Twelve Tables, around 450 BC (Leg XII Tab 5.6). According to the relevant provisions, children under the age of 12/14 could conclude contracts that were to their benefit (a rule surviving until Justinian's time, as appears from Inst Just 1.25). In all other cases, the permission of the father or *tutor* was required. Youngsters over the age of 12/14, free of *patria potestas*, were under the guidance of a *curator* and were entitled to restitution (*restitutio in integrum*) when a contract was to their disadvantage. Moreover, an *exceptio legis Laetoria*[10] could be raised when a minor was sued for a loan and when a popular action was available, that is to say, an action that could be raised by anyone, a so-called *actio popularis* against the person who had abused an

[8] For a brief survey, see M Kaser and R Knütel, *Römisches Privatrecht* 19 (2008) 334 ff.

[9] See further F Grelle, 'La "Correctio morum" nella legislazione Flavia' in H Temporini et al (eds), *Aufstieg und Niedergang der Römischen Welt, II*, 13 (1980) 340–65.

[10] Sometimes referred to as *Plaetoria* in the past, even in Roman legal sources. The *Lex (P)Laetoria* dates from 192 or 191 BC.

inexperienced minor.[11] Later, in the course of the reception of Roman law, the *tutela impuberum* and the *cura minorum* were no longer distinguished from each other, but they survived until the arrival of modern law for the protection of minors.[12]

The tutelage of women (*tutela mulieris*) was connected to the disappearance of the old form of marriage by *manus*, through which a woman came under the authority of her husband at the same level as his children. Gaius (1.144–145 = Leg XII Tab 5.1) wrote:

> Veteres enim voluerunt feminas etamsi perfectae aetatis sint, propter levitatem in tutelam esse. (For it was the wish of the old lawyers that women, even those of full age, should be in guardianship as being scatterbrained.)

However, this form of tutelage had already almost been abolished in classical Roman law, as apparent from Gaius 1.190:

> Feminas vero perfectae aetatis in tutela esse fere nulla pretiosa ratio suasisse videtur: nam quae vulgo creditur, quia leviate animi plerumque decipiuntur et aequum erat eas tutorum auctoritate regi, magis speciosa videtur quam vera; mulieres enim quae perfectae aetatis sunt, ipsae sibi negotia tractant et in quibusdam causis dicis gratia tutor interponit auctoritatem suam; saepe etiam invitus auctor fieri a praetore cogitur. (There seems, on the other hand, to have been no very worthwhile reason why women who have reached the age of maturity should be in guardianship; for the argument which is commonly believed, that because they are scatterbrained they are frequently subject to deception and that it was proper for them to be under a guardian's authority, seems to be specious rather than true. For women of full age deal with their own affairs for themselves, and while in certain instances the guardian interposes his authorisation for the form's sake, he is often compelled by the praetor to give authorisation, even against his wishes.)[13]

This text, written in about 160 AD, clearly shows that guardianship for adult women was already in decline, but it is nevertheless remarkable that a century later women were not only no longer under tutelage but apparently also very active participants in commercial transactions! That is why, in the time of Diocletian, many imperial rescripts were addressed to women. The enigmatic aspects of these rescripts and their addressees have been examined by the well-known Italian Romanist Eduardo Volterra.[14]

Persons with mental illness had a guardian on the basis of the Law of the Twelve Tables (Leg XII Tab 5.7a):

[11] JA Ankum 'Gab es im klassischen römischen Recht eine *Exceptio* und eine *Replicatio Legis Laetoriae*?'. in G Klingenberg, J-M Rainer & H Stiegler (eds), *Vestigia Iuris Romani — Festschrift Gunter Wesener* (1992) 21–33 (also in JA Ankum, *Extravagantes, Scritti sparsi di diritto romano* (2007) 243 ff).

[12] H Coing, *Europäisches Privatrecht*, Vol I (1985) 197 ff.

[13] Translation by WM Gordon *et al* (1988).

[14] E Volterra 'Les Femmes dans les 'Inscriptiones' des Rescrits Impériaux'. in E von Caemmerer *et al* (eds), *Xenion, Festschrift PJ Zepos*, Vol I (1973) 717–24. (also in E Volterra, *Scritti Giuridici*, Vol V (1993) 339–46).

> Si furiosus escit, adgnatum gentiliumque in eo pecuniaque eius potestas esto. (When a person will be mentally ill, the agnate and relative must be in control of his person and of his patrimony.)

This is called *cura furiosi*: the guardian was responsible for the administration of the assets of the person concerned. Prodigals had also been under guardianship since the time of the Law of the Twelve Tables, originally only for what they had acquired *ab intestato*. This was commonly understood as *cura prodigi* (found in Leg XII Tab 5.7c, transmitted in D. 27.10.1 pr). Tutors and guardians were appointed according to fixed rules of family law and were under the supervision of a magistrate. If necessary, a magistrate nominated tutors and guardians. When the guardianship came to an end, the tutor or curator could be forced to render an account of his administration with the *actio tutelae*. Fraud on his part committed during the period he acted as a tutor or curator was sanctioned by a criminal *accusatio suspecti tutoris*, which had far-reaching consequences for the status of those found guilty of such fraud.[15]

4. LEGAL PROTECTION THROUGH LEGISLATION AND MAGISTRATES

Apart from the above-mentioned contractual protection by Roman magistrates within the framework of *bona fides* (section 2), namely the *exceptio doli* and the *actio de dolo*, the Romans adopted legislative measures to protect socially weaker groups. Thus, one could consider the relationship between *patroni* and *liberti*, the so-called *clientela* relationship, as another form of imposed legal protection.[16] Poor Roman citizens, and also freed slaves, entered into special relationships with wealthy Roman citizens for whom they had to perform services[17] in return for social and legal protection. In addition, the *Lex Cincia* — a plebiscitum[18] of 204 BC[19] provided protection against donations made under social pressure.[20] The regime of the *Lex Cincia* was aimed at protecting a donor of lower status who might be forced by a person of higher status to make a donation. Gifts in excess of a certain amount were prohibited and could only be given to certain close relatives (*personae exceptae*). Nevertheless, the sanction was again founded in the law of procedure, in the form of an *exceptio legis Cinciae*, which could be raised against a claim for a gift, for example when someone promised to give an amount of money in the form of a formal oral *stipulatio*. The resulting *condictio* or *actio ex stipulatu* could be countered by the *exceptio legis Cinciae*. Although the *donatio*

15 Loss of status in public and private law: no possibility to be elected as a magistrate; no possibility to have a function on behalf of others in private law (*capitis deminutio*).

16 E Badian *Foreign Clientelae* (1958).

17 B Albanese, *Le Persone Nel Diritto Privato Romano* (1979) 63 ff; W Waldstein, *Operae Libertorum Untersuchungen zur Dienstpflicht freigelassener Sklaven* (1986).

18 A decision of the lower popular assembly called *concilium plebis* whose decisions were binding on all Roman citizens since the *Lex Hortensia* (287 BC).

19 F Casavola, *Lex Cincia, Contributo Alla Storia delle Origine della Donazione Romana* (1960).

20 Ibid.

was not a contract in classical Roman law, it could be the reason (*causa*) for a stipulation or a transfer of ownership.

During the Roman Principate, other forms of imposed legal protection were established by means of decisions of the Senate (*Senatus Consulta*). I will mention two decisions that played an important role in legal history after the reception of Roman law.

The *SC Vellaeanum* (46 AD) prohibited women from standing surety for other people's debts. Here it is important to observe that in Roman law personal security was far more prevalent than real security, such as pledge and mortgage. In cases where a woman had stood surety in spite of the *senatus consultum*, she was entitled to the *exceptio SC Vellaeani.*[21] The reason for this remedy was protection against possible constraint under which sensible women agreed to disadvantageous legal transactions. According to Wolfgang Ernst,[22] the protective regime of the *SC Vellaeanum* is still visible in modern consumer law. He explains this by referring to German private law, especially BGB § 138.[23] This provision indeed differs significantly from the equivalent provision in the Dutch Civil Code (Arts 3:40 and 3:44[24]), where the element of giving an advantage to a third person (in Roman terminology *intercessio*) is absent.

The *SC Macedonianum*, issued during the reign of Vespasian at the end of the first century AD, contained a prohibition on lending money to a son who was still under the authority of his father. Paternal authority in classical Roman law terminated only on the death of the father.[25] The loan was not immediately void *ipso iure*, but a legal remedy was available to protect the son against a claim by the money lender, the so-called *exceptio SC Macedoniani.*

[21] On the indirect effect of an *exceptio*, see the dissertation of JMJ Chorus, *Handelen in strijd met de wet* (1976) 37 ff, and the further discussion in Max Kaser, *Über Verbotsgesetze und Verbotswidrige Geschäfte Im Römischen Recht* (1977) passim; 'On the History of the *SC Vellaeanum*, see also D Medicus. in *Zur Geschichte des Senatus Consultum Velleianum* (1957) especially 29ff.

[22] W Ernst 'Interzession: Vom Verbot der Fraueninterzession über die Sittenwidrigkeit von Angehörigenbürgschaften zum Schutz des Verbrauchers als Interzedenten'. in R Zimmermann et al (eds), *Rechtsgeschichte und Privatrechtsdogmatik* (1999) 395–430. See also JE Spruit, 'Het Raets-besluit van Burgemeester Velleius'. in J Van der Westhuizen *et al* (eds), *Huldigingbundel Paul van Warmelo* (1984) 194–215.

[23] § 138 BGB: '(1) Ein Rechtsgeschäft das gegen die guten Sitten verstößt, ist nichtig. (2) Nichtig ist insbesondere ein Rechtsgeschäft, durch das jemand unter Ausbeutung der Zwangslage, der Unerfahrenheit, des Mangels an Urteilsvermögen oder der erheblichen Willensschwäche eines anderen sich oder einem Dritten für eine Leistung Vermögensvorteile versprechen oder gewähren lässt, die in einem auffälligen Mißverhältnis zu der Leistung stehen.' (emphasis added).

[24] BW Art. 3:40: '(1) Een rechtshandeling die door inhoud of strekking in strijd is met de goede zeden of de openbare orde, is nietig. (2) Strijd met een dwingende wetsbepaling leidt tot nietigheid van de rechtshandeling, doch, indien de bepaling uitsluitend strekt ter bescherming van één der partijen bij een meerzijdige rechtshandeling, slechts tot vernietigbaarheid etc.' BW Art. 3:44: '(1) Een rechthandeling is vernietigbaar, wanneer zijn door bedreiging, door bedrog of door misbruik van omstandigheden is tot stand gekomen, etc.'.

[25] Even a son becoming a Roman magistrate remains under the *patria potestas*! For a witty account of this *SC Macedonianum*, see D Daube 'Did Macedo Kill His Father?' (1947) Zeitschrift der Savigny Stiftung, Rom. Abt. 65, 308 ff (also in D Daube, *Collected Studies*, Vol II (1991) 193–234).

Apart from the rules of this *senatus consultum*, there was the *peculium*, a patrimony at the disposal (but not ownership) of someone who was not legally independent — a son or even a slave — that enabled him to take part in economic activities.[26] However, the rules concerning the *peculium* are not intended to protect the user of the *peculium* but rather his *pater familias*.

5. THE RULES OF MISTAKE OF LAW AS IMPOSED PROTECTION

The rules concerning mistake of law may be regarded as a form of imposed legal protection, not only in private law, including the law concerning *delicta privata* ('delicts' in Scottish and South African legal terminology), but also in criminal law, the latter being beyond the scope of this paper.[27] Under these rules, four groups of privileged persons — women, minors, farmers and soldiers — could invoke a mistake of law that others were generally not allowed to invoke. The main authority here is a rather famous passage from the Digest:

> D. 22.6.9 pr. Paulus liber singularis de iuris et facti ignorantia. Regula est iuris quidem ignorantiam cuique nocere, facti vero ignorantiam non nocere. Videamus igitur in quibus speciebus locum habere possit, ante praemisso quod minoribus viginti quinque annis ius ignorare permissum est. Quod et in feminis in quibusdam causis propter sexus infirmitatem dicitur. Et ideo sicubi non est delictum, sed iuris ignorantia, non laeduntur. (Paul in his monograph on mistake of law and of fact. It is a rule that mistake of law is harmful for everyone, but a mistake of fact is not. Let us see in which cases this rule applies, taking into account beforehand that it is permitted for persons younger than 25 years old not to know the law. And this holds also for women in certain cases because of the weakness of the female. And therefore they are not victims when there is mistake of law and no delict.)

In other texts, soldiers (*milites*) and farmers (*rustici*) were added to the group requiring special protection. Soldiers are mentioned in:

> C. 1.18.1 Imp. Antonius A Maximo militia. Quamvis cum causam tuam agreres, ignorantia iuris propter simplicitatem armatae militiae adlegationes competentes omiseris, tamen si nondum satisfecisti permitto tibi, si coeperis ex sententia convemiri, defensionibus tuis uti. [213] (Emperor Antonius Caracalla to the soldier Maximus. Although you have omitted to use available ways of defending yourself, when you were involved in a procedure by ignorance of the law through the simplicity of those

[26] There are many Roman legal texts on both these institutions in the Digest and Codex of Justinian. See JJ Brinkhof '*Een studie over het peculium in het klassieke Romeinse recht*'. (1978). The talented Leiden Romanist Egbert Koops is currently preparing a new book on *peculium*.

[27] See nevertheless the interesting text Pap. D. 48.5.39(38).2: 'Quare mulier tunc demum eam poenam, quam mares, sustinebit, cum incestum iure gentium prohibitum admiserit: nam si sola iuris nostri observatio interveniet, mulier ab incesti crimine erit excusata.' (A woman is excused from the crime of incest when it concerns a form of this crime which is only considered as such in Roman law; she is not excused from a form of incest according to natural law!)

belonging to the army, I allow you to use your ways of defence when you have not yet complied to the sentence and your opponent has started to compel you to do so. [213 AD])

Simplicity of mind (*rusticitas*) was the reason for protection in some but certainly not all other cases:

C. 2.2.2 Imp. Gordianus A Nocturno. Venia edicti non petita patronum seu patronam eorumque parentes et liberos, heredes insuper, etsi extranei sunt, a libertis seu liberis eorum non debere in ius vocari ius certissimum est; nec in ea re rusticitati venia praebeatur, cum naturali ratione honor eiusmodi personis debeatur. [239] (Emperor Gordianus to Nocturnus. When a special permission is not sought, it is very fixed law that patrons, their parents and children cannot be summoned to court by freed men or their children. And in this case there is no clemency towards simplicity of mind, for one has to pay respect towards those persons out of natural reason. [AD 239])

Particularly interesting is the appearance in this text of the *naturalis ratio*, which we find at the very beginning of the Institutes of Gaius (around AD 160)[28] as a basic principle of *ius gentium* — in Gaius's terminology 'natural law'.[29] A freed man had summoned the son of his patron to appear in court in contravention of a decree of the Senate. In this case, stupidity or ignorance was no excuse — natural reason must teach you that you have to honour your patron and his family. This is a reference to the above-mentioned *patronus-clientela* relationship (section 3).

In the Middle Ages, these persons were sometimes called *personae privilegiatae*,[30] an expression most probably coined by the glossator Bulgarus[31] at the beginning of the twelfth century, but using the old concept of *privilegium* defined by Modestinus in the third century AD:

D. 50.17.196 Modestinus libro octavo regularum. Privilegia quaedam causae sunt, quaedam personae. Et ideo quaedam ad heredem transmittuntur, quae causae sunt; quae personae sunt, ad heredem non transeunt. (Privileges are sometimes linked with a

[28] Gaius, Inst 1.1, reconstructed with the help of D. 1.1.9.

[29] LC Winkel 'Ist die Bedeutung der gaianischen *naturalis ratio* von der Zeit abhängig?. in M Avenarius *et al.* (eds), *Ars Iuris, Festschrift für Okko Behrends zum 70, Geburtstag* (2009) 603–09. See also MA Loth & LC Winkel, 'Reasonableness in a Divided Society' (2009) *De Iure* 302–15.

[30] Th Mayer-Maly 'Error Iuris' in H Miehsler & E Mock (eds) *Ius Humanitatis, Festschrift A. Verdross* (1980) 147–69; Th Mayer-Maly, 'Rusticitas' in Studi in onore di Cesare Sanfilippo, Vol I (1982) 309–47; LC Winkel, Error iuris nocet, Rechtsirrtum als Problem der Rechtsordnung, Vol. I: Rechtsirrtum in der griechischen Philosophie und im römischen Recht bis Justinian (1985) 89 ff.

[31] HU Kantorowicz *Studies in the Glossators of the Roman Law* (1938, repr 1969) 246, quotes a short treatise of the glossator Bulgarus from first half of the twelfth century, entitled Summula de iuris et facti ignorantia, where we read in lines 4–7: 'Amplius inquiritur, an persona tua privilegio sit munita, ut militis, cui contra rem iudicatam subvenitur, si nondum solverit. Similiter et minor privilegio gaudet, ut prediximus, et femina, que iuris ignara solvit, sublevatur, in quibus [casibus] veterum legum statuta declarant.' (Further, one asks whether your person is provided with a privilege, as the soldier who is helped after a sentence when he has not yet paid. In the same way a minor enjoys a privilege, as we have said before, and a woman who in ignorance of the law made a payment, is helped in the cases indicated by the provisions of the old laws.).

thing, sometimes with a person. And therefore those that are linked with a thing pass over to the heir, those that are linked with a person do not pass to the heir.)

It is not certain whether the expression *personae privilegiatae* appears in the authoritative Accursian gloss, *Glossa ordinaria*, in the mid-thirteenth century.[32]

6. LEGAL PROTECTION IN THE LEGISLATION OF JUSTINIAN AND ITS RECEPTION

In later legal history, most of the above-mentioned forms of imposed legal protection were preserved in Justinian's legislation. They were then revived during the first stages of the reception that resurrected Roman law in its Justinianic form after the eleventh century, when Roman law was taught at universities, starting with Bologna in 1088. Territorial legislation sometimes altered the age of minority, and women were generally considered to be *sui iuris*. In some regions, however, a married woman lost full legal capacity, and this was often linked to the regime of matrimonial property. Grotius (*Inleidinge* I, 5, 21–23) tells us that the overwhelming power of the husband, also over his wife's property, stems from 'oude Duitsche zeden' (old Germanic customs). Most likely her incapacity goes back at least to the *Sachsenspiegel* (I, 31, 2),[33] as Grotius indicates in the margin of the Lund manuscript of the *Inleidinge*.[34] In a country like the Netherlands, where general community of property between husband and wife was common, the legal incapacity of married women endured until 1957. Both the *SC Vellaeanum* and the *SC Macedonianum* were part of received Roman law everywhere, as were the rules for the protection of minors, prodigals and persons who were mentally ill.[35]

[32] The expression is medieval, but cannot be traced exactly, see, eg the gloss *Regula est* ad D. 22.6.9 *pr.* where it is missing. Canon law sources are more likely here. S Kuttner, *Kanonistische Schuldlehre* (1935, repr 1973) 166–67, says that Gratian already distinguishes between groups of persons. In later legal history (nineteenth century), FC von Savigny, *Das System des heutigen römischen Rechts*, Vol III (1840) 429–40 mentions the four groups, but does not use the expression *personae privilegiatae*. Bernhard Windscheid, *Lehrbuch des Pandektenrechts*, edited by Th Kipp, 9th edn (1906, repr 1984) Vol I, § 29, 123 ff, deals with the concept of *privilegium* but does not use *personae privilegiatae* either.

[33] For an account of old Germanic customary law of the first half of the thirteenth century, see JBM van Hoek *Eipe von Repgow's Rechtsboek in Beeld: Observaties omtrent de verluchting van de Saksenspiegel* (1982).

[34] F Dovring, HWFD Fischer and EM Meijers (eds) *Hugo de Groot, Inleidinge tot de Hollandsche Rechts-Geleerdheid* (1965) 21 at fn 1.

[35] A survey of the reception of Roman law in France may be found in the works of Philibertus Bugnyon, *Traicté des loix abrogées et inusitées en toutes les cours, terres, jurisdictions et seigneuries du Royaume de France* (1677) (in the collection of the University Library in Leyden) and Bernardus Autumnus, *La conference du droict François avec le droict roman, civil et canon* (1644) (in the collection of the University Library in Leyden). A survey of the reception of Roman law in the Netherlands appears in Simon van Groenewegen van der Made, De *legibus abrogatis*. Its 3rd edn from 1669 (in the collection of the University Library in Amsterdam) was translated into English by B Beinart and Margaret Hewett in three volumes (1974–87). According to Bugnyon, I, 166, women in France were not allowed to act in court, neither for themselves nor for others, the last without any doubt a

Taking into account the *histoire de longue durée*, one may say that the oldest forms of legal protection are to be found in family law but that the idea of protection spread to all areas of patrimonial law. Apart from examples of protection from the field of family law, the principle of good faith played a key role in other fields. In the *ius commune*, most probably since Donellus, all contracts gradually came under its spell, starting with contracts between merchants. However, at the end of the sixteenth century, even Grotius was still hesitant in this regard and occasionally referred to the distinction between *iudicia bonae fidei* and *iudicia stricti iuris*.[36] Nevertheless, one may generally assume that in the European *ius commune* all contracts gradually became *contractus bonae fidei*.[37]

The period of national codification resulted in a rather formal approach to imposed protection. Minors, mentally disabled persons, prodigals and – in some cases — women remained protected, but all other forms of protection were formalised under the influence of the notion of legal equality, which was one of the main consequences of the French revolution, and liberalism, which was a consequence of *liberté*. For a considerable amount of time, *l'égalité devant la loi* prevented the courts from taking forms of unequal social power into account.[38] It took nearly a century before more sociological approaches to law arose and these forms of inequality came to be studied and explained. This happened for the first time not in France or England but in the newest industrial country of Europe, the German Empire. Rudolph von Jhering,[39] Eugen Ehrlich[40] and Anton Menger,[41] all German speaking jurists, may be mentioned here. However, legal equality was not the same as social and economic equality! Special attention must be paid to the development of imposed legal protection in nineteenth-century Europe in the field of labour contracts. At that time, freedom of contract in the field of labour was unveiled as fictitious, and collective labour contracts therefore arose in place of individual ones.

consequence of the reception of the *SC Vellaeanum*. See also *Autumnus*, II, 269; Groenewegen (1669) at 486, cf Grotius, *Inleidinge*, I.4.7 with interesting references to the *Lex Langobardorum* in the surviving manuscript of Lund. See the edn edited by Dovring, Fischer and Meijers, *above* n 33, at 15 fn 2.

[36] De iure belli ac pacis II.11.6. See L Winkel 'Die Irrtumslehre'. in R Feenstra & R Zimmermann (eds), *Das Römisch-Holländische Recht — Fortschritte des Zivilrechts Im 17, Und 18, Jahrhundert* (1992) at 232.

[37] H Coing, above n 12, at 410.

[38] E Griffin-Collart, 'L'Évolution de la Notion d'Égalité de l'Utilitarisme À l'État de Providence' in L Ingber (ed), L'Égalité, Vol IV (1975) 352–71.

[39] R von Jhering, Der Zweck Im Recht (1877–1884, many reprints), See Also F *Wieacker, Privatrechtsgeschichte der Neuzeit*, 2nd edn (1967), 451ff.

[40] E Ehrlich, *Grundlegung der Soziologie des Rechts* (1929). Ehrlich was also the author of a book entitled *Beiträge zur Theorie der Rechtsquellen*, Vol. I: *Das ius civile, ius publicum, ius privatum* (1902, repr 1970); see also M Rehbinder, *Die Begründung der Rechtssoziologie durch Eugen Ehrlich* (1967) who hints at the interesting link between the study of Roman law at the end of its practical application in Germany and the birth of legal sociology.

[41] A Menger *Das Bürgerliche Recht und die Besiztlose Volksklasse*, 4th edn (1908).

7. CONCLUSIONS

Many measures of modern consumer protection may be regarded as extensions and elaborations of the old criterion of good faith (*bona fides*) in Roman contract law. The system of *causa* in contract law[42] and in the regime for the transfer of ownership, and the further development of the *causa stipulationis* in Roman law[43] and the aforementioned transfer of ownership, can serve as possible remedies for the protection of the underprivileged. In these areas, modern Dutch private law is still strongly influenced by Roman law.[44]

The old institutions in Roman family law, which were aimed at protecting weaker persons, are not only part of Dutch private law but are generally present in the legal systems of civil law countries. However, it remains unclear whether similar common law institutions can also be traced back to Roman law.

[42] In this respect, the doctrine of causa is comparable with the English concept of consideration. Still interesting is EM Meijers, 'Nieuwe bijdragen omtrent de leer der consideration en der causa' in *Meijers, Verzamelde Privaatrechtelijke Opstellen*, Vol III (1955) 301–10.

[43] JG Wolf, Causa Stipulationis (1970) especially at 76 ff.

[44] JA Ankum, 'Roman Law in the New Dutch Civil Code' (1994) Casopis pro právní vedu a praxi II, 203–25.

Index

www.ingramcontent.com/pod-product-compliance
Ingram Content Group UK Ltd.
Pitfield, Milton Keynes, MK11 3LW, UK
UKHW020139290926
15471UKWH00003B/578

9 781849 461184